DATE DUE			
		WITHDRAWN	

344.7305
Hen

Henderson, Harry.
Gun control

002438

WHEATON WARRENVILLE S HS
1993 TIGER TRAIL

487322 04496   35473D   004

LIBRARY IN A BOOK

GUN CONTROL

Revised Edition

Harry Henderson

Facts On File, Inc.

To the victims of gun violence and to responsible gun owners

GUN CONTROL, Revised Edition

Copyright © 2005, 2000 by Harry Henderson
Graphs copyright © 2005 by Facts On File, Inc.

Facts On File, Inc.
132 West 31st Street
New York NY 10001

Library of Congress Cataloging-in-Publication Data
Henderson, Harry, 1951–
Gun control/Harry Henderson. – Rev. ed.
p. cm. – (Library in a book)
Includes bibliographical references and index.
ISBN 0-8160-5660-9 (alk. paper)
1. Firearms –Law and legislation – United States. 2. Gun control – United States.
I. Title. II. Series.
KF3941.H46 2005
344.7305'33–dc22   2004050651

Facts On File books are available at special discounts when purchased in bulk quantities for businesses, associations, institutions or sales promotions. Please call our Special Sales Department in New York at 212/967-8800 or 800/322-8755.

You can find Facts On File on the World Wide Web at http://www.factsonfile.com.

Text design by Ron Monteleone

Graphs by Sholto Ainslie

Printed in the United States of America

MP Hermitage 10   9   8   7   6   5   4   3   2   1

This book is printed on acid-free paper.

CONTENTS

———————

PART III
APPENDICES

PART I

OVERVIEW OF THE TOPIC

CHAPTER 1

INTRODUCTION TO
GUN CONTROL

The issue of whether (and how) the ownership and use of firearms should be regulated has been a contentious one in recent years. In the 1990s mass shooting incidents in schools (such as Columbine High School in Littleton, Colorado) and workplaces (including a high-rise office building in San Francisco) energized the debate between advocates of gun control and gun rights advocates.

Although the number of school and workplace shootings (and the shock they brought) seems to have subsided since the 1990s, and indeed the overall rate of violent crime has continued to decline, guns continue to be the object of passionate advocacy in U.S. culture and politics. Groups such as the Brady Campaign to Prevent Gun Violence and the National Rifle Association continue their ongoing efforts to keep their issues before the public. The battle over gun control thus continues to be fought in Congress and state legislatures as well as in the courts. It is a complex and many-faceted issue.

When one gets down to details, the issue of gun control includes a wide variety of approaches to the regulation of firearm ownership and use. Some of the details of gun control proposals can be arcane and subject to interpretation, such as what exactly constitutes an "assault weapon" or a "Saturday night special." But in general, the debate over gun control involves questions such as the following:

- Should ordinary citizens who are not involved with the military, law enforcement, or security be allowed to own a gun?
- If so, what should be the requirements for owning a gun? A minimum age? Background screening? Taking a safe gun-handling course?
- Should gun shows, pawnshops, and private gun sales be subject to the same restrictions as sales from licensed dealers? Should gun sales over the Internet be banned?

- Should all guns be registered in a permanent database that police can use to track guns used in crime? Might such a database be misused by an oppressive government?
- Should people be allowed to carry guns outside the home? Carry them concealed? If so, should a permit be required? How hard should it be to get the permit?
- Should some types of guns be banned, such as high capacity semiautomatic rifles and pistols, or cheap handguns, or all handguns?
- Should some types of ammunition be banned, such as armor-piercing or "cop-killer" bullets?
- Should gun purchasers be limited to buying one gun a month? Should there be limits on the purchase of ammunition?
- Should gun manufacturers have to meet safety standards like those applied to other consumer products? Should certain safety devices such as a trigger lock or a "loaded" indicator be required?
- Should parents be held responsible when children access guns?
- Should gun manufacturers be held liable if they market or distribute their products in a way that makes it easy for criminals to get them?
- Should .50 caliber sniper rifles be banned because terrorists might use such weapons to bring down aircraft or puncture chemical tanks?
- Should the United States and other nations undertake a regulatory and enforcement campaign to dry up the burgeoning worldwide illicit market in light weapons?

DIFFICULT QUESTIONS, CONFLICTING ANSWERS

It has been hard to find lasting agreement on any of these questions. Since the federal government first began to regulate firearms in 1927, there has been a national debate between gun control advocates and gun rights advocates[1] about a variety of proposals ranging from outright bans on certain kinds of firearms to minor changes in the way prospective gun purchasers are screened.

The intensity of the gun debate has varied and tends to peak in times of social turmoil. It was fueled by assassinations and racial violence in the 1960s, an upsurge in crime in the 1970s, and a new wave of drug-related violence in the 1980s. By the mid-1990s, however, it seemed that reductions in crime rates and the passage of new federal gun legislation (the Brady Bill and the Assault Weapons Ban) might have put the gun issue on the back burner.

However, in the mid- to late 1990s, a wave of high-profile mass shooting incidents in workplaces and schools occurred. It is true that the chance of a given individual becoming a victim of such a mass shooting is considerably less than that of being struck by lightning, but on April 20, 1999, when two teenagers opened fire in Columbine High School in Littleton, Colorado, killing 15 people (including themselves), statistics seemed to be beside the point. The intense media coverage and the shock of murder and mayhem in the supposedly secure environment of suburban America has led to a renewed search for the causes and possible cures for the persistent violence in American society. The apparent growth in violent hate crimes, such as the wounding of five people by gunfire in a Jewish community center in Los Angeles, added further anguish and urgency to the debate.

The new century, and particularly the terrorist attacks of September 11, 2001, brought a new complexion to the gun debate. Gun control advocates began to stress the easy availability of guns to terrorists as a compelling new reason for gun control. Other Americans, including gun rights advocates, drew the opposite conclusion, arguing that an armed citizenry could provide an important layer in the defense against terror.

In October 2002, the Washington, D.C.-area snipers who killed 10 people and wounded four brought a new kind of gun terror to the populace. Unlike earlier mass shootings that were horrific but brief in duration, in this instance the killing of people seemingly at random went on for almost a month, with law enforcement officials appearing to be baffled and the targets essentially defenseless.

One obvious place to look for the cause of mayhem is the widespread availability of firearms, including rapid-fire semiautomatic weapons. Immediately following the Littleton tragedy, President Bill Clinton and many members of Congress promoted stricter gun controls, including raising the minimum age for firearms purchase to 21, requiring background checks for purchasers at gun shows, and requiring that all new guns be sold with trigger locks that could prevent unauthorized use.

The gun debate is especially difficult to analyze because it takes place on two levels. One level is pragmatic, concerned with the effectiveness and trade-offs involved in particular policies.

The Brady Campaign to Prevent Gun Violence believes that in order to stem the flow of handgun violence, America needs a national system of handgun owner licensing. Handguns should be treated like cars in that owners would be licensed and handguns would be registered. Congress would establish minimum standards for the licensing system, which would be implemented by the states. Without a national system, gun traffickers will continue to make mass purchases of handguns in states with weak laws and sell them into the illegal

market across the country. Minimum national standards will help to stop in-
terstate gun trafficking and ensure that everyone who buys a handgun in this
country is qualified to own one.[2]

Not surprisingly, the National Rifle Association disagrees with the gun/car
analogy:

purchase and ownership of arms is a right expressly protected by the constitu-
tion, whereas operating a vehicle on public roads is a privilege. Note that a
license and registration is not required to merely own a vehicle or operate it
on private property, only to do so on public roads. Similarly, licenses and per-
mits are not typically required to buy or own a gun, or to keep a gun at home,
but are required when using a gun to hunt publicly-owned game or to carry
a gun for protection in public places.[3]

Gun control advocates generally want to exert a maximum effort to keep
guns away from persons who are likely to use them irresponsibly. Gun rights
advocates want to use a combination of education and law enforcement to
deter gun abuse. However, people who don't have strong feelings one way
or the other might well ask: Why not compromise and do a bit more of
both?

One problem with finding a compromise is that the two sides often
don't agree on even the basic facts or their significance. For example,
Handgun Control, Inc., used to cite a study that claims that a gun fired in
the home is 43 times more likely to kill a family member or friend than to
kill in self-defense. But criminologist and gun control critic Gary Kleck
has suggested that the vast majority of successful uses of a gun to drive
away a burglar or other criminal do not include the gun being fired, let
alone result in the intruder being killed. Kleck believes that when the lives
and property saved by such defensive gun uses are balanced against the
risk of homicide or accident within the household, the balance strongly favors gun ownership.

But figures such as the number of defensive gun uses vary greatly with
definitions and methodology. Kleck has estimated about 2 million successful cases of armed self-defense per year. On the other hand, the Justice Department's National Crime Victimization Survey gave a figure of 108,000.
Is Kleck's figure too high due to inadequate sampling (as some critics suggest), or does the Justice Department's low total reflect the likelihood that
many people who drive away criminals don't feel a desire or need to inform
the police? As Philip Cook of Duke University observes: "Many of the basic
statistics about guns are in wide disagreement with each other depending on
which source you go to."[4]

Other areas of contention in the analysis of gun violence include:

- Does making it easier for law-abiding citizens to carry concealed weapons deter criminals? Will it increase the number of traffic, barroom, or other confrontations that escalate to deadly force? If both, does the benefit of the first effect outweigh the cost of the latter?[5]
- A number of studies have found that having a handgun in the home increases the risk of a family member becoming a homicide or suicide victim. Is this presence of a gun a cause of or a response to crime or social pathology?
- Will requiring trigger locks and other safety devices on guns save lives? Or might it give people a false sense of security or cause more people to be victimized by crime because they can't get to their gun in time?
- Would banning the cheap handguns called "Saturday night specials" reduce crime by drying up a source of "starter guns" for beginning criminals? Or would it deprive poor people of the most effective means of self-defense they can afford?
- Do the semiautomatic rifles and handguns commonly called "assault weapons" play a significant part in crime? Do such weapons have any legitimate uses?

PRIVILEGE OR RIGHT?

As the questions framed in the previous section suggest, gun control and gun rights advocates find it very hard to resolve the trade-offs involved in proposed gun control measures, but the conflict between gun control advocates and gun rights advocates runs even deeper when it enters the area of political philosophy. As the statement from the Brady Campaign, cited earlier notes, to gun control advocates, gun ownership is a *privilege*, as is driving. From that point of view the question of whether or how to extend that privilege is a matter of social policy. Experts should analyze whether the social utility of gun ownership outweighs the social costs. Politicians and policy makers can make proposals based on expert findings, and voters can vote for or against them in true democratic fashion.

But to most gun advocates, gun ownership is not a mere privilege; it is a *right*, as are freedom of speech or of the press. For a privilege, the question is simply whether it is socially useful to extend or restrict it; for a right, much stricter standards come into play. According to the standards of the courts, the government must show a "compelling" interest before it can restrict a right, and the proposed restrictions must be "narrowly tailored" to accomplish their objective with as little interference to free exercise of the right as possible. Thus, with regard to the First Amendment rights of expression, there can generally be no "prior restraint" on speech or writing. Of course if the speaker, to use a famous example, shouts "fire" in a crowded theater when there is no fire, he or she can be held responsible for any resulting damages. People can also be held responsible for libel or slander. Finally, there can be some restrictions as to the "place and manner" in which the right is exercised.

Generally, gun rights advocates want gun ownership to be treated in a way similar to speech or writing. Every adult citizen who does not have a criminal or mental health record should be able to own and carry the gun of his or her choice with minimal restrictions (such as banning guns in some public places like schools). Any criminal who commits a crime with that firearm, however, should be prosecuted and punished.

The gulf between privilege and right thus makes it hard for the two sides in the gun debate to even speak the same language. The gun control advocate tends to see each proposed gun ban or restriction as an issue to be resolved politically on its own merits. The gun rights advocate, however, sees each proposal as being the latest attack on a fundamental right in furtherance of an agenda leading to a total ban on gun ownership. Emotionally, the gun control advocate tends to see the gun rights advocate as uncompromising, even fanatical in opposing even the most reasonable measures. In turn, the gun rights advocate tends to see the gun control advocates as untrustworthy and manipulative, proposing reasonable-sounding measures but unwilling to admit their ultimate goals.

Most people, of course, are not activists on either side of the gun issue. Polls (see Appendix A) record a high level of generalized support for gun control, though opinion on the most extreme measures (such as a total ban on handguns) is more evenly split between supporters and opponents. Our political system, however, gives the activists who can raise campaign contributions and mobilize voters a disproportionate influence on the outcome of legislative proposals. Traditionally the National Rifle Association (NRA) has had political influence out of proportion even to its considerable membership. In recent years, however, antigun groups have become more skillful in grassroots organizing and may also benefit from what opponents call a bias in the major national media in favor of gun control.

Neither the assertion of a right to bear arms nor the legislation of controls on their ownership or use is a recent development. Gun rights and gun control are simply the latest developments in the struggle of societies to determine how weapons should be used. Thus a review of gun issues begins with a look at their historical roots and development.

ARMS AND GOVERNANCE

Each society, past and present, has a particular balance of power among its influential classes such as religious leaders, intellectuals, and the wealthy, as well as the warriors or soldiers. Clearly the hunter-warrior in a hunter/gatherer culture, an armed and armored feudal noble, and a citizen-soldier in ancient Rome, modern Switzerland, or modern Israel are all arms bearers, but they have different forms of social status and responsibilities.

WARRIOR ELITE OR ARMED CITIZEN?

Societies since ancient times have adopted two general models with regard to weapons use. In some societies, such as medieval Europe and feudal Japan, an elite group of heavily armed and highly trained warriors formed the ruling class. In an economy barely beyond subsistence, a knight together with his weapons, armor, and horse represented a tremendous investment in resources. With that investment, the warrior elite offered protection and stability to the community, but it also used its weapons and skill to enforce its claim to the share of land, labor, or harvest that it needed to perpetuate itself. Medieval society was hierarchical, but also decentralized. Although the ideology of feudalism depicted a ladder of loyalty and responsibility that extended upward to the king, the feudal elite, holding land and equipped with the same weapons as the king and his retinue, could combine to restrict this power, as the English barons did to King John I with the Magna Carta in 1215.

But serfs, peasants, and even free tradespersons were no match for the heavily equipped noble who had been trained in arms since early childhood. Thus in 1381, when these classes revolted against the English ruling class, "some carried only sticks, some swords covered with rust, some merely axes and others bows more reddened with age and smoke than old ivory, many of their arrows had only one plume."[6] The leaders of the rebellion were tricked and the followers soon routed.

As the revival of the economy in Europe made independent landowners and tradesmen wealthier, they often sought the trappings of nobility, including fine swords and fancy clothes. The nobility resisted: After all, it was the nobility who were "armigerous"—entitled to bear a coat of arms whose symbology derived from the tools and uses of war. The weapons allowed to a person generally reflected social status: A noble could have a sword, and a yeoman (freeholder) farmer might be entitled to an axe or a bow (although the use of the latter for hunting was always a touchy issue).

A different model for arms bearing is found in varying degrees in the city-states of ancient Greece and the Roman Republic. In a republic, a person who was entitled to a voice in how the state was run was also responsible for helping to defend it. But just who should control the weapons was subject to dispute. Plato believed that because the state needed to train its citizens for defense, the state should have a monopoly on arms. Citizens could not own their own weapons but would be issued them for training and war as needed. Aristotle, on the other hand, believed in widespread arms ownership as a way to balance the power of the different social classes. In his *Politics* he noted that if weapons ownership were confined to a single elite group, "the farmers have no arms, the workers have neither land nor arms; this makes them virtually the servants of those who possess arms."[7] In a republic where citizens had their own weapons, ambitious leaders could sometimes turn their popular following into a private army and engage in a coup or a civil war. On the other hand, the ability of a tyrant to rule in the face of significant popular opposition was reduced by the decentralization of weapons ownership.

GUNPOWDER AND THE NATION-STATE

The introduction of gunpowder weapons in Europe about 1300 had far-reaching effects on the social and political use of weaponry. In its first centuries, gunpowder was primarily used in siege guns that, while crude and unwieldy, could batter down the walls of castles of those who would not submit to the king. Even as artillery improved and developed into a form that could be used in field battles, it remained very expensive. The "iron argument of kings" could generally only be afforded by kings and tended to centralize power in a nation-state.

Small arms started out as cumbersome miniature "hand cannons," but with the development of improved firing mechanisms (matchlock in the 15th century; wheel lock and flintlock in the 16th century), handheld infantry guns became practicable. These weapons could not be fired rapidly because loading was an intricate, multistep process. Indeed, as late as the mid-19th century, a trained longbow user could shoot more often and to better effect than the user of a gunpowder weapon. But the gun had one big advantage: Training someone to be good with the bow took years, while a few weeks of training with a gun was sufficient. Of course early guns were also quite expensive—this was still a society of crafts, not industry.

Early guns had short range and poor accuracy. To use them effectively, soldiers had to be formed into lines and trained to fire in volleys. The individualized warfare of the knight was replaced by the machinelike precision of thousands of common soldiers drilled to act as one. By the 18th century, in Europe, the gun was the instrument of the standing army of an increasingly centralized state. Certainly, persons with the means and opportunity could have guns for hunting, and pistols were available as well. Nevertheless, the gun was not a commonplace tool of the ordinary citizen.

ARMS IN THE ANGLO-AMERICAN TRADITION

In most modern European nations, gun ownership is heavily regulated, and guns play little part in daily life. Gun control is accepted as a matter of course by the overwhelming majority of citizens. Europeans often express astonishment at widespread gun ownership in the United States and the contentiousness of the gun issue in U.S. politics.

To understand how Americans acquired a distinctive attitude toward firearms, it is important to remember that the political culture of the United States grew out of the English rather than continental European experience.

THE MILITIA AND THE RIGHT TO BEAR ARMS

Once conquered by the Normans in 1066, Britain would not be invaded again successfully. By the 16th century, British rulers saw their first line of defense as being a navy that strove always to be able to defeat any combination of opponents. Compared to the emerging powers of the European mainland (Spain, France, and later, Germany) the English standing army would always be small; for one thing, the nation lacked the population and resources to create a large military establishment. But Britain had an additional military resource that it could call on in times of crisis: the armed, organized citizen.

Earlier, Anglo-Saxon Britain had the *fyrd*, in which all free men trained with basic weapons and which could be called out in times of emergency by the sheriff. In 1181, King Henry II revived this idea in his Assize of Arms, which specified the armor and weapons that could be used by each social class—full armor and the lance for the knight and lighter armor for the tradesman. Later, Henry III expanded the Assize to include serfs, as well as requiring the establishment of a group of men to guard cities at night (a primitive police force) and requiring that citizens respond to the "hue and cry" to help subdue criminals who resisted.

As lances gave way to pike and musket, the militia tradition continued to be important. At the outbreak of the English Civil War in 1642, Parliament declared that it, not the king, had the right to regulate the militia. "By God, not for an hour!" King Charles I exclaimed. He knew that without control of the militia, "Kingly power is but a shadow."[8] Even after the monarchists prevailed and Charles II came to the throne in 1660, the militia served as a partial check on the power of the king, though its importance faded after the Glorious Revolution of 1688–89 put England on the course to a limited, constitutional monarchy.

Several provisions in the Bill of Rights that arose from that revolution noted the abuses of Charles II and James II and showed the importance attached to the right to bear arms:

> *5. By raising and keeping a standing army within this kingdom in time of peace, without the consent of parliament, and quartering [housing] soldiers contrary to law. . . . 6. By causing several good subjects, being protestants, to be disarmed at the same time when papists [Catholics] were both armed and employed contrary to law.*

In its list of remedies for these abuses, the second part of the Bill of Rights specified "7. The subjects which are Protestants may have arms for their defence suitable to their conditions and allowed by law."[9]

Andrew Fletcher, who survived a death sentence from James II and went on to help establish the new government, discussed the role of the armed citizen in *A Discourse of Government with Relation to Militias* (1698), where he said the constitution should "put the sword into the hands of the subject. . . . And I cannot see, why arms should be denied to any man who is not a slave, since they are the only true badges of liberty."[10]

EARLY ARMS CONTROL

Many of today's opponents of gun control look to the militia tradition and the English common law for their inspiration. But there is another side to this tradition: The same laws that established a right or duty to bear arms for the common defense often prescribed who could bear what kinds of arms. The Assize of Arms of Henry II in 1181 seized arms and armor from Jews to distribute to the "free men" it armed. The Glorious Revolution established a right to bear arms for Protestants, but not Catholics, and the arms to be borne were those "suitable to their conditions [social class] and allowed by law."

Crime on the streets and highways often provoked weapons regulations. The Statute of Northampton (1328) prohibited any person "great or small" from going armed in a public place, though in practice the law was generally used only against people who "terrified" others through their use of arms. Also, people of differing social status continued to be treated differently: Henry VIII, for example, barred anyone with an income of less than £300 annually from having a handgun or crossbow, in an attempt to keep such weapons out of the hands of common robbers.

COLONIAL AMERICA

At about the time the militia and the right to bear arms were becoming less important to many English people, they became essential for the colonists who were establishing settlements in America in the 1600s. As historian Daniel Boorstin notes, "Shooting small game with a bow or a gun and throwing a tomahawk became lifesaving skills when Indians attacked . . . civil and military uses of firearms dovetailed as they had not generally done in Europe."[11]

Native Americans quickly learned about the usefulness of firearms for hunting and war. They soon became subject to a gun control law:

> *Whereas the country by sad experience have found that the traders with Indians by their avarice have so armed the Indians with powder, shot, and guns . . . Be it enacted . . . that if any person . . . shall presume to trade, truck, barter, sell or utter, directly or indirectly, to or with any Indians any powder, shot, or arms . . . shall suffer death without benefit of clergy.[12]*

The rival French colonists, too, posed a military threat to the British colonies until they were defeated by a combination of British and colonial volunteer forces in the French and Indian War of 1754–63. The British government did not want to undertake the expense of maintaining and supplying large numbers of professional soldiers on a frontier 3,000 miles away. The colonists would have to take primary responsibility for their own defense. They naturally adopted and refined the historical model of the militia to the needs of a very different society.

REVOLUTION AND CONSTITUTION

Following the end of the French and Indian War, disputes over the taxation and treatment of the colonists as well as their political rights eventually boiled over into revolution. In 1777, British colonial undersecretary William Knox proposed that to forestall rebellion,

> *The Militia Law should be repealed and none suffered to be reenacted and the Arms of all the People should be taken away & and every piece of Ordnance removed into the King's Stores, nor should any Foundry or manufacturer of Arms, Gunpowder, or Warlike Stores, be ever suffered in America, nor should any Gunpowder, Lead, Arms, or Ordnance be imported into it without License; they will have but little need of such things for the future, as the King's Troops, Ships & Forts will be sufficient to protect them from danger.[13]*

Colonial activists formed the militias known as minutemen, creating a widespread network of resistance while leaders in the Second Continental Congress of 1775 debated whether to seek total American independence. But events overtook them when British officials, in the spirit of Knox's proposal, sent troops to Lexington and Concord to seize arms and ammunition. Although General Thomas Gage's forces won the first stand-up skirmish, the militias spontaneously unleashed guerrilla warfare on the returning Redcoats. In this effort, an accurate new weapon, the rifle, allowed snipers to pick off British troops from the distant cover of fences, rocks, and trees.

In the War of Independence, of the 231,771 men who served on the American side, 164,087 came from the militias. Militarily, the militias were a mixed bag, often poorly trained and ill prepared for major field battles, as well as being prone to desertion. But although it was the professional military efforts of George Washington, his colleagues, and French allies that ultimately won the war, the conflict could not have been started or sustained in its early years without the militia.

In creating its new charter of government, U.S. political leaders kept the importance of the militia and the traditional distrust of a standing army in mind. James Madison, for example, noted that liberty could be kept secure because

[To a U.S. army of about 25,000 or 30,000 men] would be opposed a militia amounting to near half a million citizens, with arms in their hands, officered by men chosen from among themselves, fighting for their common liberties, and united and conducted by governments possessing their affections and confidence.[14]

Although various wordings were proposed for the Second Amendment in the Constitution's Bill of Rights, the right to bear arms and the militia were always closely linked. The final version reads: "A well-regulated Militia, being necessary to the security of a Free State, the right of the people to keep and bear arms, shall not be infringed."

GUN CONTROL IN THE NINETEENTH CENTURY

Although Americans in the early 19th century maintained a romantic view of the militia and the frontiersman, the militias themselves soon faded into disuse, many becoming little more than armed social clubs. But state constitutions retained explicit guarantees of the right to keep and bear arms. Kentucky's constitution for example stated "The right of the citizens to bear arms in defense of themselves and the state shall not be questioned."[15] And in some cases it was not questioned: In the Kentucky case of *Bliss v. Commonwealth* (1822), for example, the court overturned a prohibition against the carrying of concealed weapons.

14

But this absolutist position would not predominate. In the Tennessee case of *Aymette v. State* (1840), the court upheld a similar law in the case of a man wearing a concealed Bowie knife. The judges looked back into English history and noted that the conditions under which arms could be owned or carried had often been regulated. They also noted the intimate connection between arms bearing and service in the militia for the common defense. They thus concluded that "The legislature, therefore, have a right to prohibit the wearing or keeping weapons dangerous to the peace and safety of the citizens, and which are not usual in civilized warfare, or would not contribute to the common defense."

As cities grew, and with them concern about urban crime, many communities passed laws against the carrying of weapons often associated with criminals, such as knives, brass knuckles, and, in some cases, handguns. Often, as in *Nunn v. State* (1846), a distinction was made between banning some kinds of guns (small, concealable handguns in this case) and banning *all* firearms. The former was ruled to be a legitimate exercise of state or local police power, but the latter was presumed to violate the right to bear arms in the state constitution.

Conditions on the frontier were obviously quite different than in cities, but contrary to Hollywood myth, the "Wild West" was not a totally lawless place where guns constantly blazed in the streets. With settlement came a need for law. Where the political organization or resources did not yet exist for regular law enforcement, members of the community often formed committees to apprehend criminal gangs. Such vigilantes were often surprisingly scrupulous in trying the suspects. Historian Richard Hofstader noted that vigilante organizations "often drew their leaders from the top levels of society . . . and their following came largely from the solid middle class."[16] And while gangs and gunfighters did exist, they killed each other, mainly, and not innocent civilians.

Post–Civil War America brought new challenges. During Reconstruction, African Americans gained citizenship and with it the right to keep and bear arms. Many militias became racially integrated, albeit often corrupt. But following Reconstruction, when white politicians or the Ku Klux Klan regained control of an area, "almost universally the first thing done was to disarm the negroes and leave them defenseless."[17] As another writer ironically notes, "The former states of the Confederacy, many of which had recognized the right to carry arms openly before the Civil War, developed a very sudden willingness to qualify that right."[18]

Federal legislation for the postwar South led the Supreme Court to its first major confrontation with the Second Amendment. The case of *United States v. Cruikshank* (1876) arose from the trial of a band of white farmers (and probable KKK members) who had attacked and burned a courthouse held by a group of armed blacks during an election dispute. The whites were tried under a Reconstruction civil rights statute and charged, among other things, with depriving the blacks of their right to bear arms. The lower court convicted them, but the Supreme Court overturned the conviction on appeal, ruling that the federal government could not enforce the right to bear arms in the Second Amendment against the states or private individuals.

In the late 19th century successive waves of immigrants flooded into U.S. cities from Italy, Ireland, Germany, and other countries. The neighborhoods in which they settled were often perceived to be crime ridden, and an increasing number of gun control measures were passed in response. Finally, in 1911, New York State enacted the Sullivan Law, which was the first state law that created a strict permit system for handgun ownership.

Thus by the early 20th century, guns remained in widespread use (particularly rifles and shotguns in rural areas). Gun control in some form existed on a state and local level in many areas. But as with many other laws, gun laws were often enforced against the poor and persons perceived to be criminally inclined, while "established citizens" could carry a concealed handgun with the blessing of the local sheriff or police chief.

GUN CONTROL IN MODERN AMERICA

As far as gun control is concerned, "modern America" can be said to have begun around 1919 when alcohol Prohibition created a raging thirst to be satisfied by the competing groups of gangsters who vied for control of the liquor business. They did so with the aid of a powerful new kind of gun, the Thompson submachine, or tommy, gun, a fully automatic weapon that would shoot as long as the trigger was held back. In the St. Valentine's Day Massacre (1929), horrified citizens were faced with newspaper photos of seven dead mobsters; their bodies had been riddled with bullets by rival gangsters who had posed as the police. In 1933, after an assassination attempt against newly elected President Franklin D. Roosevelt, gun control for the first time became a topic for national debate. Wide press coverage and growing public pressure led to a demand for national firearms regulations.

THE 1930S: FEDERAL REGULATION BEGINS

In 1927 Congress passed the first federal gun law, making it illegal to mail concealable firearms. While still in effect, the law had little practical effect on the gun trade because guns could be shipped by a variety of other means.

But the 1930s would see a more significant attempt to create national gun regulations.

The National Firearms Act of 1934 was rather modest by modern standards. It didn't actually outlaw machine guns or sawed-off shotguns, but it imposed a $200 tax on their manufacture, sale, and ownership—a rather high amount of money at that time. (Because they are short enough to conceal beneath a coat, sawed-off shotguns have long been considered a weapon of particular usefulness to criminals.) The law also required that purchasers of such weapons undergo an FBI background check.

In 1938 Congress extended the national firearm regulation system by passing the Federal Firearms Act. This law required that all manufacturers, importers, and dealers in firearms be licensed. It forbade delivery of a gun to a person who had been convicted of (or was under indictment for) a crime or who did not meet local licensing laws.

Thus by the end of the 1930s the federal government was significantly involved in firearms regulation. Control of automatic weapons became strict, though ironically very few crimes have been committed with fully automatic weapons. But the lack of systematic background checks and the existence of generally weak state laws meant that purchasers of handguns, by far the most common kind of gun used in crimes, were not tightly screened.

THE SECOND AMENDMENT DEBATE

Until the federal government began to regulate firearms in the 1930s, the Second Amendment was not a major factor in gun-related litigation. The Supreme Court as well as state courts had made it clear that whatever rights it guaranteed, the Second Amendment applied only to the actions of Congress or the federal government, not to state or local legislatures. (Under their own constitutions, state courts generally found that there was an individual right to keep and bear arms but decided to varying extents that state or local governments could regulate how arms were used, such as by banning concealed handguns.)

However, once the National Firearms Act was passed, the question of the Second Amendment's applicability to federal firearms control could no longer be escaped. The key case arose when two bootleggers, Jack Miller and Frank Layton, were accused of "unlawfully, knowingly, willingly, and feloniously transport[ing] in interstate commerce . . . a double-barrel 12-gauge Stevens shotgun having a barrel less than 18 inches in length."

A lower court ordered Miller and Layton freed, ruling that the Second Amendment prevented Congress from regulating commerce in weapons. The two bootleggers promptly disappeared into the countryside. But meanwhile, the government lawyers appealed the conviction. Because there was no longer anyone to pay for the defense, the Supreme Court heard only the government's side.

The Second Amendment begins with the phrase "A well-regulated militia, being necessary to the security of a free state" and then goes on to say "the right of the people to keep and bear arms, shall not be infringed." This rather curious phrasing leads to two major questions: (1) Does the reference to the militia simply state the framer's *purpose* in guaranteeing the right to bear arms, or does it *limit* that right to arms that can be used in the militia? (2) Does "the people" refer to a *collective* right to maintain a militia or to an *individual* right to keep and bear arms?

The Court's ruling suggests an answer to the first question that sees the militia clause as limiting or qualifying the right to bear arms. The key part of the decision said that the Court

> *can not take judicial notice that a shotgun having a barrel less than 18 inches long has today any reasonable relation to the preservation or efficiency of a well regulated militia; and therefore can not say that the Second Amendment guarantees to the citizen the right to keep and bear such a weapon.*

In other words, the Court based its decision on whether the weapon in question had military application and thus could further the development of the militia.

Ever since then, gun control advocates have argued that the Second Amendment thus applies only to bearing arms as part of an organized militia, which today is the National Guard:

> *The contemporary meaning of the Second Amendment is the same as it was at the time of its adoption. The federal government may regulate the National Guard, but cannot disarm it against the will of state legislatures. Nothing in the Second Amendment, however, precludes Congress or the states from requiring licensing and restrictions of firearms; in fact, there is nothing to stop an outright congressional ban on private ownership of all handguns and all rifles.[19]*

Gun rights advocates, however, bring up a number of objections to this view. In his influential article "The Embarrassing Second Amendment," Sanford Levinson, while a supporter of some forms of gun control, argues that if the framers of the Second Amendment had wanted only to protect the right of the states to have militias, they would have said so. Further, he notes, *militia* has a much broader historical meaning that cannot be restricted to today's National Guard. Thus George Mason, who refused to sign the Constitution because it initially lacked a Bill of Rights, declared, "Who are the militia? They consist now of the whole people."[20] Indeed, federal statutes define the militia as consisting of all able-bodied male citizens (today women would have to be included as well.) As for the question of whether the right to bear arms is intended to be individual or collective, Levinson and others have noted that in the rest of the Bill of Rights, *the people* always means *individuals*, even if they choose to act collectively—as in "the right of the people to peacefully assemble" in the First Amendment.

Levinson points out that the Second Amendment debate reveals a curious reversal of conservatives and liberals from their usual positions on civil rights. Liberals interpret the rest of the Bill of Rights broadly without worrying too much about the social cost of freeing criminals. However, they want to interpret the Second Amendment narrowly because of what they consider to be the social costs of gun ownership. Conservatives, on the other hand, often complain about the courts finding "new rights" in broad interpretations of the Bill of Rights but favor a broader interpretation where the Second Amendment is concerned.

Levinson urges that the scholarly community begin to take the Second Amendment seriously. To some extent, academic opinion has indeed shifted from a collectivist to an individualist interpretation of the Second Amendment.

But gun control advocates have a powerful bottom-line argument. Since *Miller*, the Supreme Court has not significantly revisited the Second Amendment and has not turned down any gun laws based on it. This is true even of cases involving weapons of definite military usefulness, despite the implication in *Miller* that such weapons might, unlike the sawed-off shotgun, find constitutional protection. In 1999, however, a federal district judge in the case of *United States v. Timothy Emerson* ruled that the Second Amendment did confer an individual right to keep and bear arms and that this right could not be removed without giving the defendant full due process. This ruling drew upon many of the historical arguments that scholars such as Levinson had made earlier. The decision was promptly appealed by the federal government

The federal appeals court overruled the district court with regard to the action taken against the defendant, but its decision left intact the lower court's conclusions about the Second Amendment. Meanwhile, however, other federal appeals circuits (notably the Ninth) have continued to deny the individual rights interpretation of the Second Amendment.

To add to the legal turmoil, in May 2001 U.S. attorney general John Ashcroft announced that the Justice Department would essentially adopt the individual rights approach to the Second Amendment, while at the same time saying that it would not challenge any existing federal gun laws.

Gun Control

Although the Supreme Court ultimately declined to hear the *Emerson* case, if the appeals circuits continue to issue conflicting decisions the pressure for a final resolution of the Second Amendment issue is likely to grow.

GUNS AND SOCIAL CONFLICT

The 1940s and 1950s saw little new firearm legislation. But the 1960s brought rapid change and upheaval to U.S. society. In the five years from 1963 to 1968, three national leaders were assassinated: President John F. Kennedy, civil rights leader Martin Luther King, Jr., and Senator (and Democratic presidential favorite) Robert F. Kennedy. Black militants and anti–Vietnam War protesters took to the streets and challenged the legitimacy of government and other institutions.

As the turmoil grew, many groups began to arm themselves, ranging from the Ku Klux Klan and other racist organizations to the Black Panthers, who proclaimed their rights under the Second Amendment and marched with their rifles to the California statehouse. Riots flared in the ghetto districts of Los Angeles and other large cities.

Reaction to the worst social turmoil since the 1930s led to a second great wave of federal gun legislation. Gun control advocates pointed out that Lee Harvey Oswald had obtained through the mail the rifle he had used to kill John F. Kennedy. (Such sales were already illegal under the 1927 act, but there was little practical enforcement.)

Kennedy's successor, President Lyndon B. Johnson, put his formidable political skills on the side of gun control. In his 1968 State of the Union Address, he urged Congress to pass a law to prevent "mail-order murder." He also came out for universal gun registration and licensing. A few months later, the King and Robert Kennedy assassinations gave a tremendous impetus to the gun control advocates, and their supporters in Congress were able to overcome the objections of the powerful National Rifle Association, which had begun to take a larger role in fighting gun control legislation.

Congress passed the Gun Control Act of 1968. It restricted nearly all interstate sales of firearms and tightened penalties for selling guns to minors or persons with criminal records. Every sale of a gun or ammunition had to be recorded in detail.

Gun rights advocates questioned whether these tight new laws would actually have any effect on crime. Gun control advocates endorsed a 1969 report by the National Commission on the Causes and Prevention of Violence, which had undertaken a massive study of the conditions that had led to urban riots and other violence during the preceding decade. The commission's report recommended national regulation of handguns and, echoing President Johnson's speeches, urged the requirement of registration of all guns and licensing of all purchasers.

GUNS, CRIME, AND SELF-DEFENSE

The 1960s had also marked the beginning of an overall increase in crime rates that would generally continue until the mid-1990s. Although large-scale social conflict had subsided by 1970, crime—and what to do about it—became a major political issue. An important part of that issue was the role played by guns. Did the widespread availability of guns—particularly hand-guns—contribute to the crime rate by making it easy for criminals to terrorize their victims, or did it actually reduce crime by giving law-abiding citizens the means of self-defense?

Starting in the 1970s, gun control advocates began to focus on a type of inexpensive, often poorly made handgun commonly known as a Saturday night special. They have argued that these cheap guns provided criminals with a ready supply of weapons. Gun rights advocates, however, have argued that banning cheap guns would deprive poor people—who live in the most crime-ridden neighborhoods with the least reliable police protection—of the means to defend themselves from criminals.

But the whole idea that guns were an effective means for defense against criminals would be called into question. A 1986 paper by Arthur Kellermann and Donald T. Reay in the *New England Journal of Medicine* concluded that a gun kept in the home was 43 times more likely to be used to kill a family member or friend than to kill a criminal intruder.[21] As noted earlier, however, such studies are filled with assumptions that are difficult to evaluate and have led to a war of numbers.

However, if criminologist Gary Kleck's estimate of 2 million defensive gun uses per year mentioned earlier is true, guns are used many times to defend people or property for each time they kill an innocent person. If so (and Kleck's estimates have in turn been challenged), does that mean guns do more good than harm?

Although dueling numbers play a part in the gun debate, the debate itself is often reduced in the media to a war of anecdotes in which tragic personal experience is cited by both sides. Gun control advocates see the armed citizen not as a deterrent to criminals, but as part of the problem. In 1993, Colin Ferguson used his semiautomatic handgun to shoot a number of people in a car on the Long Island Rail Road. One injury victim, a former law enforcement officer, testified at a congressional hearing that

There is no question in my mind that I would have done more damage if I had possessed such a weapon than the six deaths and the nineteen injuries that

occurred on the train . . . And with people running and knocking one another
down, if someone behind me had started firing, I dare say I would then think
I was in a crossfire.[22]

On the other hand, when George Hennard opened fire in Luby's Cafeteria in Killeen, Texas in October 1991, Suzanna Gratia, an experienced
shooter, had left her gun in the car before entering the restaurant, comply-
ing with a recently passed law. She testified before Congress that she had to
watch helplessly as Hennard killed her parents and other customers. "I had
a clear shot at him," she insisted.[23]

Generally, the war of anecdotes favors the gun control advocates. As pro-
gun criminologist John Lott has documented in his 2003 book *The Bias*
Against Guns, when guns are used to massacre people in a restaurant or
schoolyard, the media shows the carnage in full detail. But generally speaking, someone who simply brandishes a gun to drive away a criminal is not
news, nor is what *might have* happened if someone like Suzanna Gratia had
had a gun.

With legislative action in Washington, D.C., blocked by the continued
political power of the NRA, the gun control battle shifted to local government, with gun control activists trying to come in under the radar. In 1981,
Morton Grove, Illinois, passed the first total handgun ban in modern times.
The law withstood all challenges, with the court ruling that whatever rights
people might have to keep and bear arms in general, there was nothing
wrong with banning *some* types of guns.

Gun rights advocates generally react to the initiatives of the gun control
advocates, but they have sometimes taken the offensive. The National Rifle
Association has persistently and loudly pushed proposals for tough sentencing for all persons convicted of using a gun in a crime and for enforcement
of existing gun laws rather than the passing of new ones that they see as having dubious value.

The biggest pro-gun crusade in recent years, however, is found in the
debate over concealed carry laws. States differ widely in whether they
allow people to carry guns concealed in a holster within their coat or
waistband or in a container such as a fanny pack. In his overall work,
which includes his influential book *More Guns, Less Crime*, John Lott has
conducted large-scale studies that he says show that states that make it
easy for law-abiding citizens to have concealed handguns have lower crime
rates than comparable states that do not. On the other hand, the Brady
Campaign to Prevent Gun Violence issued its own study in 1999 that
claimed Lott was wrong and that crime rates in states with liberal concealed-carry laws either did not decrease as rapidly as in those with stricter
laws or actually increased. The debate moves quickly into complicated is-

sues of sampling and statistical methodology. Since the 1990s gun rights activists have had considerable success in promoting liberalization of state concealed-carry laws in such states as Missouri, despite fierce opposition from the gun control forces.

THE DRUG WAR, ASSAULT WEAPONS, AND THE NEW MILITIA

Just as bootleg liquor helped make the 1920s roar, the growing use of illegal drugs (particularly crack, a type of cocaine) brought a new wave of gangsterism in the 1980s. The focus of attention in the gun control debate became the so-called assault weapons, which had become the badge of the new gangster.

The term *assault weapon* can be confusing. Originally, it was a military term for a fully automatic rifle (such as the M-16) that could also be fired in short bursts. The purpose of these weapons (first introduced by the Germans in World War II and quickly adopted by the Soviets in the form of the AK-47), is primarily to give an infantry soldier enough firepower to cover an assault on an enemy position.

Some gun enthusiasts began to use the term to refer to civilian, semiautomatic versions of military weapons, but gun control advocates are also accused of taking advantage of the confusion in which the popular media often seem to blur the distinction between a true assault weapon or machine gun and a semiautomatic rifle or handgun. The latter shoots only one time for each pull of the trigger; it does not "spray" bullets. Gun rights advocates point out that there is no fundamental difference in operation between an Uzi or Tec-9 and the kind of semiautomatic pistols and rifles that have been in use since the 19th century. They accuse their opponents of using the scary, militarylike appearance of modern guns to create more support for gun control. Further, they point out that semiauto rifles are used in only a tiny fraction of crimes. Gun control advocates, however, point out that the ability to shoot rapid single shots and the use of a large (10 round or more) magazine (bullet holder) certainly allows a shooter to kill many more people in a short time. They point to the use of such weapons by gang members and the way in which they facilitate mass shooting incidents.

Gun control advocates (including former President Bill Clinton) have frequently argued that assault weapons have no "sporting use" or place in hunting and are not needed for defense against crime. Irritated gun rights advocates reply that "the Second Amendment isn't about hunting ducks" and that such weapons can be needed for community defense, citing how Korean merchants in Los Angeles used them to drive off a mob of looters during the L.A. riots in 1992.

Starting in the 1980s assault weapons also became associated with the gun-toting antigovernment activists in Montana, Michigan, and other states who had begun to organize private militia groups in response to what they saw as an out-of-control federal government that, among other things, was trying to disarm the people of the United States. Even though their ideological roots ranged from racist to libertarian beliefs, the members of the new militias generally said that they simply wanted to be left alone and that they were asserting the historical rights that had motivated the minutemen of the American Revolution.

Some militia activists reacted strongly to the killing of white separatist Randy Weaver's wife, son, and friend by FBI agents during a 1992 siege of his Ruby Ridge, Idaho, cabin. They accused the government of first entrapping and then targeting a man whose only crime had been selling a shotgun whose barrel was too short. They were also outraged the following year by the federal assault and siege of the church of the Branch Davidian religious sect in Waco, Texas, leading eventually to the fiery death of its leader, David Koresh, and dozens of followers, including many children. The revelation in the summer of 1999 that FBI agents had used pyrotechnic devices (capable of starting fires) during the final attack on the compound and the possible concealment of evidence of government wrongdoing led to renewed investigations but did not resolve questions of government culpability for many critics.

Some gun rights activists have pointed to these incidents to show why citizens must have the right to bear arms to deter abuses by government. Although gun control advocates, on the other hand, admitted to errors by law enforcement agencies, they considered the tragedies to be largely the fault of the gun-toting victims themselves. Since the Oklahoma City bombing of 1995, however, these militias faded from public view as concern shifted to foreign-based terrorism.

THE 1990S: BRADY AND BEYOND

Growing popular support for gun control and the efforts of the Clinton administration and many Democrats in Congress led to two substantial federal gun control laws. In 1981, James S. Brady, press secretary to President Ronald Reagan, was wounded along with Reagan in an assassination attempt by John Hinckley. Brady was badly wounded, faced a long recovery, and is confined to a wheelchair. His wife, Sarah Brady, became a crusader for gun control, joining Handgun Control, Inc. (HCI) and later becoming the organization's formidable chairperson. While lacking the resources of the NRA, HCI became adept at grassroots organizing and legal action.

Introduction to Gun Control

While gun control advocates were increasing their organization and public visibility, the NRA was becoming increasingly militant and absolutist in its opposition to gun control. In 1986, it lobbied Congress to pass the Firearms Owners' Protection Act, which permitted rifles and shotguns (but not handguns) to be sold by mail, eased dealer record-keeping requirements, and increased penalties for criminal misuse of guns. The NRA, however, also seemed to stumble in public opinion in the 1990s, such as when a widely publicized comment in a fund-raising letter about federal "jack-booted thugs" led President George H. W. Bush to cancel his membership, (Later, veteran actor Charlton Heston was appointed president of the NRA, and his popularity is credited with rehabilitating the organization's image to some extent. Heston retired in 2003.)

By the end of the 1980s, Brady and other gun control activists had mobilized considerable public support (including that of President Reagan, who had changed his mind) for a proposal to require a waiting period before a person could buy a gun. They believed that a waiting period was necessary for doing a proper background check of gun purchasers so that criminals and the mentally ill could be weeded out. They also believed that a mandatory waiting period could reduce impulsive gun purchases by people who were angry with someone and bent on violence. Gun rights advocates have suggested, however, that a person being stalked or harassed might be killed while waiting for a gun that is urgently needed for self-defense.

Although the Brady Bill failed in its first attempt at passage in 1991, Congress passed the Brady Handgun Violence Prevention Act in November 1993. The law established a five-day waiting period, after which the gun could be sold if the purchaser met an expanded list of requirements. (In addition to barring convicted felons and the mentally ill, the law also barred from gun purchase anyone who was currently under a court order for stalking or harassment.)

The Brady Act was challenged in court, but only the part requiring state officials to carry out the background checks was overturned by the Supreme Court in 1997 in *Printz v. U.S.*, on the grounds that Congress lacked the power to commandeer the services of local officials. This decision would have little impact because the Brady Act already had a provision that after five years (in 1998) the waiting period would be replaced by a computerized national instant check system that would verify a gun purchaser in much the same way that stores validate credit cards.

Another big victory for gun control advocates came in 1994 with the passage of the Violent Crime Control Act, which banned the manufacture, sale, and import of a large variety of semiautomatic weapons such as the Uzi, Tec-9, and similar "copycat" weapons. The list of banned weapons was later expanded, but weapons manufactured or imported before the ban

25

took effect can still be owned. Perhaps the culmination of a generally successful decade for gun control activists came on May 14, 2000, when the Million Mom March, organized by mother and publicist Donna Dees-Thomases, brought some 750,000 people to Washington, D.C., to advocate for gun control in the wake of recent shooting rampages.

NEW APPROACHES TO GUN CONTROL

Given the difficulty of passing gun control legislation against the opposition of the NRA and other pro–gun rights groups, gun control advocates have explored and implemented a variety of other approaches to gun control. In general, they involve the attempt to create scientific or legal models to change the behavior of gun manufacturers, dealers, and owners.

THE MEDICAL MODEL AND GUN VIOLENCE

There is little disagreement that a significant number of deaths and injuries are caused by firearms, although gun deaths peaked at about 40,000 in 1995 and then started to decline. According to the Centers for Disease Control and Prevention (CDC), firearms are the second leading cause of injury death in the United States although the overall homicide rate as well as the firearm injury rate have continued to decline.

Starting in the 1980s, a number of medical professionals including some involved with the CDC and with the *Journal of the American Medical Association (JAMA)* began to write about what they called "an epidemic of gun violence" that they said was causing up to $4 billion in medical expenses every year. They suggested that the approach taken toward traditional public health problems should also be taken toward gun violence. For example, in responding to the growing number of deaths from AIDS, doctors had to isolate the cause of the disease, identify practices that promoted infection, and devise educational and public policy strategies to contain it; similarly, these medical researchers and activists suggested that guns are the "pathogens" that promoted a growing epidemic of violence. They hoped to use their authority as medical professionals to publicize the dangers of guns in the home—in particular, the danger of accidental gun deaths, especially those involving children. They compiled studies that claimed that gun ownership increased the risk of homicide, suicide, and accidental death.[24]

Gun rights advocates (including a small group of doctors such as Edgar A. Suter) have attacked the "medicalization" of the gun issue. Philosophically, they argue that a gun is not an active organism like HIV, the virus that causes AIDS: It can't do anything by itself. Also, unlike HIV, a gun is a tool that has legitimate uses such as self-defense. Treating the misuse of tools as an "epidemic" promotes the viewpoint that people are helpless, passive victims of their impulses, and not responsible for their actions.

Gun advocates also argue that the proponents of the "gun epidemic" theory use poor statistical techniques and make many unwarranted assumptions; for example, with regard to suicide, they disagree with the conclusion that reducing the number of guns would necessarily reduce the number of suicides, noting that Japan, which has very tight gun control, has a high suicide rate. Would banning guns simply lead to people finding other means, such as jumping, gas asphyxiation, or sleeping pills?

Gun control advocates point out, however, that a gun is an "impulse weapon"—it takes only the pull of a trigger to commit an irrevocable act. Gun injuries are also much more likely to be fatal, while people who try other means of suicide often survive.

Medical and sociological gun control advocates have also pointed out that such countries as Britain and Japan, with strict firearm controls, have far lower homicide rates than the United States. Gun rights activists question whether such cross-cultural comparisons are valid, noting that European and Japanese societies are more conformist and that it is social control, not gun control, that is responsible for their low rate of violence.

"FOR THE CHILDREN"

Politics in the late 1990s seemed to be characterized by the framing of many issues in terms of how they affect children. Because people care deeply about their (and others') children, this may be good politics, though critics argue that it promotes an emotionally distorted approach to making public policy.

With regard to guns, the debate focuses on the easy access of guns to children, the potential for accidental or intentional shootings in the home, and the mass shooting incidents in schools and playgrounds (such as the five children killed and 30 wounded by Patrick Purdy in 1989 in Stockton, California, or the 15 killed in Columbine High School in Littleton, Colorado in 1999).

Although the federal Gun-Free School Zones Act (which bans gun possession in and near schools) was overturned by the Supreme Court, there are plenty of laws and policies that forbid students or others from bringing guns onto school property. John Lott suggests that the characterization of gun violence in schools is rather misleading:

> *The total number of accidental gun deaths each year is about 1,300 and each year such accidents take the lives of 200 children 14 years of age and under.*

Gun Control

However, these regrettable numbers of lives lost need to be put into some perspective with the other risks children face. Despite over 200 million guns owned by between 76 to 85 million people, the [number of] children killed is much smaller than the number lost through bicycle accidents, drowning, and fires. Children are 14.5 times more likely to die from car accidents than from accidents involving guns.

The debate over violence in the schools involves not only gun access, but the influence of violent movies, TV shows, and computer games, as well as parental neglect. Although a strong majority favor stronger gun control, there is also considerable support for regulations involving the media and its marketing practices. In the 1999 crime bill debates, opponents of stricter gun controls tried to add amendments dealing with the media, while gun rights advocates accused them of delay and diversionary tactics. (Conservative gun rights advocates tend to support restrictions on the media, while libertarians support both gun rights and freedom of speech.)

By late 1999, efforts to pass new federal gun legislation had bogged down, but gun control advocates promised to make gun control a major issue in the 2000 presidential campaign. Most Democrats saw gun control as a winning issue, while many Republicans found themselves caught between growing public pressure for gun control and a vocal, well-organized minority of gun rights advocates who see the gun issue as being, like abortion, a litmus test for political support. The actual outcome was, however, disappointing for gun control advocates. With the razor-thin margins in many states in the 2000 presidential election, many observers have suggested that Democratic candidate Al Gore's support for gun control may have cost him the election to Republican George W. Bush in relatively conservative states such as Gore's own Tennessee.

Although the extent of the problem and the efficacy of the cure are in dispute, gun control advocates make a powerful appeal when they suggest that only comprehensive gun control can stop killings in schools, workplaces, and on the streets. They hope that this appeal, combined with already strong support for gun control, will enable them to overcome the political power of the NRA and other gun rights advocates.

GUNS AND PRODUCT SAFETY

Faced with a protracted struggle in the political arena, some gun control activists launched a new offensive in the late 1990s by filing liability suits against gun manufacturers. Suing the shooter is a possibility, of course, but most criminals have little in the way of recoverable assets.

Another possibility is to sue the gun dealer who sells a firearm to a person who is obviously intoxicated or otherwise incompetent. In 1997, for example, Deborah Kitchen was shot by her ex-boyfriend, leaving her paralyzed. The boyfriend had obtained a .22 caliber rifle from a local Kmart store, despite his having, according to his testimony, consumed a fifth of whiskey and a whole case of beer during the day. The appeals court ruled that under such circumstances the store could be guilty of "negligent entrustment" of the gun.

A basic ground for suing a manufacturer is that the product has a defect or design flaw that makes it unreasonably hazardous. In the 1998 case of *Dix v. Beretta*, one teenager shot and killed another with a Beretta handgun. He had carefully replaced the loaded magazine with an empty one, not knowing that the gun held an additional round in the firing chamber. The plaintiff argued that this characteristic of the gun was a design flaw and that the gun did not have any indicator to warn that it was not empty. Beretta, however, noted that its guns did have a standard safety device that had to be disengaged before the gun could be fired. The jury refused to find Beretta liable for an industry-standard design. (Gun control advocates frequently note, however, that guns are subject to few of the safety regulations or standards that are applied to other products.)

Another legal approach is to argue that a product is inherently hazardous, despite not having a defective design. In *Addison v. Williams* the plaintiff claimed that manufacturing assault weapons was an "ultrahazardous activity" that was inherently and unreasonably dangerous and imposed an unacceptable cost on the community. But in this case and others courts have ruled that the ultrahazardous activity doctrine applies only to activities involving the use of land, such as having a leaky gas tank. The plaintiff had also charged that by being much more dangerous than ordinary handguns, assault weapons posed "an unreasonable risk of harm to the public." Pointing out that all guns are dangerous in various ways, the court in *Addison* declined that claim as well.

Kelley v. R.G. Industries dealt with a victim injured by a robber using a Saturday night special rather than an assault weapon. At first, the court started out in fashion similar to that in the *Addison* case. It dismissed the ultrahazardous activity complaint on the same grounds of it not being land related. It also dismissed the possibility that the gun was inherently defective in design. The court refused to extend strict liability to all handguns, despite agreeing that they contributed to a significant social problem. But the court then looked at the Maryland legislation concerning Saturday night specials and its characterization of the cheap, inaccurate, and poorly made guns as being of use only to criminals. The court also looked at evidence that the manufacturer was targeting poor, high-crime neighborhoods and held the company liable for the shooting injury.

Gun control advocates hail such legal efforts as an attempt to at long last hold an irresponsible industry accountable for the consequences of its marketing of dangerous products. They claim that the result will be safer guns and fewer crimes and accidents.

Gun rights advocates, however, see such efforts as an attempt to stretch reasonable concepts of liability into a form of "backdoor gun control," in effect obtaining through the courts what they could not obtain through political means. They argue that if such suits are widely successful, gun manufacturers may be forced out of business, or at least forced to market only expensive handguns, affordable only by the well-off and by criminals.

Thus, in a law journal article, Philip D. Oliver warns that

> *courts tempted to impose gun control through tort law should recognize that they are ill-suited to carry out carefully calibrated regulatory schemes, and that manifest injustice would result from imposing liability on suppliers who have done nothing that is not fully sanctioned by society . . .*[26]

The legislatures, however, may be catching up with the courts in promoting gun safety. In fall 1999, the California legislature enacted a bill that requires that all guns sold in California pass strict safety tests. However, critics (including some gun control supporters) suggest that the legislation is flawed and that it will create a large black market in used guns that can no longer be sold legally because private owners will have no way to have them tested. Meanwhile, large gun manufacturers who can afford to set up testing labs continued to sell all the guns they wanted, and police departments benefited from a loophole introduced at the last minute that exempted the Glock pistol, a very popular police weapon.

THE NEXT TOBACCO?

Gun makers soon faced an even more potent legal threat: the class-action suit. Starting in late 1998, more than 30 cities began the process of suing gun manufacturers. They argued that the guns are unsafe (lacking such safety devices as trigger locks), are negligently distributed (with no effective control to prevent guns from going into the criminal black market), and are deceptively marketed as well. If they succeed, the suits could cost the gun industry billions of dollars in claims for the medical, police, and other expenses caused by firearms injuries.

The precedent for the effort is the successful legal campaign against the tobacco industry that began in 1994. The result was a $250 billion settlement to be shared by 46 states. Gun control advocates and litigators point to similarities between the tobacco and gun industries. They argue that both industries market a product that is inherently unsafe, is advertised and marketed in a way that is deceptive, and targets vulnerable groups such as young people.

The gun industry and gun rights advocates believe the gun–tobacco analogy is flawed, however. They point out that the gun industry, unlike the tobacco industry, did not try to conceal the fact that its products could be dangerous. As noted earlier, they also argue that guns save many lives by stopping crime and that any accounting of the social costs of guns would have to be balanced against the benefits of security and successful defense. However, there is another difference between the tobacco and gun industries: The tobacco industry has much more money for fighting legal battles.

In the 1998 case *Hamilton v. Accu-Tek*, a Brooklyn jury found that 15 of the 25 gun makers sued by gun victims had some degree of negligence or liability, although only three had to pay actual damages. The jury reached their conclusion after reviewing evidence that the companies should have known that their marketing practices would lead to a disproportionate number of guns ending up in criminal hands in New York.

In April 2001, the New York Court of Appeals overturned the jury's verdict, ruling that because the guns were not defective, the manufacturer could not be sued for misuse of the product. The judges also noted that guns were heavily regulated, and that any further restrictions on the marketing should come from legislatures, not courts.

Fear of the costs of litigation prompted a major gun manufacturer, Smith & Wesson, to settle lawsuits by 17 different cities in March 2000 by agreeing to marketing restrictions and to including trigger locks with all guns. However, the agreement broke down in a dispute over whether dealers who carried Smith & Wesson firearms would also have to apply the restrictions to guns from other manufacturers. Meanwhile, gun activists had launched a boycott against the company, viewing it as a traitor to the cause.

One characteristic of the civil justice system is that it is decentralized: Different courts can and do come to different conclusions. In 2002, in the case of *Cincinnati v. Beretta* the Ohio State Supreme Court ruled that plaintiffs had adequately demonstrated that the availability of guns to criminals caused by negligent marketing represented a substantial danger to the community—a major public nuisance.

In California, though, a similar suit, *Merril v. Navegar,* was thrown out because the court found that a California law (later repealed) barred such suits. Indeed, the latest front in the legal war over guns has been opened by the gun industry and gun advocates, who have succeeded in passing laws in many states that bar suits over nondefective guns.

In early 2004, it looked like this movement would prevail at the federal level, which would have been a major blow to the legal offensive against the gun industry. A bill banning lawsuits against gun manufacturers for nondefective guns passed in the House and appeared to have the votes needed to pass in the Senate (and then be signed by President George W. Bush, who supported the legislation). However, Democrats, spurred on by gun control activists, attached amendments that would require background checks for all purchases at gun shows and that would require trigger locks on all new firearms—both were issues that seemed to have a considerable degree of bipartisan support. As a result, Republicans withdrew their support from the bill and it collapsed. Another focus of both law enforcement and civil litigation in recent years has been the use of "straw buyers" by criminals to get around gun laws. A straw buyer is someone who is legally qualified or permitted to buy a gun. After obtaining the gun (or, usually, several guns) the straw buyer then sells or transfers the guns to a criminal or juvenile who would not have been able to legally buy them from a dealer. Statistics suggest that only about 15 percent of gun dealers are involved with such straw purchases, but they provide a disproportionate number of guns used in crimes.

Lawsuits in California and other states in 2003 and 2004 have sought to show that dealers knew or should have known they were dealing with straw buyers, and that they were recklessly allowing guns to get into criminal hands. In August 2003, the California suit was settled when several major gun dealers and distributors agreed to have their workers trained in recognizing straw buyers. They also agreed to provide more information that would help law enforcement officials track down straw buyers. Another suit, in West Virginia, has resulted in a $1 million payment for the wounding of two New Jersey police officers by a gun obtained by a straw buyer.

GUN CONTROL AND TERRORISM

If the gun debate were not complicated enough, the "war on terrorism" since September 2001 has added a new dimension. Although the September 11 hijackers used no guns, about two months later the Brady Center to Prevent Handgun Violence issued a lengthy report titled "Guns and Terror: How Terrorists Exploit Our Weak Gun Laws." The report claimed that "for terrorists around the world, the United States is the great gun bazaar."[27] Indeed, it is true that the international black market in small arms and light weapons is a major source for the guns used in insurgencies, terrorism, and genocidal conflicts. However, although some terrorists apparently did enter the United States in order to take advantage of the availability of firearms and gun training, it seems doubtful that any plausible form of international gun control could really keep terrorists from obtaining and using weapons effectively.

Gun control groups also began to focus on so-called sniper rifles as another form of terrorist threat. The Washington, D.C.–area sniper shootings in October 2002 suggested the apparent ease by which an even moderately competent sniper using a car as a hunting blind could kill for some time before authorities can catch him or her. As a result, a ban on rifles such as the Bushmaster, used by now-convicted suspects Lee Boyd Malvo and John Muhammad, has been suggested.

Another target of concern for gun control advocates is heavy .50 caliber rifles, whose bullets can pierce light armored vehicles or puncture chemical storage tanks, perhaps causing a major fire or explosion. However, no such attacks have yet occurred, and it is uncertain whether single-shot heavy rifles would really be the choice of terrorists when weapons like car bombs are so easy to construct.

Gun rights activists were not slow to adapt their own agenda to the war on terrorism. Against the opposition of many in the G. W. Bush administration and in Congress, airline pilots were authorized to apply for licenses to carry firearms in the cockpit. Supporters of this proposal argued that arming the crew might well have stopped the hijackings that led to the mass casualties of September 11. Opponents, however, believe that firearms are too dangerous aboard a fragile aircraft and could distract pilots from their primary task of safely flying the plane. Despite the approval, as of early 2004 few pilots have undertaken the lengthy psychological testing and firearms training required before they can carry guns.

Gun rights advocates often argue that an armed citizenry would also provide a general defense against terrorism. They argue that no law enforcement or Homeland Security agency is able to guard all the vulnerable points in a huge nation like the United States. Properly qualified persons with concealed weapons permits, however, might be able to stop terrorists who might be seeking, for example, to set off bombs in a shopping mall. However, besides the concern that hysteria might lead to attacks on innocent people who someone thinks might be terrorists, there is the fact that even in Israel, where many citizens routinely carry firearms, numerous suicide bombings and other attacks have succeeded.

Besides the guns themselves, gun records also became the subject of confrontation. The U.S. attorney general, John Ashcroft, has refused to allow records from firearms background checks to be used by terrorism investigators. New York senator Charles Schumer (a prominent gun control advocate) has argued that "every day the FBI is barred from using this [background check] information, the investigatory trail grows colder."[28]

Ashcroft argues that the Brady Law did not permit such use, and that it would violate the privacy rights of gun owners. Many critics, though, have seen this concern for privacy to be hypocritical when the privacy of many other people (such as library users) seems to be threatened by actions under the USA PATRIOT Act.

THE FUTURE OF GUN CONTROL

By the middle of the first decade of the 21st century gun control has become a multifaceted but somewhat subdued issue. As long as Republicans control Congress, it is unlikely that major new gun control laws will pass, although there may be success with certain measures (such as eventually renewing the assault weapons ban or closing the gun show loophole) for which there is widespread and bipartisan support. On the other hand, the effort to shield the gun industry from legal liability may have stalled, at least for a time. Because of the continuing cost of defending or settling lawsuits, as well as market stagnation, the gun industry will continue to face tough times.

It is likely that gun control will be an issue in the 2004 presidential race between Democrat John Kerry and incumbent George W. Bush, but it is unlikely to be a major issue like the economy, Iraq, or the war on terrorism. This does not mean it will not be an important issue, however—in the expected close election, any issue able to motivate even a relatively small number of voters could be decisive. (Indeed, Kerry attacked Bush in September 2004 for allowing the assault weapons ban to lapse without making any real effort on its behalf.) Although not as much so as abortion or same-sex marriage, gun control is a cultural issue. The effects of such issues on political outcomes are always hard to predict.

There are two sorts of compromises that might eventually emerge in the battle over gun control. One, a pragmatic compromise, may already be in evidence. Many people on both sides of the issue would be willing to live with the current gun laws plus perhaps some enhancements to gun safety such as more comprehensive background checks and requirements for gun locks and safe gun storage.

A second type of compromise might be possible if the Supreme Court agrees that the Second Amendment conveys an individual right to keep and bear arms. Under such a scenario, the Court would likely go on to say that this right is not absolute, but is subject to certain restrictions, such as safety and training requirements. It would then depend on whether the standard of scrutiny for such restrictions were set high enough that gun owners would feel their rights would be protected by the courts. If so, it is possible that registration, licensing, and gun training requirements would be accepted as reasonable and not leading to gun confiscation.

---

[1] In the interest of even-handedness, the author has adopted the term *gun control advocates* to refer to those seeking to maintain or to increase restrictions on

firearms or their use, and *gun rights advocates* to refer to those seeking to preserve or increase rights involving firearms or their use.

[2] Quoted from "Licensing and Registration: Frequently Asked Questions." Brady Campaign to Prevent Gun Violence. Available online. URL: http://www.bradycampaign.org/facts/faqs/?page=licreg. Posted in June 2002.

[3] Quoted from National Rifle Association Institute for Legislative Action. "Fact Sheet: Firearm Safety in America 2003." Available online. URL: http://www.nraila.org/Issues/FactSheets/Read.aspx?ID=120. Posted on September 8, 2003.

[4] Philip Cook, quoted in David Phinney, et al. "Gun Fight: Seeking a Cease-Fire." ABC News online. Available online. URL: http://abcnewsgo.com/sections/us/DailyNews/guns_damage.html. Posted on June 8, 1999.

[5] Appendix A summarizes statistics relating to many of these questions.

[6] W. Marina, "Weapons, Technology and Legitimacy," in D. B. Kates, *Firearms and Violence*. Pacific Institute for Public Policy Research, San Francisco, 1984, p. 429.

[7] Aristotle, quoted in Kurschke, p. 60.

[8] King Charles I of England, quoted in David Hardy, *Origins and Development of the Second Amendment*. Chino Valley, Ariz.: Blacksmith, 1986, p. 25.

[9] Bill of Rights of 1689, William III and Mary, sess. 2, chapter 2.

[10] Andrew Fletcher, quoted in Stephen P. Halbrook, *That Every Man Be Armed: The Evolution of a Constitutional Right*. San Francisco, Calif.: Liberty Tree Press, 1984, p. 47.

[11] Daniel Boorstin, *The Americans: The Colonial Experience*. New York: Random House, 1965, p. 365.

[12] Virginia statute, quoted in Stephen P. Halbrook, *That Every Man Be Armed*, p. 56.

[13] William Knox, quoted in Benedict D. LaRosa. "Gun Control: A Historical Perspective," in Jacob Hornberger and Richard M. Ebeling, *The Tyranny of Gun Control*. Fairfax, Va.: Future of Freedom Foundation, 1997, p. 49.

[14] James Madison, *Federalist*, No. 46, quoted in Marjolijn Bijlefeld. *The Gun Control Debate*. Westport, Conn.: Greenwood Press, 1997, p. 5.

[15] See Chapter 2 for several cases involving the interpretation of state constitutions.

[16] Richard Hofstadter, "Reflections on American Violence in the United States," in Hofstadter and Wallace, *American Violence*, p. 22.

[17] Albion Tourgeé, quoted in David Kopel, *The Samurai, the Mountie, and the Cowboy*. Buffalo, N.Y.: Prometheus Books, 1992, p. 333.

[18] Clayton E. Cramer. "The Racist Roots of Gun Control." Available online. URL: http://www.magi.com/~freddo/racist.html. Posted in 1993.

[19] Roy G. Weatherup. "Standing Armies and Armed Citizens: An Historical Analysis of the Second Amendment." *Hastings Constitutional Law Quarterly 2* (Fall 1975), pp. 1000–1001.

[20] Sanford Levinson. "The Embarrassing Second Amendment." *Yale Law Journal 99* (1989), p. 637–659.

[21] See the bibliographies in Chapter 7 for summaries of these and other significant gun-related studies.

[22] Tamara L. Roleff, editor. *Gun Control: Opposing Viewpoints*. San Diego, Calif.: Greenhaven Press, 1997, p. 13.

[23] Suzanna Gratia, quoted in Tamara L. Roleff, editor. *Gun Control: Opposing Viewpoints*, p. 13.

[24] See The bibliographies in Chapter 7 for representative studies and critiques.

[25] John Lott, quoted in "An Interview with John Lott, Jr." University of Chicago Press. Available online. URL: http://www.press.uchicago.edu/Misc/Chicago/493636.html. Posted in 1998.

[26] Philip D. Oliver, "Rejecting the 'Whipping-Boy' Approach to Tort Law," *University of Arkansas at Little Rock Law Journal* 14 (1991), n.p.

[27] Quoted in Sam MacDonald, "An Antigun Firefight." *Insight On the News*, vol. 18, April 22, 2002, p. 12ff.

[28] Charles Schumer, quoted in Sam MacDonald, "Gun Control's New Language: How Anti-Terror Rhetoric Is Being Used Against the Second Amendment." *Reason*, vol. 33, March 2002, p. 16ff.

CHAPTER 2

THE LAW OF GUN CONTROL

Firearms are primarily regulated by the states, along with several important federal laws. In general, the existence of a law at a higher jurisdiction (state or federal) is not a bar to more restrictive legislation at a lower level (city or state). Therefore determining the firearms laws in force in a given locale requires study of federal, state, and county or municipal laws.

The following discussion groups firearms laws by topic. Under each topic, any relevant federal laws are given first, followed by a list of states that have legislated in that area.

For a summary of features of state gun laws as of the time of this writing, see Appendix B. For the latest information about new or pending state or federal legislation, see the web sites described in Chapter 6. Note that as of late 2004 Congress had not renewed the assault weapons ban nor agreed on legislation mandating the use of trigger locks or requiring instant background checks for purchasers at gun shows. Finally, note that state and local laws change frequently. The following material is useful for showing the extent that various types of gun laws are in force, but readers with specific legal questions should check with state or local authorities or attorneys with expertise in this area.

BANS ON SPECIFIC WEAPONS AND OTHER ITEMS

AUTOMATIC WEAPONS/MACHINE GUNS

The National Firearms Act of 1934 (P.L. No. 73–474) placed high taxes on the manufacturers, sellers, and purchasers of automatic weapons (machine guns). Fully automatic weapons made after May 19, 1986, are now banned; earlier ones can be sold by federally licensed Class III firearm dealers on payment of tax and after passing a background check.

SEMIAUTOMATIC WEAPONS/ASSAULT WEAPONS

The Assault Weapons Ban in the 1994 Omnibus Crime Bill prohibited the following specific weapons: Norinco; Mitchell and Poly Technologies Automat Kalashnikovs (i.e., AK-47 type guns; all models); Action Arms Israeli Military Industries UZI and Galil; Beretta Ar70 (SC-70); Colt AR-15; Fabrique National FN/FAL, FN/LAR, and FNC; SWD M-10, M-11, M-11/9, and M-12; Steyr AUG INTRATEC TEC-9, TEC-DC0, and TEC-22; revolving cylinder shotguns, such as (or similar to) the Street Sweeper; and Striker 12.

In addition, the law banned all semiautomatic weapons that are equipped with a detachable magazine and two or more of the following: bayonet lug, flash suppressor, protruding pistol grip, folding stock, or threaded muzzle. Magazines that hold more than 10 rounds are also prohibited. Weapons and magazines manufactured before September 13, 1994, however, are exempt.

The following states ban all or some types of assault weapons: California, Connecticut and New Jersey, as well as some jurisdictions in New York and Ohio. (Hawaii bans "assault pistols.") A number of cities have their own assault weapons bans. These include: Albany, New York; Atlanta, Georgia; Berkeley, California; Cleveland, Ohio; Columbus, Ohio; Denver, Colorado (ban on sale); Los Angeles, California; and New York City.

SHORT-BARRELED ("SAWED-OFF") WEAPONS

The National Firearms Act of 1934 placed high taxes on the manufacturers, sellers, and purchasers of short-barreled guns such as sawed-off shotguns and carbines.

SATURDAY NIGHT SPECIALS

The federal Gun Control Act of 1968 banned the import of guns "not generally recognized as particularly suitable for, or readily adaptable to sporting purposes." This has been interpreted as a ban on inexpensive handguns known as Saturday night specials, as well as certain types of semiautomatic shotguns (Street Sweepers) and some assault weapons. A number of cities such as Los Angeles, San Francisco, and Denver have also banned Saturday night specials.

HARD-TO-DETECT GUNS

The federal Undetectable Firearms Act of 1988 (P.L. 100–649) bans the manufacture, import, or sale of guns that cannot be detected by metal detectors or airport screening equipment (such as guns made mostly of plastic).

HANDGUNS (GENERAL)

Court decisions (such as *Quilici v. Morton Grove*) have generally held that cities or other jurisdictions are free to ban all handguns if they wish, though few have done so. In 1981, Morton Grove, Illinois, became the first town to do so in modern times. Washington, D.C.; Chicago; and a number of towns in Illinois also ban handguns.

REGULATED ACCESSORIES AND AMMUNITION

Under federal law, silencers are treated in the same category as automatic weapons. Armor-piercing ammunition (popularly called cop-killer bullets) were banned in 1986, with an expanded definition of banned bullets in the Violent Crime Control and Law Enforcement Act of 1994 that includes bullets made of tungsten, beryllium, depleted uranium, and other exotic materials. Other accessories can also cause a weapon to be banned (see Assault Weapons above).

RESTRICTIONS ON GUN OWNERSHIP

BASIC REQUIREMENTS

Age

Under federal law (18 U.S.C. §922(b)(1)), federally licensed firearm dealers cannot sell a handgun to a person under 21 years of age or a long gun (rifle or shotgun) to anyone under 18 years of age. Persons under 18 years of age are also prohibited from possessing a handgun (18 U.S.C. § 22(x)). The following states prohibit all sales (including private sales) of guns to persons under 21: Connecticut, Georgia, Hawaii, Iowa, Maryland, Missouri, Nebraska, Ohio, Rhode Island, and South Carolina.

Residence

An individual cannot "transfer, sell, deliver or transport" a gun to a resident of another state. Mail-order gun sales between states are prohibited. (There are some exceptions, such as for guns that have been inherited and antique firearms.)

Background

Under the Brady Act, all purchasers of guns must first pass a background check before buying. (For more details on this check, see Buying and Selling Firearms below.) Guns cannot be sold to any person who

- has been convicted of a crime with a sentence of a year or more (except for state misdemeanors with a sentence of two years or less).
- has a court restraining order based on violent activity (such as for harassment, spousal abuse, or stalking).
- has been convicted of domestic abuse.
- has been arrested for selling or using drugs.
- is a fugitive from justice.
- has been certified as mentally unstable or is in a mental institution.
- is an illegal alien or has renounced his or her U.S. citizenship.

LICENSES AND PERMITS

The following states require licenses or permits for buying a handgun: Connecticut, Hawaii, Illinois, Iowa, Kansas (in some areas), Massachusetts, Michigan, Minnesota, Missouri, Nebraska, New Jersey, New York, North Carolina, and Ohio (in some areas). Hawaii, Illinois, Massachusetts, Minnesota and New Jersey also require a permit for buying a long gun (the term used for long-barreled guns such as a rifle or a shotgun). The District of Columbia does not allow ownership of handguns.

REGISTRATION

Registration involves completing a form for the gun itself, in addition to holding the necessary license or permit. California, Hawaii, Kansas (in some areas), Michigan, Nevada (in some areas), New York, and Ohio (in some areas) require registration.

BUYING AND SELLING FIREARMS

BACKGROUND CHECK AND WAITING PERIOD

Two closely related firearms provisions are for a background check (to confirm that a prospective gun purchaser does not have a criminal, mental health, or other record that would make him or her ineligible to buy a gun) and for a waiting period, or the minimum time before a gun can be handed over to the purchaser.

Starting February 28, 1994, the Brady Handgun Violence Prevention Law (the Brady Act) required a five-day waiting period for all handguns purchased from dealers (but not private sales). This resulted in waiting periods being enforced in 32 states that did not previously have them. The federal waiting period requirement expired in November 30, 1998, and has been replaced by the National Instant Check System (NICS), which gives dealers the ability to confirm instantly a purchaser's eligibility to buy a firearm. (In cases where there are problems with confirmation, the purchase can be delayed up to five days.)

Although the federal waiting period has expired, states are still free to impose their own waiting periods. The following states have waiting periods, ranging from a few days to several months: California, Connecticut, Florida, Hawaii, Illinois, Kansas (in some areas), Maryland, Massachusetts, Minnesota, Missouri, Nevada (some areas), New York, Ohio (in some areas), Rhode Island, South Dakota, Virginia (in some areas), Washington, and Wisconsin.

LICENSING OF MANUFACTURERS

The Gun Control Act of 1968 requires that firearms and ammunition manufacturers obtain a federal license and pay a fee of $50 per year for firearms manufacturers and $10 per year for ammunition makers unless the manufacturer makes "destructive devices" or "armor-piercing ammunition," in which case the fee is $1,000 per year.

LICENSING OF DEALERS

The Federal Firearms Act of 1938 (P. L. No. 75–785) required that all dealers who buy or sell weapons across state lines hold a Federal Firearms License (FFL). The Gun Control Act of 1968 (P. L. No. 90–618) superseded the 1938 law. It increased license fees and prohibited most sales of firearms or ammunition across state lines. All gun dealers now had to be licensed and had to record all sales of firearms or ammunition so that they could be traced by police. Maximum penalties were raised to $5,000 and imprisonment for five years.

The Firearms Owners Protection Act of 1986 liberalized some of these requirements. Long guns (rifles and shotguns), but not handguns, could be sold across state lines. Guns and ammunition could be purchased through the mail subject to various restrictions. Gun dealers could sell firearms in a place other than a store (such as a flea market or a gun show). Record-keeping requirements were reduced.

The Violent Crime Control and Law Enforcement Act of 1994 made further changes to the system. License holders are now photographed and fingerprinted and are required to comply with applicable state and local laws. Dealers must report any thefts of weapons within 48 hours and must immediately respond to the federal Bureau of Alcohol, Tobacco, and Firearms requests for firearm traces.

FIREARMS IMPORTS

A number of laws regulate the importing of firearms. The Mutual Security Act of 1954 (P.L. No. 83–665) led to the establishment of import controls under the Office of Munitions Control of the Department of State. The Omnibus Crime Control and Safe Streets Act of 1968 (P.L. No. 90–351) together with the Gun Control Act of 1968 banned the import of Saturday night specials and restricted imports of automatic weapons. Further restrictions on semiautomatic assault weapons were added by the Omnibus Violent Crime Control and Prevention Act of 1994 (P.L. No. 103–322).

GUN SHOWS, PAWN SHOPS, AND PRIVATE SALES

As noted in the above sections, some federal laws apply also to private sales, but sales other than those by licensed dealers have generally been regulated (if at all) by state or local jurisdictions. As of 2003, 18 states have enacted legislation requiring background checks before purchasing guns at gun shows. However, proposals that were pending in Congress in 2004 (and likely to eventually pass in some form) would require that all purchasers at gun shows (or persons seeking to redeem firearms left at pawn shops) undergo instant background checks. Other proposals would require that all private gun sales be conducted through a licensed dealer and would ban sales of guns or ammunition via the Internet.

"ONE GUN A MONTH"

Maryland, South Carolina, and Virginia have passed laws limiting purchases to one gun per month. The city of Los Angeles also has such a law.

STORAGE AND CARRYING OF FIREARMS

CONCEALED CARRY

The following states prohibit the carrying of concealed weapons: Illinois, Kansas, Missouri, Nebraska, Ohio, and Wisconsin.

The following states "may issue" a concealed weapons permit (this is usually at the discretion of police officials; permits are often hard to obtain): Alabama, California, Delaware, Hawaii, Iowa, Maryland, Massachusetts, New Jersey, New York, Rhode Island, and South Carolina.

The following states "shall issue" a concealed weapons permit to anyone who meets basic objective requirements (such as lack of a felony or mental health record): Alaska, Arizona, Arkansas, Colorado, Connecticut, Florida, Georgia, Idaho, Indiana, Kentucky, Louisiana, Maine, Michigan, Minnesota, Mississippi, Missouri, Montana, Nevada, New Hampshire, North Carolina, North Dakota, Ohio, Oklahoma, Oregon, Pennsylvania, South Carolina, South Dakota, Tennessee, Texas, Utah, Virginia, Washington, West Virginia, and Wyoming. (The Brady Campaign notes that Colorado, while having a "shall issue" law, in practice exercises discretion by law enforcement and issues very few permits.) In recent years gun rights groups have had some success in states such as Missouri passing laws that alter wording on concealed-carry permits from "may issue" to "shall issue."

One state, Vermont, requires no permit at all for carrying a concealed weapon.

The following states require some training or experience with firearms use to receive a concealed-carry permit: Alaska, Arizona, Arkansas, Connecticut, Florida, Kentucky, Montana, North Carolina, Oklahoma, Oregon, South Carolina, Texas, West Virginia, and Wyoming. In practice, this can range from completing a fairly rigorous approved course to performing a vaguely defined "demonstration of competence" to a local sheriff.

SAFE STORAGE AND CHILD ACCESS

Legislation proposed in Congress in recent years would require that trigger locks be offered with all new handguns sold.

A number of states have enacted laws that include some or all of the following features:

- penalties for allowing a child access to a gun (in some cases, penalties do not apply if the gun is in locked storage or is obtained through a break-in),
- a requirement that dealers offer a trigger lock for sale with each handgun, and/or
- a requirement that guns be kept in locked storage or are fitted with a locking device that prevents unauthorized operation.

States with such laws are Connecticut, Delaware, Florida, Hawaii, Maryland, Massachusetts, Minnesota, Nevada, New Jersey, North Carolina, Rhode Island, Texas, Virginia, and Wisconsin. In 2003 Maryland became the first state to require that all new handguns sold include internal trigger locking mechanisms. New Jersey has passed a law requiring "smart gun" technology that allows guns to be fired only by authorized users, but the law will not actually take effect until availability of appropriate technology has been certified.

GUNS IN PUBLIC BUILDINGS (SCHOOLS, ETC.)

The Gun-Free Schools Zones Act (part of the Crime Control Act of 1990) made it illegal for anyone (other than a police officer or security guard) to have a firearm in a school zone, or to carry unloaded firearms (unless in a locked container) within 1,000 feet of school grounds. The Supreme Court overturned this law in 1995 in *U.S. v. Lopez* (see Representative Court Cases).

Oklahoma, Texas, and Utah ban the carrying of guns into schools or other public buildings, bars, sporting events, or private businesses that post "No Guns Allowed" signs. Most, if not all, school districts have rules banning guns and other weapons.

REPRESENTATIVE COURT CASES

There have been a wider variety of cases at all levels dealing with the regulation of firearms and, more recently, with civil liability of firearm manufacturers or dealers. However, because there are so many constitutional and civil issues involved in gun control litigation, the following list breaks down the decisions by topic. (Note that some cases involve more than one topic.) Cases under each topic are listed in chronological order.

TOPICAL GUIDE TO COURT CASES

Assault weapons and machine guns: *Sonzinsky v. United States; Addison v. Williams; Arnold v. Cleveland; Cincinnati v. Langan; Benjamin v. Bailey; Springfield Armory v. City of Columbus; Coalition of New Jersey Sportsmen v. Whitman*

Attainder argument: *Springfield Armory v. City of Columbus; Benjamin v. Bailey*

Commerce Clause in the U.S. Constitution: *Cases v. U.S.; U.S. v. Lopez*

Concealed weapons: *Bliss v. Commonwealth; Aymette v. State; Nunn v. State; In re Brickey*

Equal protection of the laws: *Cases v. U.S.; Cincinnati v. Langan; Benjamin v. Bailey*

Ex post facto laws: *Cases v. U.S.*

Federal Gun Control Legislation: (divided in subsections per law)

Brady Bill: *Printz v. U.S.*
Federal Firearm Act of 1938: *Cases v. U.S.*
National Firearms Act of 1934: *Sonzinsky v. United States; United States v. Miller*
Gun Control Act of 1968: *U.S. v. Warin*
Gun Free School Zones Act: *U.S. v. Lopez*
Omnibus Violent Crime Control and Prevention Act of 1994: *U.S. v. Emerson*
Federalism: *Printz v. U.S.*
"Grandfather" provision in laws: *Cincinnati v. Langan*
Handgun ban: *Nunn v. State; Andrews v. State; In re Brickey; State v. Rosenthal; Quilici v. Morton Grove; California Rifle and Pistol Association v. City of West Hollywood*
Handgun permit: *Application of Atkinson; Schubert v. DeBard*
Intoxication and weapons use: *City of Salina v. Blaksley; Kitchen v. K-Mart*
Liability (civil): (divided into subsections)
　　Gun manufacturer: *Kelley v. R.G. Industries, Inc.; Perkins v. F.I.F. Corp.; Dix v. Beretta; Hamilton v. Accu-Tek; City of Cincinnati v. Beretta USA Corporation*
　　Impact on minorities: *National Association for the Advancement of Colored People v. AccuSport et al.*
　　Negligent entrustment: *Kitchen v. K-Mart*
　　Retailer: *Kitchen v. K-Mart*
　　"Unreasonably dangerous" or "ultrahazardous" products doctrine: *Kelley v. R.G. Industries, Inc.; Perkins v. F.I.E. Corp.; Addison v. Williams*
Militia and military weapons: *Andrews v. State; Presser v. Illinois; City of Salina v. Blaksley; United States v. Miller; Cases v. U.S; U.S. v. Warin*
Ninth Amendment: *Quilici v. Morton Grove*
"Right to Bear Arms" in state constitutions: *Bliss v. Commonwealth; Aymette v. State; Nunn v. State; Andrews v. State; In re Brickey; City of Salina v. Blaksley; Arnold v. Cleveland; Benjamin v. Bailey; Schubert v. DeBard; Quilici v. Morton Grove*
Saturday Night Specials: *Kelley v. R.G. Industries, Inc.; California Rifle and Pistol Association v. City of West Hollywood*
Second Amendment:
　　Applied to states: *Andrews v. State; United States v. Cruikshank; Presser v. Illinois; In re Brickey; Quilici v. Morton Grove*
　　Applied to federal government: *United States v. Miller; Cases v. U.S.; U.S. v. Warin*

Gun Control

Supremacy and Preemption:
State over local: *State v. Rosenthal; Quilici v. Morton Grove; California Rifle and Pistol Association v. City of West Hollywood*
Federal over state/local: *Presser v. Illinois; Arnold v. Cleveland; Quilici v. Morton Grove; Printz v. U.S.*
Taxation on firearms: *Sonzinsky v. United States*
Tenth Amendment: *Printz v. U.S.*
Travel and weapons use: *Application of Atkinson*
Vagueness argument: *Cincinnati v. Langan; Springfield Armory v. City of Columbus; Benjamin v. Bailey*
Welfare Clause in the U.S. Constitution: *Sonzinsky v. United States*

BLISS V. COMMONWEALTH, 2 LITTELL 90 (KENTUCKY, 1822)

Background

The defendant (Bliss) was convicted of violating a Kentucky law that stated "any person in this commonwealth, who shall hereafter wear a pocket pistol, dirk, large knife, or sword in a cane, concealed as a weapon, unless when traveling on a journey, shall be fined in any sum not less than $100 . . ."

Legal Issues

The defendant argued that by forbidding his sword-cane, the statute violated the state constitution, which provided "that the right of the citizens to bear arms in defense of themselves and the state, shall not be questioned." The State argued that it agreed that there was a constitutionally protected right to bear arms, but that the means of doing so could be regulated, including by regulating the carrying of concealed weapons.

Decision

The court suggested that the constitutional provision is "as well calculated to secure to the citizens the right to bear arms in defense of themselves and the state, as any that could have been adopted by the makers of the constitution." The court noted that later in the Constitution "it is expressly declared, 'that every thing in that article is excepted out of the general powers of government, and shall forever remain inviolate; and that all laws contrary thereto, or contrary to the constitution, shall be void.'"

The court declared, ". . . to be in conflict with the constitution, it is not essential that the act should contain a prohibition against bearing arms in every possible form; it is the right to bear arms in defense of the citizens and the state, that is secured by the constitution, and whatever restraint [of] the full and complete exercise of that right, though not an entire destruction of it, is forbidden by the explicit language of the constitution." The statute was therefore declared unconstitutional.

Impact

Although not involving a firearm, this is one of the earliest state decisions relating to weapon laws and the most absolute in its insistence on a totally unfettered right to bear arms. Its precedent is not followed in most subsequent decisions, which find at least some arms regulations (such as the prohibition of concealed weapons) to be compatible with the constitutional right to bear arms.

AYMETTE V. STATE, 2 HUMPHREYS 154 (TENNESSEE, 1840)

Background

William Aymette was convicted of carrying a concealed bowie knife, in violation of a state law providing that "if any person shall wear any bowie knife, or Arkansas tooth-pick [a type of bowie knife], or other knife or weapon, that shall in form, shape, or size resemble a bowie knife or Arkansas tooth-pick, under his clothes, or keep the same concealed about his person, such person shall be guilty of a misdemeanor." He appealed the conviction.

Legal Issues

Aymette argued that a ban on such weapons is a violation of the provision of the Tennessee constitution "that the free white men of this state have a right to keep and bear arms for their common defense." He claimed that the decision of what weapons to carry and how to carry them is an individual one, beyond the power of the legislature to regulate.

Decision

The appeals court pointedly rejected the absolute right declared in *Bliss v. Commonwealth* above. It examined the history of the right to bear arms in English law because the framers of the state legislation had used that tradition. It noted, for example, that an act passed by Parliament during the reign of Charles II had declared that the people may have arms "suitable to their condition and as allowed by law," which implied a regulatory power. Further, the right to bear arms in English law was tied to a *common* defense of the people (against tyranny or disorder). The court concluded, "The legislature, therefore, have a right to prohibit the wearing or keeping weapons dangerous to the peace and safety of the citizens, and which are not usual in civilized warfare, or would not contribute to the common defense." Aymette's conviction was thus upheld.

Impact

Although it involves a knife rather than a gun, this case illustrates two continuing themes that will be applied to firearm regulation: (1) the question of whether the right to bear arms is collective or individual, and (2) the application of the "police power" of the state to the types of weapons people may have and the manner in which they may be carried. This case cast an early vote for the "collective" position and upheld the state's police power.

NUNN V. STATE, 1 KELLY 243 (GEORGIA, 1846)

Background

Hawkins H. Nunn was indicted and convicted "for having and keeping about his person, and elsewhere, a pistol, the same not being such a pistol as is known and used as a horseman's pistol, under an act of the General Assembly of the State of Georgia, entitled 'An Act to guard and protect the citizens of this State against the unwarrantable and too prevalent use of deadly weapons.'" (The law, an early example of strict gun control, also banned the sale of a variety of weapons, including bowie knives and concealable pistols. The "horseman's pistol" is a larger, hard-to-conceal weapon, usually kept in a saddle holster.) Nunn's appeal reached the Georgia Supreme Court.

Legal Issues

Nunn challenged his conviction on several grounds, some of which related to the indictment process and are not relevant here. He asserted that the law under which he was convicted violated both the U.S. Constitution and the Constitution of the State of Georgia by infringing the right to keep and bear arms for self-defense.

Decision

The court first observed that the statute in question was badly written and vague. As for the plaintiff, "It is not pretended that he carried his weapon secretly, but it is charged as a crime, that he had and kept it about his person, and elsewhere. And this presents for our decision the broad question, is it competent for the legislature to deny to one of its citizens this privilege? We think not."

After reviewing similar cases in other states, the court ruled that "so far as the act of 1837 seeks to suppress the practice of carrying certain weapons secretly, that it is valid, inasmuch as it does not deprive the citizen of his natural right of self-defence, or of his constitutional right to keep and bear arms. But that so much of it, as contains a prohibition against bearing arms openly is in conflict with the Constitution, and void . . ."

Impact

This decision suggests that the state and federal constitutions convey an individual, not merely a collective, right to keep and bear arms for their defense. The state or a local jurisdiction can use its police power to ban the carrying of concealed arms as dangerous to the community or can make other regulations, so long as they do not destroy the efficacy of the right to self-defense and they still permit the effective exercise of constitutional rights.

ANDREWS V. STATE, 50 TENN. 165 (TENNESSEE, 1871)

Background

The case of James Andrews was combined with several other cases for appeal purposes. Altogether, the cases involved the violation of a Tennessee law prohibiting "any person to publicly or privately carry a dirk, swordcane, Spanish stiletto, belt or pocket pistol or revolver."

Legal Issues

The appellants argued that the weapons laws violated both the Second Amendment to the U.S. Constitution and the Tennessee Constitution. They noted that in the *Aymette* case the court ruled that the knife could be banned because it was not a weapon of war that would be protected by the constitution's interest in promoting the common defense. A pistol, they argued, was a weapon that could be used in war, and the state could not make a regulation that amounted to a prohibition of such a weapon.

The State argued that the Second Amendment did not apply to the states. Further, even "if [the State] can not prohibit carrying arms, they may, by regulation, determine what arms may be carried, what shall be proscribed; may declare where they may be carried, and when they may be carried, as well as declare the mode. If weapons of warfare are protected by the

Constitution, still they are subject, by the exception, to regulation in respect to times, places and modes."

Thus according to the State, even if a pistol were considered a military weapon, the allowable conditions for carrying it could be specified by regulation.

Decision

The court reiterated the collective nature of the right to bear arms for defense as found in English law, asserting "It was this great political right that our fathers aimed to protect; not the claims of the assassin and the cutthroat to carry the implements of his trade. They would as soon have protected the burglar's jimmy and skeleton key." They also noted that English precedent did not object to specifying allowable weapons according to the class or condition of the person.

The Second Amendment argument was disposed of quickly by declaring that the amendment restrained only Congress and had no application to the states. (This indeed was the generally accepted view about all provisions of the Bill of Rights until the 20th century when the process of incorporating some rights into the Fourteenth Amendment and applying them against the states gradually took hold.)

The court noted that the Tennessee Constitution specified "That the citizens of this State have a right to keep and bear arms for their common defense. But the Legislature shall have power by law, to regulate the wearing of arms, with a view to prevent crime." In interpreting this, the court focused on the language about "common defense" and the importance of the militia expressed elsewhere in the state constitution. In this context the constitution protects "the usual arms of the citizens of the country, and the use of which will properly train and render him efficient in defense of his own liberties, as well as of the State. Under this head, with a knowledge of the habits of our people, and of the arms in the use of which a soldier should be trained, we would hold, that the rifle of all descriptions, the shot gun, the musket, and repeater, are such arms; and that under the Constitution the right to keep such arms, can not be infringed or forbidden by the Legislature."

However, the court noted that constitutional reference to the prevention of crime meant that "a man may well be prohibited from carrying his arms to church, or other public assemblage, as the carrying them to such places is not an appropriate use of them, nor necessary in order to his familiarity with them, and his training and efficiency in their use. As to arms worn, or which are carried about the person, not being such arms as we have indicated as arms that may be kept and used, the wearing of such arms may be prohibited if the Legislature deems proper, absolutely, at all times, and under all circumstances."

The court left it to a factual examination to determine whether a revolver might be considered a military weapon whose carrying was protected by the constitution (although the manner of carrying could still be regulated in any case).

Impact

This decision continues in the tradition of the keeping of arms being an individual right, but one exercised in the context of promoting a collective defense (the well-trained militia). The state's police power can prohibit weapons that are not suitable or customary for this purpose. The keeping of military weapons cannot be banned, but the manner of bearing them can be regulated.

UNITED STATES V. CRUIKSHANK, 92 U.S. 542 (1876)

Background

The background in this case is somewhat unclear, but it seems to have arisen from the killing of two African Americans by a group of Ku Klux Klan members in Louisiana. They were charged with banding together "unlawfully and feloniously . . . to injure, oppress, threaten, and intimidate," which was in violation of a federal civil rights statute called the Enforcement Act. The act was part of the apparatus set up during the Reconstruction period in an attempt to protect the rights of blacks in the South.

The indictment goes on to charge the defendants with trying to "hinder and prevent in their respective free exercise and enjoyment of their lawful right and privilege to peaceably assemble with each other and with other citizens of the said United States for a peaceable and lawful purpose." The second count charges them with hindering the black citizens in their exercise of their "right to keep and bear arms for a lawful purpose." (To note in passing, laws that prevented blacks from carrying weapons, either directly or indirectly—such as by banning the cheaper weapons that they could afford—were a common part of the strategy for regaining white control in the South in the latter part of the 19th century.) Other counts involved interference with other rights, such as the right to vote. The defendants (including one William Cruikshank) were convicted and appealed. The Supreme Court agreed to hear their appeal directly.

Legal Issues

The relevant and underlying issue is whether the federal government has the right to prohibit citizens in the states from violating basic constitutional rights such as the freedom of assembly (First Amendment) or the right to keep and bear arms (Second Amendment). In other words, does the specification of rights in the U.S. Constitution restrain only the federal government and its agents, or does it also restrain state and local governments or the actions of private citizens?

Decision

The Court declared that as with the right of assembly in the First Amendment, the right to bear arms for a peaceful purpose as specified in the Second Amendment "is not a right granted by the Constitution. Neither is it in any manner dependent upon that instrument for its existence. The Second Amendment declares that it shall not be infringed; but this, as has been seen, means no more than that it shall not be infringed by Congress." The Second Amendment therefore cannot be used as the basis for a law enforced against the states or individual citizens. The Court overturned the other counts of the indictment on various grounds (including vagueness), and the defendants were ordered released.

Impact

This decision is rather confusing. Some gun control advocates say that it means that the right to bear arms is not protected at all by the Second Amendment. Gun rights advocates, however, say that it is simply a statement of the basic doctrine that the Constitution does not create rights but declares or affirms rights arising out of the common or natural law.

What is undisputed is that the Supreme Court decided that the Second Amendment, whatever sort of right it declared, was a restraint only on Congress, not on the states, localities, or citizens. As noted earlier, many parts of the Bill of Rights would later be "incorporated" into the Fourteenth Amendment and enforced against the states (notably, to protect the civil rights of African Americans and other minorities), but to date the Second Amendment has not been included in this process.

PRESSER V. ILLINOIS, 116 U.S. 252 (1886)

Background

The military code of the state of Illinois specifies: "It shall not be lawful for any body of men whatever, other than the regular organized volunteer militia of this State, and the troops of the United States, to associate themselves together as a military company or organization, or to drill or parade with arms in any city, or town, of this State, without the license of the Governor thereof . . ."

Herman Presser was indicted for violating this statute as part of a German-American social and military society called the Lehr und Wehr Verein ("Education and Defense Society"). The group was incorporated under Illinois law with the stated purpose "of improving the mental and bodily condition of its members so as to qualify them for the duties of citizens of a republic." In December 1879, the group, led by Presser, engaged in a march and drill, armed with rifles, without the required license from the governor.

Legal Issues

Presser argued that the Second Amendment gave him and his group the right to bear arms in keeping with its goal of maintaining a well-trained militia. He said that the state cannot restrict that right to the official, organized militia (the Illinois National Guard) because under Article I, Section 8 of the U.S. Constitution, only Congress has the power "To provide for organizing, arming, and disciplining the militia, and for governing such part of them as may be employed in the service of the United States, reserving to the States, respectively, the appointment of the officers, and the authority of training the militia, according to the discipline prescribed by Congress . . ."

The State made the usual argument that the Second Amendment was not applicable to the states. It also argued that the prohibition of private militias was not in conflict with the power of Congress to oversee the organization of state militias.

Decision

The Court sided with the State's argument. There is no constitutionally protected right to march as part of a private armed militia. The Second Amendment does not apply to the states.

Impact

This decision gained some recent relevance with the formation of many private militias in the 1980s. Gun control advocates see *Presser* as denying any constitutional protection to such organizations, as well as reaffirming that the Second Amendment is not a bar to state or local gun regulations.

Gun rights advocates, however, point to the following part of the decision as affirming that the right to bear arms usable in connection with the official militia is an individual right that cannot be infringed: "It is undoubtedly true that all citizens capable of bearing arms constitute the reserved military force or reserve militia of the United States as well as of the States, and in view of this prerogative of the general government, as well as of its general powers, the States cannot, even laying the constitutional provision in question out of view, prohibit the people from keeping and bearing arms, so as to deprive the United States of their rightful resource for maintaining the public security, and disable the people from performing their duty to the general government."

IN RE *BRICKEY,* 8 IDAHO 597 (1902)

Background

The Territory (not yet a state) of Idaho had a law against carrying a deadly weapon within the limits of a city. The defendant was convicted and imprisoned in county jail for having carried a loaded revolver in violation of the law. (The gun had been carried openly; it was not concealed.) He filed a writ of habeas corpus with the Idaho Supreme Court, arguing that the law was unconstitutional.

Legal Issues

The basic issue was whether the weapons law violated either the Second Amendment or the Idaho constitution. The latter states that "The people have the right to bear arms for their security and defense, but the legislature shall regulate the exercise of this right by law."

Decision

The court sided with the petitioner, ruling: "Under these constitutional provisions [federal and state], the legislature has no power to prohibit a citizen from bearing arms in any portion of the state of Idaho, whether within or without the corporate limits of cities, towns, and villages. The legislature may, as expressly provided in our state constitution, regulate the exercise of this right, but may not prohibit it. A statute prohibiting the carrying of concealed deadly weapons would be a proper exercise of the police power of the state. But the statute in question does not prohibit the carrying of weapons concealed, which is of itself a pernicious practice, but prohibits the carrying of them in any manner in cities, towns, and villages. We are compelled to hold this statute void."

Impact

The decision suggests that the state's police power can be used to regulate how weapons can be carried but not completely prohibit it. It is also one of the relatively few decisions that seems to also apply the federal Second Amendment to the state, though it can be viewed as superfluous to the state constitution.

STATE [OF VERMONT] V. ROSENTHAL, 75 VERMONT 295 (1903)

Background

The defendant was convicted of carrying a loaded pistol within the limits of the city of Rutland, Vermont, in violation of an ordinance that "provides that no person shall carry within the city any steel or brass knuckles, pistol, sling shot, stiletto, or weapon of similar character, nor carry any weapon concealed on his person, without permission of the mayor or chief of police, in writing." He appealed to the Supreme Court of Vermont.

Legal Issues

The defendant argued that the city ordinance conflicted with state law, which did not prohibit the carrying of an unconcealed firearm, except at a school. State law should take precedence.

Decision

The court agreed with the defendant that the local law conflicted with that of the state because "unless a special permission is granted by the mayor or chief of police for that purpose, a person is prohibited from carrying such weapons in circumstances where the same is lawful by the Constitution and the general laws of the state," and conversely, "there is nothing in the ordinance to prevent the granting of such permission, notwithstanding it be in circumstances to constitute a crime under the general laws" (e.g., such as by allowing a gun to be carried in a school).

Impact

In recent years many cities have passed firearms laws more restrictive than those of the state. This frequently leads to the issue of "state preemption"—whether any aspect of firearms law specified by the state precludes a city or county from making its own legislation in that area. This issue is fought out on a state-by-state basis and depends on the relationship between the language of the conflicting laws and the intentions expressed by the legislature.

CITY OF SALINA V. BLAKSLEY, 72 KANSAS 230 (1905)

Background

James Blaksley was convicted by the police court of Salina, Kansas, for "carrying a revolving pistol within the city while under the influence of intoxicating liquor." His conviction was upheld by the district court and was then appealed to the Supreme Court of Kansas.

Legal Issues

The defendant argued that his conviction violated his right to keep and bear arms under the Kansas Constitution, which states "The people have the right to bear arms for their defense and security; but standing armies, in time of peace, are dangerous to liberty, and shall not be tolerated, and the military shall be in strict subordination to the civil power."

Decision

The court noted: "The power of the Legislature to prohibit or regulate the carrying of deadly weapons has been the subject of much dispute in the courts. The views expressed in the decisions are not uniform, and the reasonings of the different courts vary. It has, however, been generally held that the Legislatures can regulate the mode of carrying deadly weapons, provided they are not such as are ordinarily used in civilized warfare."

Further, "The provision in section 4 of the Bill of Rights 'that the people have the right to bear arms for their defense and security' refers to the people as a collective body. It was the safety and security of society that was being considered when this provision was put into our Constitution." The court went on to point out that the provisions for the maintenance of the state militia implied that the state could regulate the way in which weapons were to be carried.

The constitutional provision is thus ". . . a limitation on legislative power to enact laws prohibiting the bearing of arms in the militia, or any other military organization provided for by law, but is not a limitation on legislative power to enact laws prohibiting and punishing the promiscuous carrying of arms or other deadly weapons."

Impact

This view of the state constitutional provision is close to the viewpoint of most modern gun control advocates with regard to the Second Amendment: Only the right of the state to form and operate a militia is protected; the legislature is free to regulate or even prohibit the individual carrying of weapons. Certainly few people would assert that anyone has the right to carry a weapon while drunk.

SONZINSKY V. UNITED STATES, 300 U.S. 506 (1937)

Background

The previously discussed cases all dealt with state or local laws regulating firearms. In 1934, however, the federal government entered the arena when

The Law of Gun Control

Congress passed the National Firearms Act in response to public concern about the machine-gun-toting gangsters of the Prohibition era. This law banned certain highly destructive devices (such as bombs and grenades) outright, but it did not ban the machine guns. Instead, it placed a tax of $200 on every sale of a machine gun, sawed-off shotgun, or rifle with either a barrel shorter than 18 inches or a silencer. (This was a rather large amount of money at that time, both in absolute terms and in relationship to the market value of the weapon.) In addition, all firearm dealers would have to be registered and pay a $200 annual "special occupational tax." The case arose when a dealer was convicted for not paying the tax. The appeal came to the Supreme Court.

Legal Issues

The appellant raised several arguments. He argued: "The Constitution made no grant of authority to Congress to legislate substantively for the general welfare, and no such authority exists, save as the general welfare may be promoted by the exercise of the powers which are granted. . . . The power of taxation which is expressly granted may be adopted as a means to carry into operation another power also expressly granted, but resort to the taxing power to effectuate an end which is not legitimate, not within the scope of the Constitution, is obviously inadmissible." In other words, Congress could only tax to raise revenue to pay for some activity for which it has a power enumerated (listed) in the Constitution.

Furthermore, the petitioner argued that the National Firearms Act was constructed and written in a way that made it clear that it was not intended to raise revenue but rather to discourage dealing in the specified weapons. He also argued that if the purpose of the tax was really to exercise a form of police power, that power belonged not to Congress but to the states. "Congress is not empowered to tax for those purposes which are within the exclusive province of the States."

The government replied that the taxes in the National Firearms Act were authorized by Congress's broad power in Article 1, Section 8, clause 1 of the Constitution "To lay and collect taxes, duties, imposts and excises to pay the debts and provide for the common defense and general welfare of the United States." Further, "It is no objection that the size of the tax tends to burden and discourage the conduct of the occupation of petitioner. . . . Nor is it material that Congress may have anticipated and even intended such an effect. Where a tax is laid on a proper subject and discloses a revenue purpose, it is of no consequence that social, or moral, or economic factors may have been considered by Congress in enacting the measure."

Decision

The Court rejected the petitioner's argument, agreeing with the government's contention that the tax was legitimate and the motives of Congress irrelevant. The conviction was affirmed subject to factual review by the lower court.

Impact

This case is interesting in that the petitioner's argument relied not on the Second Amendment or some similar clause in a state constitution but ultimately on a theory that the powers of Congress are limited to those spelled out in the Constitution and that the power to tax is thus similarly limited. Although this was largely the intention of the framers of the Constitution, the power of Congress had been allowed to expand greatly by the 1930s and indeed was the subject of a number of cases challenging Franklin Roosevelt's New Deal legislation. Although of considerable philosophical interest, this line of argument has not prevailed in modern times.

UNITED STATES V. MILLER, 307 U.S. 174 (1939)

Background

This case began with an indictment that charged that two suspected bootleggers, Jack Miller and Frank Layton, "did unlawfully, knowingly, wilfully, and feloniously transport in interstate commerce from the town of Claremore in the State of Oklahoma to the town of Siloam Springs in the State of Arkansas a certain firearm, to-wit, a double barrel 12-gauge Stevens shotgun having a barrel less than 18 inches in length" without paying the $200 tax required under the National Firearms Act of 1934.

The lower court judge threw out the case on the grounds that the law violated the Second Amendment. The government appealed. Meanwhile, the bootleggers disappeared. When the case was finally heard in the Supreme Court, only the government was represented.

Legal Issues

There are two legal issues: Does the federal firearms tax encroach on powers reserved to the states, and does it infringe on the right to keep and bear arms specified in the Second Amendment?

Decision

The Court quickly disposed of the issue of the taxation power, citing its previous decision of *Sonzinsky v. U.S.* As for the Second Amendment, the Court simply noted that it "can not take judicial notice that a shotgun having a barrel less than 18 inches long has today any reasonable relation to the preservation or efficiency of a well regulated militia; and therefore can not say that the Second Amendment guarantees to the citizen the right to keep and bear such a weapon."

Impact

This short, rather cryptic decision has been interpreted in two different ways in the continuing debate over the meaning of the Second Amendment. Gun control advocates cite it as clearly stating that the Second Amendment must be interpreted in terms of the militia clause and does not give individuals the right to keep and bear any sort of firearm they want.

Gun rights advocates suggest that the same reference to the militia might imply that an individual would have the right to carry a weapon that *is* of a military nature (such as a fully automatic AK-47 or M-16 rifle). They also note that the defendant was not represented and that, therefore, the judges heard only one side of the case. (They also note in passing that short-barreled shotguns and carbines were in fact military weapons used by some cavalry units.)

Gun control advocates observe, however, that the Court has not directly revisited the issue of the scope and applicability of the Second Amendment in the more than 60 years since *Miller* was decided. However, the case of *U.S. v. Emerson* (1999) does set up a conflict between appeals circuits over interpretation of the Second Amendment.

CASES V. U.S., 131 F.2D 916 (1ST CIR. 1942)

Background

In 1938 Congress passed another Federal Firearms Act. Among its provisions, it prohibited a convicted felon from purchasing or otherwise receiving a gun or ammunition. José Cases Velazquez of the U.S. territory of Puerto Rico was convicted of violating the Federal Firearms Act "by transporting and receiving a firearm and ammunition" while being a convicted felon. Cases's appeal was heard by the U.S. District Court of Appeals.

Legal Issues

As the court noted in its opinion, the defendant contends that the Federal Firearms Act is unconstitutional because (a) it is an ex post facto law; (b) it violates the Second Amendment by infringing the right of the people to keep and bear arms; (c) it is an undue extension of the commerce clause; (d) it creates an unreasonable presumption of guilt; and (e) it denies equal protection of the laws.

Decision

The court rejected all five of the defendant's arguments. It declared that the Federal Firearms Act of 1938 was not an ex post facto ("after the fact") law—that is, it didn't punish someone for an act committed before the law took effect—rather, "it is abundantly plain that in enacting it Congress was in no way interested in imposing an additional penalty upon those who at some time in the past had been convicted of a crime of violence. In the act Congress sought to protect the public by preventing the transportation and possession of firearms and ammunition by those who, by their past conduct, had demonstrated their unfitness to be entrusted with such dangerous instrumentalities . . ."

With regard to the Second Amendment, the court cited the recent Supreme Court case of *U.S. v. Miller* to indicate that the amendment did not convey an absolute or unqualified right to keep and bear arms. The court noted the reference in *Miller* to a sawed-off shotgun not being a military weapon but did not conclude that Cases's pistol might be such a weapon and be protected by the Constitution: "Apparently, then, under the Second Amendment, the federal government can limit the keeping and bearing of arms by a single individual as well as by a group of individuals, but it cannot prohibit the possession or use of any weapon which has any reasonable relationship to the preservation or efficiency of a well regulated militia. However, we do not feel that the Supreme Court in this case was attempting to formulate a general rule applicable to all cases. The rule which it laid down was adequate to dispose of the case before it and that we think was as far as the Supreme Court intended to go."

The court went on to note: "While the weapon [the pistol] may be capable of military use, or while at least familiarity with it might be regarded as of value in training a person to use a comparable weapon of military type and caliber, still there is no evidence that the appellant was or ever had been a member of any military organization or that his use of the weapon under the circumstances disclosed was in preparation for a military career."

The court declared that the commerce clause of the Constitution (allowing Congress to regulate interstate commerce) did apply to Puerto Rico as a U.S. territory. It also disposed of the due process and equal protection arguments, citing the rational and practical need for lawmakers to make assumptions based on a person's prior conviction for a crime.

Impact

This case illustrates a possible path that the Supreme Court might take if it ever revisits its view of the Second Amendment in *Miller v. U.S.* The decision here implies that the Supreme Court's rejecting constitutional protection for a nonmilitary weapon doesn't necessarily mean that possession by an individual of a military weapon outside an organized military context would be protected. Gun rights advocates view such an approach as contradictory and as a failure to honor the intent of the Constitution's framers.

U.S. V. WARIN, 530 F.2D 130 (6TH CIR. 1976)

Background

The defendant, a firearms designer, was convicted of possessing a "9-millimeter prototype machine gun" in violation of the National Firearms Act as amended by the Gun Control Act of 1968. The two sides stipulated that "9-millimeter submachine guns have been used by at least one Special Forces Unit of the Army in the Vietnam War, although they are not in general use. 9-millimeter submachine guns have been used by the military forces of the United States on at least one occasion during the Vietnam war. . . . [T]hat submachine guns are part of the military equipment of the United States military and that firearms of this general type, that is, submachine guns, do bear some relationship, some reasonable relationship to the preservation or efficiency of the military forces."

Legal Issues

The defendant argued that because the weapon was a military weapon and he was a member of the "sedentary" (or reserve) state militia, he was entitled under the Second Amendment to have it, as implied by the Supreme Court rejecting the shotgun in *U.S. v. Miller* as not being a military weapon.

Decision

The court disagreed:

> *In Miller the Supreme Court did not reach the question of the extent to which a weapon which is "part of the ordinary military equipment" or whose "use could contribute to the common defense" may be regulated. In holding that the absence of evidence placing the weapon involved in the charges against Miller in one of these categories precluded the trial court from quashing the indictment on Second Amendment grounds, the Court did not*

hold the converse—that the Second Amendment is an absolute prohibition against all regulation of the manufacture, transfer and possession of any instrument capable of being used in military action.

The court went on to reiterate the common themes of the Second Amendment being a collective, not an individual, guarantee and that the common law has long recognized the right of the state to regulate the details of weapon ownership and use.

Impact

By dealing with what was clearly a military weapon, the circuit court in *Warin* seemed to be making an even stronger statement that courts are unwilling to draw the conclusion that the Second Amendment gives individuals an unqualified right to carry at least military weapons.

APPLICATION OF ATKINSON, 291 N.W.2D 396 (MINNESOTA, 1980)

Background

The plaintiff, Berton Atkinson, had been carrying a pistol in the glove compartment of his car "while traveling appreciable distances away from [his] home on public roads and highways." In 1975, the city of Bloomington, Minnesota, passed an ordinance requiring that persons wishing to carry or possess a pistol in a public place to obtain a permit from a police chief or county sheriff. Further, the applicant had to demonstrate that he or she had "an occupation or personal safety hazard requiring a permit to carry." Atkinson's permit was denied on the grounds that he had not satisfied that requirement. He appealed that decision to the court.

Legal Issues

The court saw two issues being raised by this case: Does the constitution or common law give individuals an absolute right to carry a loaded gun on a public highway? And failing that, does travel on a public highway automatically constitute the "personal safety hazard" required by the statute?

Decision

The court concluded that neither the common law nor the Constitution conveyed an "absolute" right to carry weapons for individual self-defense. Therefore, there was scope for the state to exercise its police power in regulating the carrying of weapons. Further, the court [found] "it difficult to believe that such travel [on highways] was intended by the legislature to be a personal safety hazard. . . . The hazard plaintiff has identified is vague, general, and speculative. He has not made the showing of real and immediate danger, which the statute requires in order to justify issuance of a handgun permit. The permit was properly denied."

Impact

This decision is an example of a court upholding what is called a discretionary gun permit. Gun rights advocates often argue that such laws amount to gun control for everyone except well-connected and favored persons who have an inside track with the police chief or sheriff. Accordingly, they have sometimes organized successful campaigns to remove the element of "discretion" from gun permit laws.

SCHUBERT V. DEBARD, 398 N.E.2D 1339 (INDIANA, APP. 1980)

Background

In June 1975, Joseph L. Schubert applied for a license to carry a handgun. He had previously held a handgun permit and had held commissions from two police agencies. All had expired. When his new application was denied, he made an administrative appeal.

The Indiana licensing statute provided:

The officer to whom the application is made shall conduct an investigation into the applicant's official records and verify thereby the applicant's character and reputation, and shall in addition verify for accuracy the information contained in the application, and shall forward this information together with his recommendation for approval or disapproval . . . to the superintendent who may make whatever further investigation he deems necessary. In addition, whenever disapproval is recommended, the officer to whom the application is made shall provide the superintendent and the applicant with his complete and specific reasons, in writing, for the recommendation of disapproval. If it appears to the superintendent that the applicant has a proper reason for carrying a handgun and is of good character and reputation and a proper person to be so licensed, he shall issue to the applicant either a qualified or an unlimited license to carry any handgun or handguns lawfully possessed by the applicant.

Schubert had claimed that he needed the gun to protect himself from threats and presented as evidence "a copy of a picture of a pig with appellant's name written above it." The other was a letter, signed "The Assassinater's," demanding $1,250 or "Pig, you are dead." However, he apparently had not contacted police about these threats. The court record also notes: "A report summarizing a background investigation made of appellant when he applied for a private detective's license in 1971 was admitted without objection. That report concluded that appellant was a 'chronic liar' suffering from a 'gigantic police complex.'"

The superintendent of the Indiana state police upheld the permit denial, saying that Schubert "did not have a proper reason."

Legal Issues

The Indiana Constitution says "The people shall have a right to bear arms, for the defense of themselves and the State." According to the court record, "Schubert contends . . . that the Indiana Constitution affords him the right to bear arms for his own defense. Thus, he urges that where self-defense is properly asserted as the reason for desiring a firearms license, and the applicant is otherwise qualified, the license cannot be withheld upon an administrative official's subjective determination of whether the applicant needs defending."

Decision

The court concluded that "the [police] superintendent [had] decided the application on the basis that the statutory reference to 'a proper reason' vested in him the power and duty to subjectively evaluate an assignment of 'self-defense' as a reason for desiring a license and the ability to grant or deny the license upon the basis of whether the applicant 'needed' to defend himself." The majority of the court found that "Such an approach contravenes the essential nature of the constitutional guarantee. It would supplant a right with a mere administrative privilege which might be withheld simply on the basis that such matters as the use of firearms are better left to the organized military and police forces even where defense of the individual citizen is involved."

Acknowledging that there had been legitimate concerns about Schubert's suitability to receive a permit, the court ordered a new administrative hearing.

Impact

Some "discretionary" gun laws have been overturned, and others upheld. There are a number of factors that may come into play in such decisions: whether the state constitution has an unequivocal guarantee of the right to carry arms for self-defense, the specificity and apparent rationality of the permit statute, and the extent to which a court might defer to its own beliefs about the carrying of firearms as a matter of social policy.

QUILICI V. VILLAGE OF MORTON GROVE, 695 F.2D 261 (7TH CIR. 1982)

Background

Depending on one's point of view, the village of Morton Grove, Illinois, became either famous or notorious when it enacted an ordinance that banned, among other weapons, "Any handgun, unless the same has been rendered permanently inoperative." This total ban on handguns was challenged in a civil action by Victor D. Quilici in state court. The village of Morton Grove had the case transferred to federal court, where it was joined to two other cases.

The district court rejected Quilici's suit (*Quilici v. Village of Morton Grove*, 532 F. Supp. 1169 [N.D. Ill. 1981]). The plaintiffs then appealed to the circuit court.

Legal Issues

The original district court proceeding and the review of that decision by the circuit court had the following main issues:

1. Did the Morton Grove ordinance conflict with the clause in the Illinois Constitution that states "Subject only to the police power, the right of the individual citizen to keep and bear arms shall not be infringed"? The appellants conceded that "laws which require the licensing of guns or which restrict the carrying of concealed weapons or the possession of firearms by minors, convicted felons, and incompetents are valid." They argued, however, that a total ban on hand guns was not reasonable and that it might well lead to a situation where some towns banned handguns, others permitted them with certain restrictions, and still others had no laws. This would create a chaotic situation and make it too easy for travelers to fall afoul of the law. Morton Grove contended that the constitution, in referring to "arms" in general, could be satisfied as long as *some* arms were permitted, and the town ordinance did allow the keeping of some types of rifles and shotguns.
2. Did the Second Amendment to the U.S. Constitution apply to this local law? The appellants argued that the Supreme Court case *U.S. v. Presser* implied that firearms ownership, through its connection to

"national citizenship" and the ability of the national government to ensure public security through the militia, could not be interfered with so radically by local governments. Morton Grove, however, pointed to the straightforward statement in *Presser:* "The Second Amendment declares that it shall not be infringed, but this . . . means no more than that it shall not be infringed by Congress. This is one of the amendments that has no other effect than to restrict the powers of the National government . . ." For the circuit appeal, the appellant added an argument that the statement in *Presser* was no longer valid because many provisions of the Bill of Rights had later been incorporated into the Fourteenth Amendment's guarantees of the rights of citizens that could be enforced against the states.

3. Finally, the appellant raised the issue of whether the Morton Grove ordinance conflict with a fundamental right to self-defense implied in the Ninth Amendment to the U.S. Constitution. The amendment says that "the enumeration in the Constitution, of certain rights shall not be construed to deny or disparage others retained by the people."

Decision

In looking at the Illinois Constitution, the circuit court disagreed with Morton Grove's contention that handguns were not contemplated in the constitutional protection of the right to keep and bear arms. However, the court said: "We agree with the district court that the right to keep and bear arms in Illinois is so limited by the police power that a ban on handguns does not violate that right." In coming to that conclusion they were guided partly by statements by delegates at the state constitutional convention, such as one named Foster who said that the constitutional provision "would prevent a complete ban on all guns, but there could be a ban on certain categories." Finally, the court noted that under the doctrine of "Home Rule," municipalities could enact whatever legislation they wished so long as it was not in conflict with a "positive constitutional guarantee." Any problems that might be caused by conflicting local laws were not legally relevant.

The court found no evidence that the Second Amendment had been applied to the states by the Supreme Court and that "The Supreme Court has specifically rejected the proposition that the entire Bill of Rights applies to the states through the Fourteenth Amendment." Further, the court agreed that "As the Village [of Morton Grove] correctly notes, appellants are essentially arguing that *Miller* was wrongly decided and should be overruled. Such arguments have no place before this court. Under the controlling authority of *Miller* we conclude that the right to keep and bear handguns is not guaranteed by the Second Amendment."

The Ninth Amendment argument was quickly dismissed as lacking any convincing precedents. "Appellants may believe the Ninth Amendment should be read to recognize an unwritten, fundamental, individual right to own or possess firearms; the fact remains that the Supreme Court has never embraced this theory."

The circuit court thus upheld the Morton Grove statute as being constitutional.

Impact

The Morton Grove decision shows the general tendency to construe constitutional guarantees of the right to keep and bear arms narrowly, while it gives wide scope to a legislature's exercise of police power, extending even to banning whole classes of firearms. So far, however, a total ban on *all* firearms and all circumstances of possession has not been tested in the courts.

KELLEY V. R.G. INDUSTRIES, INC., 497 A.2D 1143, 304 MD. 124 (MARYLAND, 1985)

Background

Olen J. Kelley was shot and injured during an armed robbery at the store where he worked. The gun used was assembled and sold by R.G. Industries, a subsidiary of the West German firm Rohm. Kelley sued both firms. Rohm and R.G. Industries had the case transferred to the U.S. district court in Maryland and asked that it be dismissed. (Rohm argued that "the [p]laintiffs' contentions [must] fail because the handgun performed as it was supposed to perform and because Rohm Gesellschaft is not responsible for the criminal and tortious acts of Mr. Kelley's assailant." Not finding a "controlling precedent on the strict liability issue" the district court "certified" it and transferred it to the Maryland State Court of Appeals.

Legal Issues

The Maryland court addressed the following issues:

1. *Is the manufacturer or marketer of a handgun, in general, liable under any strict liability theory to a person injured as a result of the criminal use of its product?*

2. *Is the manufacturer or marketer of a particular category of small, cheap handguns, sometimes referred to as Saturday night specials and regularly used in criminal activity, strictly liable to a person injured by such handgun during the course of a crime?*

3. Does the Rohm Revolver Handgun Model RG38S, serial number 0152662, fall within the category referred to in question 2?

Decision

The court said that under Maryland law, gun manufacturers could not be held liable under the first theory because this kind of liability applied only to the misuse of land (for example, having buried fuel tanks that leak and cause injury or damage to neighbors). The activity of making or shooting a gun has nothing to do with land. "Therefore, the abnormally dangerous activity doctrine does not apply to the manufacture or marketing of handguns."

But could the gun itself be defective and "unreasonably dangerous" even if the manufacturer took all reasonable care in selling it and even if the person who uses it had not bought it directly from the manufacturer? Noting that the product had to be defective in design (not just dangerous), the court ruled that "A handgun manufacturer or marketer could not be held liable under this theory. Contrary to Kelley's argument, a handgun is not defective merely because it is capable of being used during criminal activity to inflict harm. . . . For the handgun to be defective, there would have to be a problem in its manufacture or design, such as a weak or improperly placed part, that would cause it to fire unexpectedly or otherwise malfunction."

Moving from the gun itself to its use, the court said: "The fact that a handgun manufacturer or marketer generally would not be liable for gunshot injuries resulting from a criminal's use of the product, under previously recognized principles of strict liability, is not necessarily dispositive. This Court has repeatedly said that 'the common law is not static; its life and heart is its dynamism—its ability to keep pace with the world while constantly searching for just and fair solutions to pressing societal problems.'" Looking at Maryland's handgun regulations, the court concluded, however, that because some kinds of handgun use were permitted, it would not be appropriate to assign liability to use of all types of handguns.

However, the court recognized that Congress and state legislators had identified a particular category of handguns popularly known as Saturday night specials, characterized "by short barrels, light weight, easy concealability, low cost, use of cheap quality materials, poor manufacture, inaccuracy and unreliability." The court said such guns were of use only to criminals and not for legitimate purposes of sport or self-protection.

Turning to Rohm's product, the court observed: "Moreover, the manufacturer or marketer of a Saturday night special knows or ought to know that he is making or selling a product principally to be used in criminal activity. For example, a salesman for R.G. Industries, describing what he termed to be a 'special attribute' of a Rohm handgun, was said to have told a putative handgun marketer, 'If your store is anywhere near a ghetto area, these ought to sell real well. This is most assuredly a ghetto gun.' The R.G. salesman allegedly went on to say about another R.G. handgun, 'This sells real well, but, between you and me, it's such a piece of crap I'd be afraid to fire the thing.'"

Because ". . . the manufacturer or marketer of a Saturday night special knows or ought to know that the chief use of the product is for criminal activity. Such criminal use and the virtual absence of legitimate uses for the product are clearly foreseeable by the manufacturers and sellers of Saturday night specials . . . it is entirely consistent with public policy to hold the manufacturers and marketers of Saturday night special handguns strictly liable to innocent persons who suffer gunshot injuries from the criminal use of their products."

The court returned the case to the district court for determination of whether the gun used met the definition for a Saturday night special and, if so, for trial.

Impact

This decision begins by concluding that handguns in general are not inherently defective or unreasonably dangerous, but then the decision uses findings from legislators to conclude that a particular kind of handgun, the Saturday night special, is so and that a manufacturer can be held liable for use of such guns in criminal activity. This illustrates the fact that courts can create new criteria for liability and that gun control advocates may be able to further their goals by filing civil suits that end up making more categories of guns subject to liability. Gun rights advocates would argue, however, that the court is going beyond its proper role and is, in effect, legislating.

PERKINS V. F.I.E. CORP., 762 F.2D 1250 (5TH CIR. 1985)

Background

On September 18, 1981, Claude Nichols fought with someone in a bar parking lot. He went into the bar, shooting wildly at his opponent with a .25 caliber revolver. Three bystanders were wounded, including Joseph Perkins, who, as a result of the gunfire, became permanently paralyzed from the waist down. Nichols was convicted of aggravated battery and sentenced to five years at hard labor. Perkins sued F.I.E. Corporation, the manufacturer of the handgun used by Nichols. The suit was transferred to federal court.

Gun Control

Legal Issues

The district court noted: "The plaintiff admitted in answers to interrogatories—that there was no defect in the design of the gun, no defect in the manufacture or assembly of the component parts of the gun, no statutory prohibition to the manufacture or distribution of the gun, and that Claude Nichols was not at the time of the shooting an agent, employee, or servant of F.I.E. Corp." The plaintiff (Perkins) thus did not claim any of these traditional causes of possible liability for the manufacturer.

However, Perkins claimed that the pistol "is defective in that it is unreasonably dangerous in normal use, that the hazard of injury to human beings exceeds the utility of the pistol and this defect constitutes a proximate cause [of the injury]."

According to the court: "The plaintiffs present two theories of recovery. First, they argue that the marketing of a dangerous weapon to the general public is an ultrahazardous activity giving rise to absolute liability under Louisiana law. Second, they argue that the handgun used in the two crimes is an unreasonably dangerous product giving rise to strict products liability . . . because of its small size, enabling it to be easily concealed, coupled with marketing of it to the general public."

Decision

The district court rejected both the strict product liability and the ultrahazardous activity theory in Perkins's suit and granted summary judgment in favor of the gun manufacturer. In a similar case, *Richman v. Charter Arms Corp.* (involving a robbery, rape, and murder committed using a .38 caliber handgun), the court granted summary judgment to the defendant on product liability but not on ultrahazardous activity. The two cases were then combined in an appeal to the U.S. Circuit Court of Appeals, Fifth District.

The circuit court observed that the doctrine of "ultrahazardous activity" had only been applied to activities involving the use of land or property in a way that was inherently dangerous: for example, building a dangerous high-pressure gas line, blasting, using hazardous chemicals, and so on. The court, however, noted a general standard that had emerged from the case of *Langlois v. Allied Chemical* where the Louisiana Supreme Court had advised that: "The activities of man for which he may be liable without acting negligently are to be determined after a study of the law and customs, a balancing of claims and interests, a weighing of the risk and the gravity of harm, and a consideration of individual and societal rights and obligations." This would seem to allow for an argument that small handguns were "ultrahazardous." However, the circuit court decided that this statement of suggested methodology did not determine what sorts of cases it should be

70

applied to. The court concluded that to be ultrahazardous, "1. The Activity Must Be An Activity Relating to Land or to Other Immovables. . . . 2. The Activity Itself Must Cause the Injury and the Defendant Must Have Been Engaged Directly in the Injury-Producing Activity. . . . 3. The Activity Must Not Require the Substandard Conduct of a Third Party to Cause Injury."

Clearly, manufacturing a handgun has nothing to do with the use of land. The manufacturing of a handgun does not directly cause injury, and indeed, it requires that a third party (the shooter) be involved. The court thus declared that manufacturing a handgun is not an ultrahazardous activity, granting summary judgment in favor of the manufacturer.

Impact

Although decided under Louisiana's French-inspired laws, unique among U.S. states, the decision here reflects a widespread rejection of the theory that simply manufacturing a gun is an "ultrahazardous activity" comparable to setting off explosives on one's land. (However, note that *Kelley v. R.G. Industries* concluded that certain types of handguns—Saturday night specials— could be considered unreasonably hazardous.) Some later firearms liability has also focused on the possibility that the way some handguns are *marketed* constitutes an unreasonable risk or danger to the community. This approach has met with some success. In *Cincinnati v. Beretta* (2002) the Ohio State Supreme Court overturned the dismissal of the city's suit based on negligent marketing. The court found the city's showing of danger and harm created by the ready availability of guns to criminals and children to be credible.

The California Supreme Court dismissed a similar case in *Merril v. Navegar* (2001), ruling that the suit was barred by a California law. The law in turn was repealed in September 2002.

ADDISON V. WILLIAMS, 546 SO.2D 220
(LOUISIANA APP. 1989)

Background

According to the court record, "on New Year's Eve 1986, shortly before midnight, Cody Wayne Williams caused a disturbance at the Hub Lounge in Bossier City. Employees of the lounge took a handgun from him, and he was ordered to leave the premises. To protect themselves, customers and employees closed and locked the two steel doors to the lounge. Williams returned to the lounge with a Colt AR-15 model SP1 semiautomatic rifle and opened fire on the lounge, firing 56 rounds of .223 caliber ammunition into the building through the steel doors. Bullets and bullet fragments struck six of the occupants of the lounge, fatally injuring one person and injuring five others. Williams later pled guilty to first degree murder and is serving a life sentence in the state penitentiary."

Several lawsuits were filed on behalf of the victims against Colt Industries (manufacturer of the gun) and Olin Corporation (maker of the ammunition), and other gun manufacturers. Colt and Olin filed to have the suit dismissed for lack of a valid cause of action, and the district court agreed. The plaintiffs appealed.

Legal Issues

The appeals court reviewed the following theories of liability:

1. *the manufacturing and marketing of the AR-15 assault rifle and its ammunition to the civilian public is an ultrahazardous activity rendering defendants absolutely liable;*

2. *the weapon and its ammunition are unreasonably dangerous and defective per se rendering defendants liable under strict products liability;*

3. *the manufacturing and distribution of the products presented an unreasonable risk of harm, amounting to negligence and rendering defendants liable under LSA-C.C. Art. 2316; and*

4. *assuming defendants had a legal right to distribute the products to the public, defendants are liable because they abused that right.*

Decision

The court rejected the "ultrahazardous" and "unreasonably dangerous" theories, citing the earlier decisions of *Strickland v. Fowler* and *Perkins v. F.I.E. Corp.*, which concluded that the manufacturing or marketing of handguns was not ultrahazardous (because it did not apply to activities involved with use of land) nor unreasonably dangerous. Also, "Strickland and Perkins likewise correctly dealt with and disposed of the contention that the manufacturer was liable under a theory of strict products liability. In general, to recover in a products liability case the plaintiff must prove that the product was defective, that is, unreasonably dangerous to normal use, and that the plaintiff's injuries were caused by reason of the defect."

The court then dealt with another possibility, that

> *there is a distinction with legal effect to be drawn between the manufacture and sale of handguns and the manufacture and sale of assault rifles. Plaintiffs argue that comparing a handgun to an assault rifle is like comparing a firecracker to dynamite. It is argued that handguns are primarily defensive weapons and assault rifles are primarily offensive weapons, and that while*

there may be some social utility for handguns there is none for assault rifles. Plaintiffs emphasize the greater power, penetrating capabilities, and rapid fire of the assault rifle. It is argued that the manufacture of assault rifles and the manner in which they are marketed create an atmosphere of violence and an increased risk beyond that presented by other guns, thereby rendering this product unreasonably dangerous and defective and presenting an unreasonable risk of harm to the public.

However, the court (unlike *Kelley v. R.G. Industries* with regard to Saturday night specials) declined to characterize a particular kind of gun as creating inherent liability. "We recognize the difference in physical characteristics and capabilities of assault rifles as compared to handguns or other guns. However, all guns are dangerous and have the capacity to kill. Each type of gun has characteristics that make it more dangerous than another type, depending on the circumstances of its use. A handgun can be concealed and in that sense is more susceptible to criminal misuse than larger guns. . . . Thus, attempting to characterize one type of gun as presenting a greater risk of harm or as being more susceptible of criminal misuse than another type becomes extremely tenuous." Therefore, "The manufacturers of the weapon and the ammunition used in it are not liable for injuries resulting from the intentional criminal misuse of the gun."

Impact

This is a case where the court chose not to "legislate" beyond traditional product liability law. There has been a great increase in gun liability litigation in recent years, and it is far from clear whether most courts will eventually follow the approach in *Kelley* or the one here.

ARNOLD V. CLEVELAND, 67 OHIO ST.3D 35 (OHIO 1993)

Background

In 1989 the city council of Cleveland, Ohio, passed an ordinance banning "assault weapons"—basically, semiautomatic rifles or shotguns with high-capacity magazines. Harry W. Arnold and others appealed to the courts to overturn this law as being unconstitutional.

Legal Issues

The appellants argued that the Cleveland law placed too great a restriction on rights specified in Section 4, Article 1 of the Ohio Constitution, which states: "The people have the right to bear arms for their defense and security; but standing armies, in time of peace, are dangerous to liberty, and shall not be kept up; and the military shall be in strict subordination to the civil power." They argued that this section referred to a fundamental individual right to bear arms.

They also argued that the law interfered with a federal civilian marksmanship program created by the U.S. code by banning certain rifles used by that program. Under the doctrine of supremacy, a local or state law that conflicts with constitutionally valid federal law is void.

Decision

The lower appeals court rejected the argument based on the Ohio Constitution, saying that the ordinance "was a valid exercise of the police power." It did agree that part of the law did conflict with the U.S. code. The appellants then appealed to the Ohio Supreme Court.

That court began by noting: "The question as to whether individuals have a fundamental right to bear arms has, seemingly, been decided in the negative under the Second Amendment to the United States Constitution," citing *Cruikshank, Presser, Miller, Quilici v. Morton Grove* and other cases. "These decisions signify, and history supports the position, that the amendment was drafted not with the primary purpose of guaranteeing the rights of individuals to keep and bear arms but, rather, to allow Americans to possess arms to ensure the preservation of a militia."

The court did note, however, that state courts were free to interpret their state constitutions in ways that offered greater liberties or rights than those founded by the U.S. Supreme Court in the federal Bill of Rights. The Ohio Constitution refers to a specific right of the people "to bear arms for their defense and security." The court asserted that "The right of defense of self, property and family is a fundamental part of our concept of ordered liberty. To deprive our citizens of the right to possess any firearm would thwart the right that was so thoughtfully granted by our forefathers and the drafters of our Constitution."

Thus, the court said that the individual citizens of Ohio have a right to possess firearms for their self-defense and security. The court then quoted the great British legal scholar William Blackstone: "And we have seen that these rights consist, primarily, in the free enjoyment of personal security, of personal liberty, and of private property. So long as these remain inviolate, the subject is perfectly free; for every species of compulsive tyranny and oppression must act in opposition to one or other of these rights, having no other object upon which it can possibly be employed. To preserve these from violation, it is necessary that the constitution be supported in its full vigor."

However, the court then stated that "the people of our nation, and this state, cannot have unfettered discretion to do as we please at all times. Neither the federal Bill of Rights nor this state's Bill of Rights, implicitly or explicitly, guarantees unlimited rights." The court gave the famous example that freedom of speech does not allow one to falsely shout "fire!" in a crowded theater. Each right may be restrained in certain ways to secure the safety of society. Therefore, "we find that Section 4, Article I of the Ohio Constitution confers upon the people of Ohio the fundamental right to bear arms. However, this right is not absolute."

The court then discussed the "police power" as embodied in a community's right to "exercise all powers of local self-government and to adopt and enforce within their limits such local police, sanitary and other similar regulations, as are not in conflict with general laws." The court stated that "Laws or ordinances passed by virtue of the police power which limit or abrogate constitutionally guaranteed rights must not be arbitrary, discriminatory, capricious or unreasonable and must bear a real and substantial relation to the object sought to be obtained, namely, the health, safety, morals or general welfare of the public."

Finally, the court applied this test to the assault weapons law. It quoted the part of the law that expresses the city council's reasons for enacting it: "The Council finds and declares that the proliferation and use of assault weapons [are] resulting in an ever-increasing wave of violence in the form of uncontrolled shootings in the City, especially because of an increase in drug trafficking and drug-related crimes, and pos[e] a serious threat to the health, safety, welfare and security of the citizens of Cleveland. The Council finds that the primary purpose of assault weapons is antipersonnel and any civilian application or use of such weapons is merely incidental to such primary antipersonnel purpose. The Council further finds that the function of this type of weapon is such that any use as a recreational weapon is far outweighed by the threat that the weapon will cause injury and death to human beings. Therefore, it is necessary to establish regulations to restrict the possession or sale of these weapons. It is not the intent of the Council to place restrictions on the use of weapons which are primarily designed and intended for hunting, target practice, or other legitimate sports or recreational activities."

The court concluded that the Cleveland City Council's purposes in banning assault weapons were reasonable and bore a reasonable relationship to the goal of promoting public safety. It suggested that a ban on all firearms might, though, be unacceptable. Finally, the decision stated that the city ordinance did not interfere with the federal Civilian Marksmanship program because residents can practice marksmanship without using types of rifles banned by the city. The city ordinance was thus upheld.

Gun Control

Impact

This decision is interesting in that it begins with a sweeping declaration of fundamental rights and even classifies the bearing of arms for personal protection as a fundamental individual right. It then, however, interprets the police power to allow the banning of a whole class of firearms. Gun rights advocates have argued that this is contradictory: If gun ownership is a fundamental right as is free speech, then the "strict scrutiny" test should have been applied, requiring a "compelling" state interest and a "narrowly tailored" means to accomplishing it rather than the broader "rational basis" test applied here.

CINCINNATI V. LANGAN, 94 OHIO APP.3D 22, REVIEW DENIED, 70 OHIO ST.3D 1425 (1994)

Background

In another Ohio case, Peter Langan was convicted of violating an assault weapons ban similar to that in Cleveland mentioned in the previous case. He appealed the conviction on various grounds, and the case went to the Ohio Court of Appeals.

Legal Issues

The defendant's arguments relevant to gun control were that the Cincinnati ordinance infringed the right to bear arms in the Ohio Constitution, that the ordinance was "unconstitutionally vague" in its description of the banned weapons, and that by "grandfathering" (allowing residents who had such guns prior to the law's taking effect to keep them) it denied later residents the equal protection of the laws.

Decision

The court quickly disposed of the first constitutional argument by citing its earlier decision of *Arnold v. Cleveland*, where it had held that an assault weapons ban was a reasonable exercise of the city's police power. It ruled that the law was not vague because it clearly described specific weapons as well as general features of weapons that would be banned. Finally, the court concluded that because the law did not violate a fundamental right, its grandfathering feature need only be judged as being reasonable: "The fact that persons who did not possess semiautomatic firearms on a certain date are not allowed to possess them thereafter, while persons who did possess semiautomatic weapons prior to that date do not have to surrender those weapons they legally owned prior to the enactment of the statute, does not violate the equal protection rights of one who did not previously possess a semiautomatic weapon. The fixing of a date by which to prohibit the influx of semiautomatic weapons into the city is rationally related to the city council's goal to protect its citizenry from violent crimes and the use of semiautomatic weapons and, thus, the resulting classification contained within the ordinance is neither arbitrary nor unreasonable." Langan's conviction was upheld.

Impact

Because arguments based on the Second Amendment or similar provisions of a state constitution seem to have little chance of succeeding in modern litigation, gun rights advocates have relied more on arguments such as unconstitutional vagueness. However, a law that is both narrow and specific in describing banned weapons is unlikely to be judged vague. The idea of arguing that a group of people can be discriminated against "chronologically" by grandfathering also seems to be ineffective.

SPRINGFIELD ARMORY V. CITY OF COLUMBUS, 29 F.3D 250 (6TH CIR. 1994)

Background

A firearms dealer and two prospective purchasers joined together to challenge the constitutionality of a ban on assault weapons enacted by the city of Columbus, Ohio.

Legal Issues

According to the court: "The ordinance defines 'assault weapon' as any one of thirty-four specific rifles, three specific shotguns and nine specific pistols, or '[o]ther models by the same manufacturer with the same action design that have slight modifications or enhancements.' . . ." The plaintiffs claimed that because the law referred only to specific models by specific manufacturers (or possible future models by the same manufacturers), it was an unconstitutional "bill of attainder." (A bill of attainder is a law that punishes specific individuals without trial.) The plaintiffs also argued that the law was unconstitutionally vague.

Decision

The U.S. District Court of Appeals rejected the attainder argument but said that parts of the law were vague with regard to its descriptions of two of the weapons it listed. The plaintiffs appealed to the U.S. Court of Appeals, Sixth Circuit.

This court agreed that the Columbus law was "fundamentally irrational and impossible to apply consistently by the buying public, the sportsman, the law enforcement officer, the prosecutor or the judge. [It] outlaws assault weapons only by outlawing certain brand names without including within the prohibition similar assault weapons of the same type, function or capability. The ordinance does not achieve the stated goal of the local legislature—to get assault weapons off the street. The ordinance purports to ban 'assault weapons' but in fact it bans only an arbitrary and ill-defined subset of these weapons without providing any explanation for its selections."

The court also agreed with gun manufacturers who complained that the law gave no idea of what "slight modifications" of the named weapons would cause them to also be banned, such as a faster trigger pull, different ammunition capacity, or different caliber of ammunition. The court declared the Columbus law to be "invalid on its face."

Impact

As the court itself noted, communities can draft assault weapons bans that specify general characteristics of banned weapons rather than naming specific models and using vague language about "modifications." Laws drafted in that way are much less likely to be overturned as being unconstitutionally vague. (Note that because the court rejected the law on vagueness grounds, it did not decide the question of whether or not the law was a bill of attainder.)

U.S. V. LOPEZ, 115 S.CT. 1624 (1995)

Background

In 1990 Congress passed the Gun-Free School Zones Act, which "forbids any individual knowingly to possess a firearm at a place that [he] knows . . . is a school zone." The defendant, a 12th grade student, was convicted of violating this law by carrying a concealed handgun into his school.

The defendant appealed his conviction, arguing that the Gun-Free School Zones Act was an unwarranted intrusion on an area traditionally regulated by the states. The district court denied his appeal, ruling that the law "is a constitutional exercise of Congress' power to regulate activities in and affecting commerce." However, the defendant then appealed to the U.S. Circuit Court, which overturned the conviction on the grounds that the law had not been established as a proper exercise of Congress's power to regulate interstate commerce. The government appealed, and the case went to the U.S. Supreme Court.

Legal Issues

Article I, Section 8, Clause 3 of the U.S. Constitution gives Congress the power "[t]o regulate Commerce with foreign Nations, and among the several States, and with the Indian Tribes." The original intention for giving this power to Congress was primarily to allow Congress to create uniform regulations to prevent clashes between conflicting state laws and to prevent states from passing laws that discriminated against imports from other states.

However, starting during the New Deal era of the 1930s, the Supreme Court began to take an increasingly broader view of the Commerce Clause. In the 1935 case *A. L. A. Schecter Poultry Corp. v. United States*, the Court said that Congress could regulate commercial activities directly involved in interstate commerce but not activities that had only an indirect effect on the economy. However, as political pressure on the Court increased, the Court seemed to change its criteria and upheld New Deal legislation. Finally, in the case of *Wickard v. Filburn*, the Court declared, "[E]ven if appellee's activity be local and though it may not be regarded as commerce, it may still, whatever its nature, be reached by Congress if it exerts a substantial economic effect on interstate commerce, and this irrespective of whether such effect is what might at some earlier time have been defined as 'direct' or 'indirect.'" Thus, in *Wickard*, the Court upheld a wheat quota even in a case where the farmer consumed all the wheat he grew rather than selling it. By not having to buy any wheat, they ruled, the farmer was reducing the demand for wheat and thus affecting commerce.

Such a broad standard would seem to give Congress almost unlimited power to regulate just about any sort of activity that had any economic effect. But did possession of a gun in a school meet even that very liberal standard?

Decision

The Court noted "Even *Wickard*, which is perhaps the most far reaching example of Commerce Clause authority over intrastate activity, involved economic activity in a way that the possession of a gun in a school zone does not." The Court also concluded that the law was not a necessary part of a legitimate scheme to regulate commerce. Further, Congress had not established a reasonable relationship between this legislation and commerce, and the law had no mechanism for determining whether a particular case of gun possession had the necessary "nexus" or connection with interstate commerce. For all of these reasons the Supreme Court overturned the

Gun-Free School Zones Act as not being a proper exercise of congressional power.

Impact

This case has a number of important features. From the point of view of challenging gun control, it should be noted that the Second Amendment played no part in the challenge. Unless the Supreme Court revisits its view of the Second Amendment, challenges to federal gun control laws are likely to be based on the Commerce Clause or federalism (the division of powers between the federal government and the states, as in *Printz et al. v. U.S.*).

Beyond gun control, this decision may signal the willingness of the Supreme Court to rein in its interpretation of the Commerce Clause. In a concurring opinion Justice Clarence Thomas indeed urges the Court to consider doing so. In dissent, Justices John Paul Stevens and Stephen Breyer, however, believe the majority was wrong in not seeing the vital link between education and the future success of commerce as being a reason for a federal ban on guns in schools.

Finally, it should be noted that Congress has a way to get around such limitations on its power. Congress can appropriate money for a purpose such as helping to fund educational programs and then require that states adopt certain policies (such as a ban on guns in schools) to receive the funds.

BENJAMIN V. BAILEY, 662 A.2D 1226, 234 CONN. 455 (CONNECTICUT, 1995)

Background

This case is a challenge to a Connecticut assault weapons ban brought by DeForest H. Benjamin and a variety of other plaintiffs, including a gun manufacturer called Navegar, which was doing business as Intratec. The ban involved both a list of specific weapons (such as the AK–47) as well as specifying similar weapons such as AK–47-type guns. The trial and appeals courts rejected the suit, which was then appealed to the Connecticut Supreme Court.

Legal Issues

There were three major issues: (1) Did the assault weapons ban violate the state constitution's guarantee of the right of a person "to bear arms in defense of himself and the state"? (2) Did the ban violate "equal protection" principles by treating gun owners differently based on hard-to-distinguish characteristics of their weapons? (3) Was the law an unconstitutional "bill of attainder" because it punished the owners of specific weapons but not owners of others that were functionally equivalent?

Decision

The Connecticut Supreme Court upheld the lower courts in rejecting all three challenges. The court ruled that the state could not ban *all* guns because this would make the right of defense in the constitution ineffective, but it could ban *some* types of guns—such as assault weapons, as a reasonable exercise of its police power. The court rejected the equal protection argument because the gun ban did not violate a fundamental right (as previously noted), nor did it deal with a "suspect class" of persons (such as a racial or religious group). Therefore, the law need only "be rationally related to some legitimate government purpose in order to withstand an equal protection challenge . . ." Finally, the law was not a bill of attainder because it does not directly "punish" anyone, nor did it apply only to a specified individual or class of individuals. Rather, it prohibited *anyone* from selling the banned weapons.

The court also threw out a "vagueness" challenge accepted by a lower court, ruling that it was not too vague to refer to something like AK–47-type weapons because a person of normal intelligence would understand what was meant.

Impact

If the approach shown by the Connecticut court continues to predominate, a carefully written state assault weapons ban is likely to withstand all legal challenges.

KITCHEN V. K-MART CORP., 697 SO.2D 1200 (FLORIDA, 1997)

Background

As stated in court records,

On the night of December 14, 1987, petitioner Deborah Kitchen was shot by her ex-boyfriend, Thomas Knapp, and rendered a permanent quadriplegic, shortly after Knapp purchased a .22 caliber bolt-action rifle from a local K-Mart retail store. Knapp testified that he had consumed a fifth of whiskey and a case of beer beginning that morning and up until he left a local bar around 8:30 P.M. Knapp drove from the bar to a local K-Mart store where he purchased a rifle and a box of bullets. He returned to the bar and, after observing Kitchen leave in an automobile with friends, followed in his truck. He subsequently rammed their car, forcing it off the road, and shot Kitchen at the base of her neck.

Kitchen sued Kmart for damages, and the jury agreed that Kmart had been negligent in selling a firearm to an intoxicated person. Kmart appealed, and the appeals court overturned the verdict, ruling that as in cases involving incompetent or drunk driving, existing statutes covering the offense precluded the claim of negligence.

Legal Issues

The case came for review before the Florida Supreme Court, which was asked to answer the following question: "Can a seller of a firearm to a purchaser known to the seller to be intoxicated be held liable to a third person injured by the purchaser?"

Decision

The court noted that the existence of a law governing an activity doesn't automatically mean that there can't also be civil liability for that act. "Where a defendant's conduct creates a foreseeable zone of risk, the law generally will recognize a duty placed upon defendant either to lessen the risk or see that sufficient precautions are taken to protect others from the harm that the risk poses." Further, "as the risk grows greater, so does the duty, because the risk to be perceived defines the duty that must be undertaken." Because firearms are so dangerous, the duty of the seller is quite substantial.

The generally accepted doctrine of "negligent entrustment" says that part of that duty involves not giving a dangerous object (or *chattel*) to someone known to be incompetent to use it safely. "One who supplies directly or through a third person a chattel for the use of another whom the supplier knows or has reason to know to be likely because of his youth, inexperience, or otherwise, to use it in a manner involving unreasonable risk of physical harm to himself and others whom the supplier should expect to share in or be endangered by its use, is subject to liability for physical harm resulting to them."

Therefore, the court ruled that Kitchen could pursue her claim for "negligent entrustment" against Kmart.

Impact

Few people would argue that a person selling or giving a firearm to a person known to be intoxicated or otherwise incompetent should not be subject to criminal and civil penalties. From a gun control perspective, the decision suggests that legislatures enacting gun regulations should not fear that doing so would preclude civil liability. Gun rights advocates, however, have responded to increased litigation by promoting state legislation that would limit the liability of gun dealers in other circumstances, such as a shooting by a legally qualified purchaser.

The Law of Gun Control

PRINTZ V. U.S., 521 U.S. 98 (1997)

Background

The federal Brady Handgun Violence Prevention Act ("Brady Bill") of 1994 required the "chief law enforcement officer" of each local jurisdiction to conduct background checks of all persons wishing to buy a firearm, but no federal money was appropriated for the purpose. Two sheriffs, Jay Printz of Ravalli County, Montana, and Richard Mack of Graham County, Arizona, filed separate suits that challenged this provision of the Brady Act, claiming that forcing sheriffs to perform the checks at their own expense went beyond the powers of Congress as restricted by the Tenth Amendment to the U.S. Constitution.

In both cases, the district courts of appeals ruled that the background check provision was unconstitutional, though other parts of the law (such as the waiting period) could remain in force. However, federal attorneys appealed to the Circuit Court of Appeals, Ninth Circuit, which ruled that the background checks were constitutional. The sheriffs' appeals, now combined, came to the U.S. Supreme Court.

Legal Issues

The key issue was whether the Constitution allows Congress to enact legislation that forces local law enforcement officials to carry out a federal mandate (in this case, running background checks on firearms purchasers).

The federal government argued that "the earliest Congresses enacted statutes that required the participation of state officials in the implementation of federal laws." They also pointed to the Constitution's Supremacy Clause, which states that "the Laws of the United States . . . shall be the supreme Law of the Land; and the Judges in every State shall be bound thereby." Finally, they argued that portions of *The Federalist* (writings considered to reveal the intentions of the Constitution's framers) implied that in the structure of the new government, the federal government would be able to require the assistance of state officials for the carrying out of constitutionally valid federal legislation.

Decision

The Court did not agree that the Supremacy Clause and historical experience could be applied to local sheriffs. The justices pointed out that any precedent applied only to state judges, not law enforcement officers. They found no evidence, at least until recent times, that Congress had asserted a power to "commandeer" local officials. Further, "None of [the statements in *The Federalist*] necessarily implies—what is the critical point here—that Congress could impose these responsibilities without the States' consent."

Instead, the Court pointed to the concept of dual sovereignty, implied by the Tenth Amendment to the Constitution, which states: "The powers not delegated to the United States by the Constitution, nor prohibited by it to the States, are reserved to the States respectively, or to the people."

In view of this, the Court noted: "The Framers rejected the concept of a central government that would act upon and through the States, and instead designed a system in which the State and Federal Governments would exercise concurrent authority over the people. The Federal Government's power would be augmented immeasurably and impermissibly if it were able to impress into its service—and at no cost to itself—the police officers of the 50 States."

Thus, by a narrow 5-4 majority, the Supreme Court voided the requirement that state officials perform the background checks.

Impact

The immediate impact of the decision is limited. First, all other provisions of the Brady Act remain intact. Second, the background check provision would expire in November 1998, to be replaced by a federal system to be used directly by gun dealers.

In the long term, however, the decision may limit the ability of Congress to create "unfunded mandates" (requirements that are imposed by a higher legislature but paid for by local jurisdictions). It is also relevant to the growing interest in the Tenth Amendment by activists who are attempting to restrain the exercise of federal power in favor of local control. Of course, Congress can always require that certain procedures be carried out if a state wishes to receive federal money for law enforcement or other purposes.

DIX V. BERETTA, USA CORP., (ALAMEDA COUNTY, CALIFORNIA, 1998)

Background

Young Kenzo Dix was at the home of Michael S., a 14-year-old friend. Michael took his father's 9-millimeter Beretta pistol from a camera bag. He removed the loaded magazine and replaced it with an empty one. He then pointed the gun at Kenzo and pulled the trigger. Unfortunately, he did not know that in addition to the magazine, the gun can hold one round in the firing chamber. The gun fired, killing Kenzo.

With the assistance of Handgun Control, Inc., Kenzo's parents, Griffin and Lynn Dix, filed suit against Beretta, charging that the gun was defectively designed. They also sued the shooter's parents, charging that they had stored the gun unsafely. The latter case was settled out of court for $100,000, but the case against Beretta went to trial in Alameda County, California.

Legal Issues

The plaintiff argued that the Beretta pistol was defective in design because it did not have an indicator that would show when there was a round in the firing chamber. They also said the gun should have a lock to prevent an unauthorized person from using it. Beretta, they argued, should have foreseen that their product was liable to be misused in a way that could lead to tragic accidents.

Beretta replied that the gun already had a safety device that the young shooter had to disengage before firing. They also argued that trigger locks and locked gun cases were readily available, but Michael's parents had not chosen to use such devices. Finally, Beretta pointed out that the manual that came with the gun mentioned safety practices such as storing the weapon unloaded, separate from ammunition, and inaccessible to children.

Decision

The jury determined that Beretta's product was not defective and that the company was not responsible for Kenzo's death. (The jury foreman was later quoted as saying: "It's really the consumer buying the gun, I feel, who has ultimate responsibility for storage and safety.")

Kenzo's parents won a new trial in 2003 because of the actions of a juror showing bias toward the gun maker. The second trial ended in a mistrial when the jury deadlocked. Finally, in 2004, a third jury found in favor of Beretta USA Corp. after a brief deliberation.

Impact

So far, juries have usually not found that guns as normally designed are defective. However, this may change as cities and other jurisdictions file more suits and as there are more demands for safer guns.

CALIFORNIA RIFLE AND PISTOL ASSOCIATION V. CITY OF WEST HOLLYWOOD, 66 CAL. APP. 4TH 1302 (CALIFORNIA, 1998)

Background

The city of West Hollywood, California, passed a law banning handguns on a list of inexpensive guns often referred to as Saturday night specials. Two local store owners, aided by the California Rifle and Pistol Association and joined by the NRA and California attorney general Dan Lungren, sued to overturn the local ordinance on the grounds that it was "preempted" by state law. A variety of progun and antigun organizations lined up on either side of the case.

Legal Issues

According to the appeals court, "The primary legal issue is whether the Legislature has completely preempted the field of regulation of handgun sales. In the absence of state preemption, every municipality is authorized by the California Constitution to exercise its police power to deal with local situations." The idea of preemption is that a lower jurisdiction (such as a city) cannot make a law that deals with a matter that a higher jurisdiction (such as the state) has already definitively covered. The lower court found that the local ordinance was not preempted.

Decision

The appeals court agreed with the lower court: "Although it is clear that the Legislature could preempt all local ordinances regarding handgun sales, it is equally clear that the Legislature has not done so. Instead, the Legislature has studiously avoided comprehensive preemption of such local laws despite several legislative opportunities to enact a complete preemption. Since the Legislature has avoided preemption of all local regulation of handgun sales, the City continues to enjoy at least some of its constitutional right to regulate handgun sales. The ordinance in question here does not directly conflict with any state statute, and the question of whether to have such an ordinance is a decision within the authority of local elected legislators."

Impact

In general, courts find that a local law is preempted by the state only when at least one of the following is true: (1) the state and local laws contradict each other; or (2) the state law says it intends to preempt or effectively does so by exhaustively covering the subject matter. Gun rights advocates have sometimes tried (with only modest success) to enact state laws with more moderate gun controls, hoping to prevent municipalities from passing stricter controls.

HAMILTON V. ACCU-TEK, 13 F.SUPP.2D 366 (E.D. NEW YORK 1998)

Background

The success of massive class action suits against tobacco companies has encouraged litigators to try a similar approach against firearms manufacturers.

The Law of Gun Control

In this case, a shooting victim (and the surviving family members of six other victims) in Brooklyn, New York, joined together to sue Accu-Tek and 24 other gun manufacturers for negligent marketing that they said contributed to the victimization of their loved ones by criminals. (Although the case was originally filed in 1995, it went through a number of preliminary appeals before going to trial in 1998.)

Legal Issues

The plaintiffs argued that the gun manufacturers deliberately marketed their products in a way that they should have known increased the danger that the guns would be misused, leading to injuries or deaths. For example, they charged, an effort was made to sell more guns in areas in the southern states that had weak gun control laws; they said that the manufacturers should have known that such guns were more likely to get into the black market and thus into the hands of criminals in urban areas such as New York City.

The defendants urged the judge to dismiss the case because someone should not be liable for selling a nondefective product in a legal manner. The judge refused this request and sent the case to the jury.

Decision

After evaluating contracts and sales policies from the manufacturers, the jury decided that three of the manufacturers were both negligent and liable and ordered them to pay $560,000. Six companies were found to be negligent and liable but did not have to pay damages. Six other companies were found to be negligent, but their negligence was not determined to be the cause of the plaintiffs' injuries. Finally, 10 companies were found to be neither negligent nor liable.

The defendant appealed the ruling, and in April 2001 the New York Court of Appeals unanimously reversed the lower court, ruling that because there was no question of the firearm being defective, the manufacturer cannot be sued for someone's criminal misuse of its product. Further, the court noted that "Federal law has already implemented a statutory and regulatory scheme to ensure seller 'responsibility' through licensing requirements and buyer 'responsibility' through background checks."

Impact

As of late 2004 the situation with regard to negligent marketing claims remains mixed. More than two dozen cities have filed suits against gun manufacturers or distributors on this or other grounds; about half of the suits were dismissed before trial. In March 2000 Smith & Wesson (a major handgun manufacturer) signed a comprehensive agreement to settle lawsuits by 17 cities, but the agreement soon broke down.

U.S. V. EMERSON, CRIMINAL ACTION NO. 6:98-CR-103-C (U.S. DISTRICT COURT FOR THE NORTHERN DISTRICT OF TEXAS, SAN ANGELO DIVISION, 1999)

Background

When defendant Timothy Emerson's wife filed for divorce, she applied for a restraining order against him, seeking financial restrictions and a prohibition against his making threats or doing violence against his wife or family. In the hearing for the order, she claimed that Emerson had threatened a man with whom she had been carrying on an affair. Although no actual evidence of a threat was presented, the order was granted as a routine precaution.

One consequence of the order of which Emerson was apparently unaware was that under a 1994 federal law (18 U.S.C. § 922(g)(8)) he was now prohibited from possessing a firearm. He did not dispose of his gun, and he was indicated for violating this law.

Legal Issues

Emerson argued that the federal law violated the Constitution's Commerce Clause as well as the Second, Fifth, and Tenth Amendments. He said the law was not a proper exercise of the power of Congress to regulate interstate commerce because possession of a gun had nothing to do with commerce and that it also violated the Tenth Amendment by intruding on the power of the states. Emerson also argued that the law violated his rights under the Second Amendment, which he said gave him a personal right to bear arms that could not be removed by the simple act of issuing a restraining order in a proceeding that lacked due process and in which no evidence was presented. Similarly, he argued that the lack of due process in taking away an important right violated the Fifth Amendment.

Decision

Judge Sam R. Cummings rejected the Commerce Clause challenge, noting that a superior court had already ruled that the law did not violate that part of the Constitution. By implication, if the law had been passed under a valid power of Congress, it could not violate the Tenth Amendment, which assigns all powers not specified to Congress to the states or the people, nor had Congress violated the proper sovereignty of the states.

The Law of Gun Control

However, in a ruling that was quickly hailed by gun rights advocates, Judge Cummings ruled that the law did violate the Second Amendment. In a decision that reads like a minitutorial on the original intent and historical background of the amendment, he agreed with legal scholars such as Sanford Levenson who insist that the Second Amendment guarantees an individual right to keep and bear arms. Citing a parenthetical part of the Supreme Court decision *United States v. Verdugo-Urquidez*, (494 U.S. 259, 265, 1990) he noted that the Court held that the phrase *the people* throughout the Bill of Right was intended to refer to individuals, not merely a collective group.

Cummings also decided that the Supreme Court's ruling in *U.S. v. Miller*, with its reference to a sawed-off shotgun not having been shown to have military use, was a very narrow decision that did not resolve the question of whether the Second Amendment guaranteed an individual right to keep and bear arms. In his view, this gave him room to make such a determination. He therefore ruled that the law violated Emerson's Second Amendment rights, declaring that:

> *It is absurd that a boilerplate state court divorce order can collaterally and automatically extinguish a law-abiding citizen's Second Amendment rights, particularly when neither the judge issuing the order, nor the parties nor their attorneys are aware of the federal criminal penalties arising from firearm possession after entry of the restraining totally attenuated from divorce proceedings makes the statute unconstitutional. There must be a limit to government regulation on lawful firearm possession. This statute exceeds that limit, and therefore it is unconstitutional.*

Cummings suggested that what this law attempted to do was different from depriving a felon, who had been convicted in a full proceeding under rules of evidence, of the right to own a gun. Further, he agreed that the defendant's Fifth Amendment rights had also been violated by the lack of due process and noted that at the time the restraining order was issued no one had informed him about this rather obscure law.

On appeal, the Fifth Circuit Court of Appeals confirmed by a 2-1 majority that the Second Amendment conferred an individual right. However, the judges found that the right was not absolute, and that restricting it in cases of domestic abuse was reasonable.

Impact

Gun control supporters have argued that the opinion of the appeals court concerning the Second Amendment is just "dicta," or incidental commentary not having any legal effect. Gun rights advocates, on the other hand, believe that the opinion sets up a conflict within the appeals courts between the Fifth Circuit and others (such as the Ninth) that adhere to the idea that the Second Amendment involves only a collective right.

The Supreme Court did not take up the Emerson case. If further decisions show a continuing conflict over interpreting the Second Amendment, the Supreme Court might eventually feel compelled to make a final decision.

COALITION OF NEW JERSEY SPORTSMEN V. WHITMAN, 44 F. SUPP. 2D 666 (1999)

Background

The Coalition of New Jersey Sportsmen, a group of gun clubs, as well as some gun manufacturers and dealers, sued the governor of New Jersey to overturn the state's ban on assault weapons. This law specified particular makes and models of semiautomatic weapons that could no longer be possessed, but guns that were "substantially identical" to the listed guns could also be banned. (This was an attempt to prevent manufacturers from simply changing model names or making minor cosmetic modifications in order to get around the ban.)

Legal Issues

The plaintiffs argued that the gun law was unconstitutionally vague in that it did not adequately specify which guns were banned or might be banned in the future. They also argued that the law violated free speech by simply naming certain guns without regard to defining their characteristics, thus preventing manufacturers from using those names in the future. Further, plaintiffs argued that singling out manufacturers by name was arbitrary and violated their right to equal protection of the law.

Decision

The federal district court ruled that the statute was not vague, because it "addresses an understandable core of banned guns and adequately puts gun owners on notice that their weapon could be prohibited." The Court also ruled that the law did not violate anyone's equal protection rights; any burden on those rights was acceptable "because the rationality of the link between public safety and proscribing assault weapons is obvious." Finally, under the lesser standards protecting commercial speech under the First Amendment, no violation of free speech rights was found.

The plaintiffs appealed the ruling to the Third Circuit Court of Appeals. However, in 2001 that court unanimously upheld the lower court's ruling.

Impact

A similar California case (*Kasler v. Lockyer,* Cal. 4th [2000]) also included a claim that the state's assault weapons law violated the Second Amendment. However, the Ninth Circuit Court of Appeals in upholding the law also ruled that "because the Second Amendment does not confer an individual right to own or possess arms, we affirm the dismissal of all claims brought pursuant to that constitutional provision."

Because this is the position that seems to be prevalent in the various appeals circuits, the usual result in such cases is to apply the lower "rational basis" test to state firearms laws, as was done in the New Jersey case. In most cases involving assault weapons or gun safety it is likely the courts will find that the state did have a rational basis in enacting the law.

Currently only the Fifth Circuit (see *U.S. v. Emerson*) has upheld an individual right to keep and bear arms in the Second Amendment. If the Supreme Court should eventually resolve the conflict between the circuits in favor of this interpretation, a stricter test would presumably be applied to state gun laws. Of course, some regulations might still pass such scrutiny.

CITY OF CINCINNATI V. BERETTA USA CORPORATION,
95 OHIO ST 3D 416 (2002)

Background

The city of Cincinnati, Ohio, sued Beretta and a variety of other handgun manufacturers, on the grounds that their products were being sold negligently in such a way as to make them easily accessible to criminals. This was creating a public nuisance that was causing serious harm to the community and causing the city to spend considerable sums relating to gun violence, including providing medical treatment to victims and undertaking criminal prosecutions. (There were some other claims brought by the city, including fraud, deceptive advertising, and unjust enrichment, but these claims were dismissed or dropped in the course of litigation.)

Legal Issues

Although a variety of claims were discussed at various stages in the litigation, the most important questions were: Is the manufacturer liable for negligence because of the way guns are being sold? Is there a public nuisance for which the city can collect compensation?

Gun Control

Decision

The defendant sought dismissal of the suit before trial. The lower court agreed, finding that the complaint failed to state a valid cause of action, that the city was too "remote" to sue for damages caused by gun violence, and that a city was not allowed to sue for compensation for providing public services such as policing and hospital treatment. Further, the court ruled that a public nuisance must involve some abuse of real property or violation of regulations that endangered public health, welfare, or safety. A product whose design might be dangerous or harmful does not fit within this definition.

The lower appeals court agreed with these findings, but on further appeal the Ohio Supreme Court reversed the lower courts' rulings. First, the Supreme Court said that the lower court had not shown that there was no set of facts upon which a claim might be based, so the case should not have been dismissed for failure to state a claim. The court also agreed with a broader definition of public nuisance that encompassed "unreasonable interference" that "includes those acts that significantly interfere with public health, safety, peace, comfort, or convenience." A product whose defective design has such effects can create liability for creating a public nuisance. Further, it is for the negligent marketing or distribution of the guns, not their actual misuses by criminals, that the companies are held liable. The companies could also be held liable for their negligence without their having owed some "special duty" to the city.

The court also held that the city was not too "remote" from the harm caused by guns to have standing to sue, because of police, hospital, and other costs, as well as the possible loss of tax revenue because of damage to property values caused by the prevalence of crime. Finally, because these costs are not incidental but ongoing, the city should be allowed to try to recover damages for them. The court therefore ruled that the city's suit proceed in the lower court.

Impact

There are many conflicting opinions in state courts regarding suits against gun manufacturers. In *Spitzer v. Sturm, Ruger & Co.* (2003) the New York Supreme Court rejected a similar public nuisance claim. The court noted that firearms were already heavily regulated and that legislatures were much more suited than courts to deal with the problems caused by guns.

If the result in the Cincinnati case proves to be more typical, however, defendants may increasingly be unable to stop such suits in their tracks by getting a ruling that a municipality has no standing to sue in gun liability cases. Juries tend to be more favorable toward claims by gun victims than are judges, so if more cases go to trial, firearms manufacturers may experience increasing pressure to modify their sales and distribution practices.

NATIONAL ASSOCIATION FOR THE ADVANCEMENT OF COLORED PEOPLE V. ACCUSPORT ET AL. (E.D. N.Y., 2003)

Background

The National Association for the Advancement of Colored People (NAACP) sued Sturm, Ruger & Co., and 65 other gun manufacturers or distributors in federal district court in New York, charging that the gun manufacturers had created a public nuisance. Further, blacks had been disproportionately victimized by the negligent marketing of handguns. Rather than monetary damages, the NAACP sought an order restricting gun sales to storefront dealers only (rather than gun shows) and limiting individual purchases to one handgun a month.

Legal Issues

The NAACP argued that federal data showed—and manufacturers knew—that a disproportionate number of guns were getting into criminal hands in minority communities. The defendants argued that manufacturers were not liable for criminals obtaining and misusing their product, and that they had no control over the secondary market in guns.

Decision

The jury found that 45 defendants had not been negligent with regard to the gun sales in minority neighborhoods. The jury was unable to come to a decision regarding the remaining 23 defendants. However, federal judge Harvey Weinstein, who had announced earlier that he would make the final decision in the case, then dismissed the suits, noting that

> The NAACP proved that its members and potential members—now predominantly African-Americans—did suffer relatively more harm from the nuisance created by the defendant through the unnecessary illegal availability of guns in New York. . . . It failed, however, to show that its harm was different in kind from that suffered by other persons in New York.

That last sentence meant that the NAACP had failed one of the requirements of New York's law of public nuisance.

Gun Control

Impact

Because of the disproportionate effects of crime on blacks and other minorities, some advocates believe that gun control might be a civil rights issue—although the specific claim is of public nuisance. The problem with adding the element of race is that it complicates the question of why effects on one community should be treated differently from those in others. Judge Weinstein did suggest, however, that an approach in which a city sues based on damage to the whole community (as in cases in Cincinnati and elsewhere) might be more appropriate.

CHAPTER 3

CHRONOLOGY

This chapter provides a chronology of important events relating to gun issues. Some historical events are included because they are often cited by gun control or gun rights advocates in support of their positions.

871

- King Alfred of Saxon England's laws give every man the right to keep and bear arms but prohibit murder and other crimes.

1020

- England's King Cnut's laws recognize the right to keep and bear arms, the right to self-defense, and the right to hunt on one's own land.

1181

- In his Assize of Arms, King Henry II gives "every knight and freeman" the right to have weapons and armor. Arms holders had to swear to obey the king and defend the kingdom. The result is a kind of protomilitia.

1215

- King John is forced by barons to recognize their right to bear arms as part of the Magna Carta, which later becomes a model for the American colonists in their struggle against the English monarchy. The militia is restored.

1252

- Under Henry III, the arming of citizens is extended. An "arming of the whole people" rather than a large standing army gradually becomes the basis for England's defense.

Gun Control

1300s

- Gunpowder, already in use in China, is introduced into Europe. At first it is used primarily in crude siege cannons that can blow holes in castle walls, enforcing the power of the monarch over the nobles.

1328

- In response to rowdiness by knights and others, Edward III issues the Statute of Northampton. It prohibits "persons great or small" from carrying weapons in public, though it allows for defense of the home. The law is widely disobeyed, and, in practice, courts applied it only to those who used arms to "terrify the good people of the land."

1485

- King Henry VII forbids hunting in an attempt to reduce the number of people with weapons who could start a rebellion against the Crown.

1500s

- Portable firearms such as the arquebus become more common on the battlefield. At first the unwieldy guns are fired from tripodlike supports, but versions that can be fired from the shoulder soon appear.
- King Henry VII implements "crossbow control," decreeing that no one may shoot a crossbow in hunting or otherwise, except to protect his property and land.

1511

- King Henry VIII places tighter controls on crossbows but orders that all fathers should teach their sons to shoot the longbow, which had been a devastating weapon against French knights in earlier wars.

1541

- King Henry VIII restricts the lengths of guns that citizens may possess. People are allowed to keep other guns in their homes but not carry them in their travels on the king's highways.

1557

- Under Queen Mary I, a statute details exactly which weapons people can and must possess for the defense of the state. The kind and amount of weapons a person may have depends on the kind and amount of property they own.

1600s

■ Permanent British settlement in America begins. The colonists use firearms daily for hunting as well as in ongoing conflicts with Native Americans and French colonists.

1642

■ The English Civil War between the king and Parliament breaks out. One of the issues of contention is control of the militia, the trained bands of armed citizens who make up an important part of the nation's military power.

1659

■ With Oliver Cromwell dead and the English Civil War coming to an end, a London ordinance requires that every householder give the government a list of all arms and ammunition owned. Weapons owned by Catholics or others who had fought against Parliament or by other "dangerous" persons could be seized. Later, King Charles II continued the seizing of weapons from such persons.

1670

■ King Charles II restricts guns and bows to large landowners (who make up the nobility), thus disarming the emerging middle class and the poor. At its time, this was the most restrictive English weapons control law ever passed.

1686

■ Sir John Knight is accused of entering a church while armed. The judge acquits him because the law in question specified persons who went armed "to terrify the King's subjects."
■ In his work *Two Treatises on Government*, philosopher John Locke maintains the "natural" right of citizens to have arms for their individual and collective defense.

1688

■ In the bloodless "Glorious Revolution," William and Mary defeat English King James II, abolish the standing army, and restore—to Protestants only—the right to keep and bear arms.

Gun Control

1689

- The British Bill of Rights includes a condemnation of previous kings for disarming the people and specifies that henceforth "The subjects which are Protestants may have arms for their defence suitable to their conditions and allowed by law."

1698

- Philosopher Algernon Sidney in his book *Discourses Concerning Government* states that "the body of the People is the Public defense, and every man is armed and disciplined." American colonists soon put the idea in practice in the form of local militias.

1700s

- Two new kinds of long guns come into use: The smoothbore musket has a short range and can be fired about four times a minute by well-trained soldiers. The rifle with its grooved barrel takes longer to load but has greater range and accuracy. Both kinds of guns must be loaded by hand, one shot at a time.

1739

- In the British court case of *Rex v. Gardner,* the judge holds that the game laws did not forbid a person from mere possession of a gun for purposes of self-defense. Several later cases have similar verdicts.

1770

- British soldiers fire on unarmed Americans in Boston, leading to an upsurge of revolutionary sentiment. The British respond by beginning to raid colonial homes and gatherings to seize guns and ammunition.

1775

- The American War of Independence is ignited when British troops under General Thomas Gage attempt to seize guns and ammunition from colonists at Lexington and Concord. Although faced down initially by the trained British troops, the American Minutemen militia begins a relentless fire, aided by accurate long-range rifles.

1776

- In addition to declaring independence, the various states write constitutions that include bills of rights. In general they refer to the danger of standing armies, the reliance on a well-regulated militia, and the right to keep and bear arms.

1777

■ British colonial undersecretary William Knox presents a proposal concerning what to do with the colonies if they are subjugated and returned to British control. His proposals include the repeal of the militia laws, the confiscation of all arms held by the people, and the prohibition of the manufacture or importation of guns or powder in America.

1789

■ The Bill of Rights to the U.S. Constitution is approved. It includes the Second Amendment, which guarantees the right to keep and bear arms to maintain a strong militia as a protector of liberty.

1792

■ The Militia Act is passed. It recognizes both an unorganized ("enrolled") militia and an organized militia.

1822

■ In the Kentucky case of *Bliss v. Commonwealth*, the court holds that the state constitution prohibits any interference with the right to keep and bear arms, even concealed weapons.

1836

■ U.S. inventor Samuel Colt's revolver is patented. Because it can fire six shots without reloading, it represents a formidable increase in firepower for close combat and helps settlers repel Indian raids.

1837

■ Georgia passes the first ban on handguns. It is later overturned in *Nunn v. State* as a violation of the Second Amendment.

1840

■ The court in the Tennessee case of *Aymette v. State* upholds some measure of gun control by letting stand a ban on carrying concealed weapons. It bases its decision on English laws that had specified conditions under which weapons could be held.

1846

■ In the Georgia case of *Nunn v. State*, the court says that the state can use its police power to ban some kinds of weapons (such as concealable handguns) but not all firearms. This marks a general trend where courts uphold gun control measures that can be justified as an exercise of the police power.

1850

■ Some southern states argue that black slaves do not have the Second Amendment right to keep and bear arms because they are "not citizens."

1857

■ In *Dred Scott v. Sanford*, Supreme Court Chief Justice Taney declares that the Bill of Rights had not been written to protect blacks and that doing so would mean that, among other things, they could "keep and carry arms wherever they went."

1865

■ Following the Civil War, Black Codes are enacted to restrict the rights of the newly freed slaves. Prohibiting them from keeping and carrying firearms is a common provision.

1866

■ The Winchester repeating rifle lets its user fire up to 15 shots by working a lever every few seconds. It will become known as the gun that won the West.
■ The Fourteenth Amendment, the Freedman's Bureau Act, and the Civil Rights Act of 1866 all include the Second Amendment right to keep and bear arms among the rights that the states are prohibited from taking from any citizen.

1871

■ The National Rifle Association (NRA) is established. It initially focuses on improving marksmanship to ensure proper national defense.

1876

■ In *U.S. v. Cruikshank* a group of Ku Klux Klansmen are convicted of depriving "persons of color" their right to keep and bear arms. The

Chronology

Supreme Court overturns the conviction, declaring that this right is independent of the Second Amendment and that the latter cannot be used against individuals or states, only against the federal government.

1886

- In *Presser v. Illinois*, the Supreme Court reaffirms its ruling in the *Cruikshank* case but also says that states cannot abolish the right of citizens to keep and bear arms because it would deprive the United States of the pool of citizens who make up the "reserve militia."

1908

- New York becomes the first state to require hunting licenses.

1911

- New York City enacts the Sullivan Act, which becomes the prototype for handgun registration laws. The law may have been passed by the Tammany Hall political machine in response to fear of growing crime associated with Italian immigrants.

1919

- U.S. Congress enacts the first tax that applies to weapons. It is promoted as a revenue-raising tax rather than as a gun control measure.

1920s

- A newly developed military weapon, the Thompson submachine gun, or tommy gun, finds an unforeseen application as the gangster's gun of choice. Its devastating firepower spurs demands for a federal gun control law.

1927

- A federal law prohibits the mailing of concealable firearms in the United States.

1934

- The National Firearms Act of 1934 is passed. The law includes a variety of taxes on the manufacture, sale, and transfer of automatic weapons and certain short-barreled weapons, as well as requiring an FBI background check and the consent of local law enforcement officials for any purchase. The law does not apply to handguns.

Gun Control

1938

- Congress passes the Federal Firearms Act of 1938. It requires that manufacturers, importers, and dealers in firearms (and ammunition for pistols and revolvers) obtain licenses. The law also prohibits delivery of a gun to a known criminal, to someone under indictment, or in violation of local licensing laws.

1939

- In *U.S. v. Miller* the Supreme Court rejects an appeal by stating that it had been given no evidence that a sawed-off shotgun was suitable for use in a militia, and because it is not, carrying it would not be protected by the Second Amendment. Because the decision also implied an individual right to bear military-type arms, it would be cited by both supporters and opponents of gun control.

1958

- The Federal Aviation Act is passed. It prohibits the carrying of firearms "on or about" any passenger flying on a commercial aircraft.

1963

- The assassination of President John F. Kennedy begins what many will see as an era of heightened violence and social tension.

1966

- The nation is shocked when Charles Whitman kills 16 people with a rifle from the top of a tower at the University of Texas. He is killed by police.

1967

- As crime rates continue to increase, the President's Commission on Law Enforcement includes among its recommendations national registration of handguns and the prohibition of interstate sales of handguns.

1968

- Following the assassination of Dr. Martin Luther King, Jr., and Senator Robert Kennedy, Congress passes the Omnibus Crime Control and Safe Streets Act of 1968. It includes the Gun Control Act of 1968, which prohibits nearly all interstate gun sales, requires licensing of all gun dealers, and requires the recording of details about gun sales.

Chronology

1969

- The National Commission on the Causes and Prevention of Violence issues a report that includes recommendations for laws for the national registration of handguns and the licensing of handgun purchasers.

1972

- Senator Birch Bayh of Indiana proposes a bill that would prohibit the manufacture and sale of "nonsporting" handguns. It passes in the Senate but dies in the House. A similar bill will be passed by the Senate in 1974.

1973

- The National Advisory Commission on Criminal Justice Standards and Goals sets a goal of banning all private ownership of handguns by 1983.

1977

- In *Moore v. East Cleveland* the Supreme Court states (in passing) that the right to keep and bear arms is one of the "specific guarantees" contained in the Constitution of the United States, but this ruling is not applied to gun control cases.
- The District of Columbia imposes a ban on the acquisition, purchase, or possession of handguns.

1980s

- The 1980s introduces deadlier weapons to America's streets, including such semiautomatic pistols as the Glock and Tec-9 and, to a lesser extent, semiautomatic ("assault") rifles such as the AK-47. Media exposure to such weapons in drug- and gang-related violence helps to spur support for gun control in general and a ban on semiautomatic assault weapons in particular.

1980

- In *Lewis v. U.S.*, the Supreme Court holds that the federal government denying felons the right to possess firearms does not infringe on the provisions of the Second Amendment right to keep and bear arms nor on the equal protection clause of the Fourteenth Amendment.

1981

- President Ronald Reagan and James Brady, his press secretary, are wounded in an assassination attempt by John Hinckley. Brady and his wife

Sarah later join Handgun Control, Inc., to lobby for effective handgun control legislation.
- The village of Morton Grove, Illinois, passes an ordinance that bans individual possession of a variety of weapons including handguns, automatic weapons, and short-barreled shotguns. A U.S. district court holds that the ordinance is constitutional. In 1983 the U.S. Court of Appeals, Seventh Circuit, confirms the lower court decision in *Quilici v. Morton Grove*. The Supreme Court declines to hear the case.

1982

- California voters defeat Proposition 15, which would have imposed strict handgun controls, including registration and a freeze on the total number of guns available.

1984

- U.S. Congress passes the Armed Career Criminal Act, amending the Gun Control Act of 1968. It imposes stiff fines and prison terms for felons and other prohibited classes of persons who receive, possess, or transport a firearm. An appropriation bill passed by Congress eliminates probation or suspended sentences for persons committing a federal felony with any firearm and imposes an add-on 15-year sentence for possession of a firearm by a robber or burglar who is a repeat offender.

1986

- Writing in the *New England Journal of Medicine*, researchers Arthur Kellermann and Donald T. Reay report a survey showing that a gun kept in the home was 43 times as likely to kill a family member or friend than to kill a criminal intruder. Speaking of "an epidemic of firearms violence," a number of other medical writers begin to urge stricter gun control and education. Criminologist Gary Kleck disputes such findings, citing his own survey that says that armed citizens successfully drive off criminals more than 2 million times a year, usually without firing a shot.
- Congress passes the Firearms Owners Protection Act, a law that rolls back some provisions of earlier federal firearms legislation. For example, it reduces "paperwork" violations for firearms dealers from a felony to a misdemeanor and allows the interstate sale of long guns by dealers. However, it also increases penalties for drug traffickers who possess firearms and incorporates an amendment that essentially bans the purchase of automatic firearms by civilians if the guns were manufactured after the enactment of the law.

Chronology

- The Law Enforcement Officers Protection Act is passed. It bans the manufacture or importation of so-called cop-killer bullets that can pierce officers' bulletproof vests.

1988

- Congress passes the Terrorist Firearms Detection Act. It bans firearms (such as plastic handguns) that cannot be detected by security equipment such as airport X-ray machines.

1989

- A deranged gunman opens fire on a playground in Stockton, California, killing five schoolchildren. Such school shootings will become a major spur to gun control efforts in the 1990s.
- California adopts the Roberti-Roos Assault Weapon Act. It bans many types of semiautomatic weapons and bans sales by unlicensed dealers.
- In what becomes a growing trend, Florida enacts a law requiring a background check for persons buying a gun from a dealer and a law requiring gun owners to keep their guns locked so that children cannot get access to them.

1990

- The Indiana Supreme Court rules that the mayor of Gary, Indiana, violated the state constitution when he denied gun permits to city residents. The court cites the 1871 Civil Rights Act, which had been passed to counter the actions of Ku Klux Klan members.
- More states, such as California, Connecticut, and Iowa, pass tougher gun control regulations, requiring background checks and longer waiting periods for gun purchasers.
- In *United States v. Verdugo-Urquidez*, the Supreme Court notes in passing that *the people* has a consistent meaning of "individuals" when used in the Constitution, including the Second Amendment.

1991

- Twenty-three people are killed in a Texas cafeteria by George Hennard, Jr., who then kills himself. A woman named Suzanna Gratia later tells a congressional committee that she probably could have shot Hennard with her own gun if the law had allowed her to bring it into the building.

1992

- The wife and son of Randy Weaver, an avowed white separatist, are killed by FBI agents in a siege of his remote cabin, where he had fled after being charged with selling a sawed-off shotgun. The incident galvanizes antigovernment radicals. Weaver is later acquitted of the most serious charges and wins a settlement from the government. Congress holds hearings that question the "rules of engagement" used by the FBI.

1993

- Colin Ferguson opens fire on a Long Island Rail Road commuter train, killing five people and injuring 19.
- Gian Ferri uses an assault weapon to kill eight and injure six people in a San Francisco office tower. Gun control activists (including some relatives of shooting victims) refer to such incidents in demanding stricter gun controls, including a ban on assault weapons. Gun rights activists suggest that armed citizens could save many lives during such incidents.
- *April:* The FBI ends its siege of Branch Davidian sect leader David Koresh and his followers by battering their compound with tanks and injecting tear gas. The building is consumed by fire, killing Koresh and most of his followers, including dozens of children. This incident fuels the antigovernment militia movement and is cited by some gun rights advocates as showing the need for citizens to have guns to resist tyrannical government.
- *November:* Congress passes and President Bill Clinton signs the Brady Handgun Violence Prevention Act. This law establishes nationwide background checks and a five-day waiting period for all handgun purchases.

1994

- In another major victory for gun control advocates, Congress passes the Assault Weapons Ban Bill, which bans 19 semiautomatic firearms described as "assault weapons."

1995

- In *United States v. Lopez,* the Supreme Court strikes down the federal Gun-Free School Zones Act. The Court rules that Congress did not show a sufficient relationship between the gun ban and its constitutional power to regulate interstate commerce. (The Second Amendment is not mentioned.)
- *April:* Timothy McVeigh sets off a truck filled with explosives, destroying the federal building in Oklahoma City, killing 168 people, and injuring hundreds more. Although not directly involving firearms, the incident contributed to public anxiety and promoted demands for gun control, while seeming to quiet the most radical antigovernment groups.

Chronology

1998

- Veteran movie actor Charlton Heston is elected president of the National Rifle Association, in what is viewed by many gun control advocates as an attempt to rehabilitate the organization's somewhat tarnished image.
- In the case of *Dix v. Beretta* a jury refuses to hold the gun maker liable when a teenager fires a gun that he thinks is unloaded. The plaintiff had claimed that the gun was defectively designed. That same year, however, in the Brooklyn, New York, case of *Hamilton v. Accu-Tek*, a jury does find some gun makers liable for marketing and distributing guns recklessly, making it easy for guns to reach the hands of criminals.
- By the end of the year, more than 20 cities file class action suits against gun makers, adopting a strategy similar to that used successfully against the big tobacco companies.

1999

- *April:* Two students, Dylan Klebold and Eric Harris, kill 15 people (including themselves) at Columbine High School in Littleton, Colorado, with several guns and many homemade bombs. The tragedy immediately spurs a demand for new gun control measures, as well as calling into question the role of parents and the media in creating violent, disaffected teens. The uproar also stalls attempts by gun advocates to liberalize concealed-carry laws in a number of states.
- *June:* Congress fails to agree on a package of gun control measures as part of a new criminal justice bill. One sticking point is whether to impose a 24-hour or a 72-hour waiting period for purchases made at gun shows. Gun control advocates want the longer period to ensure that background checks are complete and also to serve as a "cooling off" period for possibly disturbed purchasers. Gun rights advocates believe that the instant background check now in place for dealer sales be used instead. Other proposals include a ban on importing high-capacity ammunition clips and a requirement that guns be sold with trigger locks.
- *August 10:* Buford Furrow, an avowed racist, kills an Asian-American postal worker and opens fire on a Jewish community center in Los Angeles, wounding five people, including three young children. He later pleads guilty.
- *August 10:* A report released by the federal Department of Education says that about three-quarters of the states have experienced a decline in the number of students expelled for gun possession. At least part of the decline is attributed to stronger security measures instituted in schools following the Columbine shootings in April.
- *August 28:* California enacts some of the nation's toughest new gun laws. New safety test requirements are expected to stop the sale of most

inexpensive handguns. Gun show promoters will have to obtain licenses, and all new handguns sold in California must include trigger locks. Earlier in the year, California had strengthened its assault weapons ban and limited buyers to buying one gun per month.

- **September 30:** A California appeals court rules that victims of a 1993 mass shooting in a San Francisco office building can sue gun manufacturers.
- **October 8:** An Ohio judge throws out Cincinnati's lawsuit against gun manufacturers, ruling that only the legislature has the authority to regulate product design, and that "the risks associated with the use of a firearm are open and obvious and matters of common knowledge." Instigators of a California state gun lawsuit believe that the ruling will not affect their case, which is brought on different grounds.
- **October 11:** The venerable Colt firearms company announces that it will no longer sell handguns to consumers, except as collector's items. The company is believed to have acted to reduce its potential liability in future lawsuits and because fear of lawsuits has begun to drive suppliers, lenders, and investors from the consumer firearms market.
- **October 15:** A U.S. district judge in Los Angeles overturns the county's ban on gun shows. He rules that state law preempts the county from legislating in this area, and that the county action poses an "undue hardship" to promoters who had sponsored the gun show for 22 years.

2000

- **January:** In his State of the Union Address, President Bill Clinton calls on states to register handgun owners, requiring them to have a background check, photo ID, and proof that they meet safety requirements. The White House also announces it would seek $280 million in funding to enforce existing gun laws.
- **January:** The U.S. Conference of Mayors meets in Washington, D.C. They display a blackboard listing nearly 3,100 fatal gun victims since the Columbine shootings and call for Congress to pass the legislation on gun sales and shows that had stalled the previous year.
- **January:** Officials in the cities of San Francisco and Oakland, California, propose municipal ordinances that would ban the sale of so-called ultra-compact handguns that can be easily carried in people's pockets. (Due to their good quality construction, such guns are not covered under existing legislation banning "Saturday Night Specials.")
- **March:** Smith & Wesson, a major handgun manufacturer, enters into an agreement with a number of local governments to settle pending lawsuits. The gunmaker agrees to a variety of provisions including required safety and "personalization" devices, childproofing, and restrictions on distribution and

sale of guns. However, the agreement soon breaks down over the question of whether the conditions also apply to products not manufactured by Smith & Wesson that are handled by the distributors.

- *May 14:* On Mother's Day, the Million Mom March, the largest pro-gun control demonstration in history, fills the Mall in Washington, D.C., with an estimated 750,000 people.
- *June 27:* New York becomes the first state to sue gun manufacturers, based on a new state law that declares illegal guns to be a "public nuisance." More than 30 cities and counties are already suing gun makers under a negligence theory.
- *November–December:* After the recounting and the court battles arising from the 2000 presidential election are done, Republican George W. Bush gains the presidency over Democratic contender Al Gore. Some observers suggest that Gore's advocacy of gun control may have cost him some swing states. However, gun control forces win some electoral victories, closing the "gun show loophole" in Colorado and Oregon and strengthening gun laws in Maryland and New York.
- *December:* Smith & Wesson enters into a legal settlement with the city of Boston. It resolves some of the issues in the earlier failed agreement, and is restricted only to Smith & Wesson's products. However, a number of gun advocacy groups organize a boycott of Smith & Wesson to protest what they view as caving in to antigun forces.

2001

- *January 17:* At his confirmation hearing, U.S. Attorney General John Ashcroft reiterates the Bush administration's support for extending the ban on assault weapons when it comes up for renewal.
- *April:* A New York appeals court overturns a verdict against three gun manufacturers for negligent marketing. The court cites the fact that the guns were not defective and were already heavily regulated by law.
- *May 17:* In a letter to NRA chief lobbyist James Jay Baker, U.S. Attorney General John Ashcroft announces a radical shift in Justice Department policy in which it will accept the individual rights theory of the Second Amendment. However, subsequent statements imply that the Justice Department will not seek to overturn any existing federal firearms laws on Second Amendment grounds.
- *May 28:* *Fortune* magazine names the National Rifle Association as the top lobbying organization in the United States, citing its success in the 2000 elections.
- *June:* Senators John McCain (R-Ariz.) and Joe Lieberman (D-Conn.) introduce a bill that would require that all purchasers at gun shows go

through the same background checks as people who buy guns at gun shops.

- *June 14:* Handgun Control, Inc., changes its name to the Brady Campaign to Prevent Gun Violence. A related group, the Center to Prevent Handgun Violence, is renamed the Brady Center to Prevent Gun Violence.
- *August:* The California Supreme Court overturns a negligence lawsuit based on the use of the Navegar TEC-9 assault pistol in the 100 California Saint shootings in 1993 in San Francisco. The court rules that the suit was barred by California law.
- *September 11:* Terrorists linked to al-Qaeda destroy the World Trade Center in New York and damage the Pentagon in Washington, D.C., killing about 2,800 people. Although no guns were used in hijacking the airliners used in the attack, the disaster will be used both to justify and oppose new gun control measures.
- *October:* The Court of Appeals for the Fifth Circuit issues its ruling in *U.S. v. Emerson.* While agreeing with the lower court that the Second Amendment conveyed an individual right to own a gun, the justices also said that restricting that right in domestic abuse cases was reasonable. The U.S. Supreme Court has thus far declined to resolve the conflicting interpretations of the Second Amendment among the circuit courts.
- *October 1:* The Million Mom March organization merges with the Brady Center to Prevent Gun Violence.

2002

- *April 26:* Robert Steinhauser, a German teenager who had been expelled from an Erfurt, Germany, high school, enters the school with a handgun and a shotgun. He kills 16 people (mainly teachers and school officials) and injures 10. His guns had been acquired legally.
- *June:* The Ohio Supreme Court allows a suit against 15 gun manufacturers to proceed. Overturning a lower court decision, it accepts the city's claim that gun marketing practices created a substantial danger by making guns too easily available to criminals and children.
- *September:* California becomes the first state to repeal a law granting gun manufacturers immunity from lawsuits.
- *October:* Ten random persons are killed and three injured by Washington, D.C.-area anonymous snipers. The shootings, revealed later to have been done with a high-powered Bushmaster rifle by Lee Boyd Malvo and John Allan Muhammad, are used by gun control advocates to argue for extending and expanding the bans on such weapons.

Chronology

2003

- *January:* Maryland becomes the first state to require that new handguns be equipped with internal locking mechanisms.
- *April:* The Bush administration through spokesperson Scott McClellan affirms its continuing support for the assault weapons ban and for renewing the law.
- *April:* Wal-Mart suspends gun sales in its 118 California stores after spot checks reveal that salespeople in six stores failed to properly complete federally required background checks or released guns to customers before the end of the 10-day waiting period. Meanwhile, New York State Attorney General Eliot Spitzer sues Wal-Mart for allegedly selling toy guns that lack the markings needed to distinguish them from real firearms.
- *April 29:* Minnesota changes the wording in its policy on concealed firearms carry permits to "shall issue," meaning that citizens must be given such permits unless they don't legally qualify. More than 30 states now have "shall issue" laws.
- *July 22:* A lawsuit charging that the killing of a disproportionate number of blacks by illegal guns was the responsibility of gun manufacturers is dismissed by a New York federal court.
- *August 7:* A Michigan state appeals court rules that a state law passed in 2000 barred the city of Detroit and Wayne County from suing gun makers for the criminal misuse of firearms.
- *August 21:* Eleven California cities and towns settle a lawsuit involving alleged reckless practices by several gun dealers and distributors. The businesses agree to have workers trained in spotting "straw buyers" who obtain guns for criminals, and to share additional sales information with law enforcement officials.

2004

- *March 2:* A bill to shield gun manufacturers and dealers from lawsuits is overwhelmingly defeated in the Senate. The Republicans had withdrawn their support for the bill after Democrats had succeeded in adding amendments that would renew the ban on assault weapons, require child safety locks on all handguns, and require background checks on gun purchases at gun shows.
- *March 9:* John Allan Muhammad, considered the mastermind behind the Washington, D.C.-area sniper killings in October 2002, is sentenced to death. The following day his young accomplice, Lee Boyd Malvo, receives a life sentence without possibility of parole.

- *June 10:* In the case of *Mosby v. McAteer*, the Rhode Island Supreme Court rules that the state's discretionary concealed gun carry law (restricting permits to persons who have a "legitimate need") does not violate the state constitution.
- *July 6:* Former presidents Gerald Ford, Jimmy Carter, and Bill Clinton appeal to President George W. Bush to take action to prevent the federal assault weapons ban from lapsing. However, Congress is expected to end the current session without further action.
- *August 3:* In the third and final trial in the case of *Dix v. Beretta*, the jury finds in favor of the gun maker.
- *September 13:* The federal assault weapons ban expires. In the presidential campaign, Democrat John Kerry charges that President George W. Bush had bowed to NRA pressure in declining to make any effort to renew the law.
- *October 4:* The U.S. Supreme Court declines to review a 9th Circuit appeals court decision uploading the Alameda County, California, ban on gun shows at county fairgrounds. The lower court had said that neither the First nor the Second Amendment had been violated by the ban.

CHAPTER 4

BIOGRAPHICAL LISTING

This chapter briefly introduces individuals who have played an important part in the gun control debate, including political leaders, researchers, writers, and activists.

John Ashcroft, Attorney General of the United States (2000–). A former governor of Missouri and then senator, as head of the Justice Department Ashcroft has angered gun control advocates by resisting efforts to allow access by criminal and antiterrorism investigators to data gathered for firearms background checks. He has defended his actions by saying that the Brady law prohibits such access and that it would violate the privacy rights of gun owners. Liberals decried what they saw as Ashcroft's hypocrisy in being so solicitous of the rights of gun owners while invading the privacy of many other people in the name of fighting terrorism. In May 2001 Ashcroft wrote a letter declaring that the Justice Department recognized the Second Amendment as conveying an individual right to keep and bear arms—an interpretation that gun control advocates decried as being out of step with 60 years of federal court rulings.

Massad F. Ayoob, prolific author and trainer in armed self-defense and gun handling. Ayoob is the founder and head of the Lethal Force Institute in Concord, New Hampshire. His books include *In the Gravest Extreme: The Role of the Firearm in Personal Protection* (1980), *Gunproof Your Children: Handgun Primer* (1986), and the *Gun Digest Book of Combat Handgunnery* (5th ed., 2002). Ayoob also writes columns and articles for publications such as *Shooting Industry*. His works emphasize the seriousness of the responsibility involved in using a gun in violent situations, and the psychological and practical factors faced even by police and other professionals.

Michael Bellesiles, controversial Emory University historian of the use of firearms in the United States. When his book *Arming America: The Origin of a National Gun Culture* was published in 2000, many gun control advocates hailed its revisionist view of the role of firearms in early American life. Bellesiles concluded from his study of gun ownership (primarily through probate, business, and military records) that, contrary to the myth of a frontier society where a rifle or musket was a daily companion for most people, most Americans before the Civil War did not own firearms and seemed to have little interest in them. He sees the modern gun culture (and its founding myth) as arising from the government letting Union soldiers keep their guns after the Civil War and a burgeoning gun industry that took advantage of romantic myths about the Old West and frontier heroes. If this is true, it would undercut support for the historical intent of the Second Amendment and the importance of the right to keep and bear arms to the first generations of Americans. However, as other historians began checking the records cited by Professor Bellesisles they found numerous discrepancies, omissions, and misattributions. An investigation by Emory University found serious problems with the work, and the officials who had awarded Bellesiles the prestigious Bancroft Prize withdrew it. Bellesisles has continued to maintain that the essential findings of his research are correct, and argues that his errors have been exaggerated.

Barbara Boxer, U.S. senator from California, elected to the Senate in 1992 after having served 10 years in the House. In addition to working for women's issues and health care, Boxer has been a strong advocate in the Senate for gun control, including the Brady Bill, the Assault Weapons Ban, and the attaching of gun control provisions to more recent crime bills.

James Brady, gun control activist. He had a distinguished career during the 1970s as a Republican political consultant and press secretary in a variety of political and corporate settings. In January 1981, he was appointed White House press secretary to the newly elected President Ronald Reagan. On March 30, 1981, he was seriously wounded in an assassination attempt on President Reagan. While struggling to recover, he joined with his wife Sarah in gun control efforts, becoming particularly involved in the leadership of Handgun Control, Inc.

Sarah Brady, gun control activist. Starting in the 1960s, Brady was a schoolteacher and Republican Party worker. In 1981, her husband was seriously wounded (along with President Reagan) in an assassination attempt. This experience spurred Brady into becoming a full-time gun control activist. Sarah Brady and her husband, Jim, continue to play a prominent role in the campaign for gun control. In their honor, in 2001 Handgun Control, Inc., was renamed the Brady Campaign to End Gun Violence and the Center to Prevent Gun Violence became the Brady Center to Prevent Gun Violence. Her most significant achievement thus far has been the passage in November 1993 of the Brady Bill, named in honor of her husband. This law established waiting period and background check requirements for all handgun purchases. Brady has received numerous public service awards.

George Herbert Walker Bush, president of the United States, 1989–1993. Bush had a moderate stance on gun control issues, leading to some criticism from the NRA and gun rights advocates. Bush supported some controls on assault weapons, including banning further imports of such weapons. When NRA executive vice president Wayne LaPierre issued a fund-raising letter in 1995 that referred to federal agents as "jack-booted thugs," Bush resigned his NRA membership.

George W. Bush, president of the United States (2001–) Bush campaigned as a "compassionate conservative" and a moderate supporter of gun rights. The president had said he supported the assault weapons ban, which came up for renewal in fall 2004. However, the Bush administration has also promoted a bill shielding gun manufacturers from liability claims. When Democrats succeeded in attaching the renewal of the assault weapons ban and the closing of the "gun show loophole," to the bill in March 2004, Republicans dropped their support for the bill, leading to an apparent stalemate on new gun legislation. (The assault weapons ban expired in September 2004.) The Justice Department under the Bush administration has also declared its support for the position that the Second Amendment guarantees an individual the right to keep and bear arms.

William Jefferson Clinton, former Arkansas governor and president of the United States, 1993–2001. Clinton was a strong supporter for gun control measures such as the Brady Bill. Following the Littleton shootings in April 1999, Clinton called for closing loopholes in gun laws by requiring background checks for purchasers at gun shows, as well as supporting waiting periods and requiring the sale of trigger locks with guns. In his rhetoric, Clinton often distinguishes between hunting/sporting use of guns and the use of assault weapons.

John Coale, trial lawyer who has specialized in suing on behalf of children and other victims of unsafe products or practices. He has sued school boards for their overuse of drugs to treat students with Attention Deficit Disorder, sued Ford Motor Company for designing unsafe school buses, and, in his biggest case to date, played a key role in a class action suit that won a $200 billion settlement from tobacco companies for the health costs caused by their products. In October 1998 his legal consortium, the Castano Group, filed the first of wave of lawsuits against gun makers, charging them with selling unsafe guns and with reckless marketing. His flamboyant style and savvy use of the media have given him a high profile.

Donna Dees-Thomases, mother and publicist who organized the Million Mom March on May 14, 2000, when an estimated 750,000 people participated in the largest gun control demonstration in history. An assistant to news anchor Dan Rather, Dees-Thomases' resolve to work for tougher gun laws began on August 10, 1999, as she was watching news reports about the shooting of five people at the Jewish Granada Hills Day Camp in California, which was later linked to a white supremacist. She conceived of the idea of a mass demonstration to show popular support for gun control. Following the actual march, the Million Mom March continued as an organization with 235 chapters in 46 states. Today, Dees-Thomases continues a busy life as a mother, publicist, and activist. Although she has been accused of "wanting to take away everyone's guns," Dees-Thomases has replied that she just wants guns to be subject to the consumer standards and required licensing and training appropriate for such deadly devices.

Dianne Feinstein, senator and gun control advocate. Feinstein was a member of the San Francisco Board of Supervisors during the 1970s. Although rebuffed two times in running for the office, she became the first woman mayor of San Francisco in November 1978 following the assassinations of Mayor George Moscone and Supervisor Harvey Milk by disgruntled former supervisor Dan White. During her nine years as mayor, she was credited with reducing crime and social unrest in the city. In 1992 she began her career as a senator from California. She has been a strong advocate for gun control, particularly for the successful passage of a ban on assault weapons.

Alan M. Gottlieb, prominent gun rights activist; chairman of the Citizens Committee for the Right to Keep and Bear Arms and founder of the Second Amendment Foundation. Gottlieb has written many articles on the Second Amendment and on gun rights. He is publisher of two magazines, *Gun Week* and *Gun News Digest*. Among his books are the *Gun Owners Political Action Manual* and *The Gun Rights Fact Book*. He has also been active in the environmental "wise use" movement, a movement that promotes compromises between economic and environmental considerations.

Stephen P. Halbrook, professor of philosophy, attorney, and writer on constitutional law, specializing in the Second Amendment. His book *That Every Man Be Armed: The Evolution of a Constitutional Right* is influential in the Second Amendment debate. In support of a suit by the NRA, Halbrook argued against the California assault weapons ban in 1990. Halbrook continued his advocacy through the 1990s and beyond. In 1995 he successfully argued before the Supreme Court in *Printz v. United States* that Congress lacked the authority to compel local law enforcement officials to conduct federal firearms background checks. In *Castillo v. United States* (2000) Halbrook also prevailed, winning a ruling that survivors of the destruction of the Branch Davidian compound in Waco could not be sentenced for offenses involving machine guns when the jury had made no finding. In recent years his attention has turned toward the role of firearms in European history, such as in his 2003 book, *Target Switzerland*, which examines the role of firearms and the militia in deterring a Nazi attack on the country.

Orrin Hatch, veteran senator from Utah. Hatch came from a working-class Mormon background and has worked for labor reform and religious freedom from a generally conservative free-enterprise standpoint. He was a strong supporter of the Americans with Disabilities Act and is a frequent opponent of gun control legislation. He argues from the history and original intent of the Constitution in favor of a robust interpretation of the Second Amendment that would be comparable to that generally given to the First Amendment by liberals. On the other hand, in 1997 he proposed a criminal justice bill that would provide for a minimum five-year sentence for those convicted of criminal gang activity. Although gun advocates generally favor tough penalties for crime (especially gun-related crime), the bill was criticized by both civil libertarians and some gun owners for its expansive definitions of crime that could ensnare innocent gun owners and dealers.

David Hemenway, professor of health policy at the School of Public Health at Harvard University. The major emphasis of Hemenway's research has been on finding ways to prevent injury. In the early 1980s he worked with Ralph Nader and Consumers Union on issues involving unsafe products. However, the importance of violent crime as a source of injury and the particular lethality of firearms attracted Hemenway's attention. Among his numerous influential studies in this field were those in which he found that unsafe storage of guns was a major source of injury and that guns were often ineffective or even counterproductive when used in self-defense. (Scholars who support gun rights, such as John Lott, have criticized that conclusion and pointed to the underreporting of defensive gun use that does not involve firing the gun. Hemenway has in turn argued that his opponents exaggerate the number of defensive gun uses.)

Charlton Heston, Academy Award-winning movie actor, best known for his star roles in *Ben-Hur* and *The Ten Commandments*. Elected president of the National Rifle Association in 1998. In electing him president, the NRA probably wanted to harness Heston's appeal as a moral icon and patriarch, particularly to older and more conservative Americans. Heston roused the crowd at annual NRA meetings by holding up a rifle and shouting "from my cold, dead hands!" By most accounts he was an effective spokesperson and fund-raiser for the organization. In 2002 the 78-year-old Heston was diagnosed with Alzheimer's disease and announced he would retire from his position with the NRA when his one-year term ended.

Don B. Kates, Jr., an activist in the civil rights struggle of the 1960s while a student at Yale Law School. He later worked in legal assistance programs and then became a professor of law and an attorney in private practice in the San Francisco area. Kates provides consultation on firearms legislation for police departments and legislative committees. He is also a prolific advocate of gun rights who has written many articles and books as well as the article on the Second Amendment in the *Encyclopedia of the American Constitution.*

Arthur R. Kellermann, director of Emory University's Center for Injury Control. In the 1980s he published a series of studies in the *New England Journal of Medicine* that supported tougher gun control, claiming that a gun kept in the home was 43 times more likely to kill a family member or friend than to kill a criminal intruder and that restricting access to guns could prevent many murders and suicides. Kellermann's writings became part of a growing body of literature created by activist physicians and medical researchers who came to view gun violence as an epidemic that should be treated as a serious public health problem. Critics such as Gary Kleck and Don Kates point to what they see as serious flaws in such studies, such as their ignoring or underestimating the impact of widespread use of firearms by citizens to scare off criminals.

Gary Kleck, professor of criminology at Florida State University. A strong civil libertarian and member of the ACLU, his reexamination of the Second Amendment led him to change from being a gun control supporter to an advocate of gun rights. In 1983 he wrote an article for the Michigan Law Review that, together with the work of Stephen Halbrook and Sanford Levinson, led many scholars to support an individual rights interpretation of the Second Amendment. His books include *Point Blank: Guns and Violence in America.*

Neal Knox, director of the Firearms Coalition and First Vice President of the NRA. He is a frequent candidate for head of the NRA, leading the more radical wing of that organization while trying to soften its public image. Moderates often accuse him of heavy-handed tactics. Knox began his struggle to radicalize the NRA in 1977 when incoming president Harlon Carter appointed him head of the organization's political arm, the Institute for Legislative Action. He was ousted in 1982 in a disagreement over lobbying practices but returned to the leadership in 1991. Knox has remained an influential leader in the organization, as well as continuing his active campaigning on gun issues in print and broadcast media.

David B. Kopel, former Manhattan assistant district attorney and firearms law expert. Kopel has written numerous pro–gun rights works including *The Samurai, The Mountie, and the Cowboy,* a cross-cultural analysis of gun control laws that concludes that the European approach to gun control would be ineffective and incompatible with the United States's cultural roots. He has authored numerous papers challenging the premises behind proposals such as bans on semiautomatic assault weapons. Much of Kopel's exploration of gun rights in the legal record is found in a 2003 publication, *Supreme Court Gun Cases*, coauthored with Stephen Halbrook and Alan Korwin.

Wayne LaPierre, CEO of the National Rifle Association and a vigorous gun rights advocate. He is the author of *Guns, Crime, and Freedom*, a comprehensive attack on the opponents of gun rights and what he views as a media biased against gun owners. In recent years he has emphasized the prosecution and jailing of criminals who misuse guns, pointing out that while the Clinton Administration claimed to have stopped 400,000 criminals from buying guns under the Brady Bill, virtually none were prosecuted. Some civil libertarians have criticized LaPierre's "tough on crime" proposals as draconian and lacking in flexibility and due process.

Sanford Levinson, McCormick Professor at the University of Texas. Although he remains generally politically liberal, Levinson's studies of the Second Amendment led him to the conclusion that it did protect an individual right to keep and bear arms and that it should be taken seriously by constitutional scholars. His 1989 paper "The Embarrassing Second Amendment" helped touch off a renewed debate about the amendment's meaning and the suggestion that it should be, like the First and Fourth Amendments, incorporated into the Fourteenth Amendment and applied to the states.

John R. Lott, criminal law and economics teacher at the University of Chicago, where he is the John M. Olin Visiting Law and Economics Fellow. In 1988–89 he was the chief economist at the U.S. Sentencing Commission. He has written many articles for academic journals and has written a book, *More Guns, Less Crime: Understanding Crime and Gun Control Laws*. Together with David Mustard, he has published studies that claim that crime decreases in proportion to the number of law-abiding citizens who carry concealed weapons. However, these claims have been disputed on methodological grounds and Lott has been accused of misusing survey data. (Lott and coauthor Mustard have defended their work vigorously.) An embarrassing moment came when Lott was revealed to have made up an online persona, "Mary Rosh," to post glowing reviews of his book *More Guns, Less Crime*. Lott's most recent book, *The Bias against Guns*, makes a detailed case that the mainstream media exaggerates gun risks and ignores most defensive uses of guns.

Fernando Mateo, New York City carpet store owner who founded Goods for Guns, a private organization that sponsors programs through which people can turn in guns and receive certificates for toys, sporting goods, food, and other rewards. A number of similar programs have been started by sports teams, recording companies, and celebrities such as hip-hop stars. Mateo says he got his idea when, after watching news accounts of murder and suicide victims, his son said that he would give up all of his Christmas presents if it would get one gun off the street. Some gun rights advocates have criticized such programs as being more symbolic than truly effective, with many of the guns being turned in unlikely to be involved with crime.

Carolyn McCarthy, congresswoman from Long Island and former licensed practical nurse. Her husband was killed and her son badly wounded in the Long Island Rail Road (LIRR) shooting in 1993. She gained national attention as she devoted her efforts to her son's difficult rehabilitation. She also studied gun issues, learning that the gun Colin Ferguson (the LIRR killer) had used in the shooting had been bought in California and illegally taken to New York and that its high-capacity (15-round) magazine was legal. She began to work for tougher gun laws. When the Republican representative in her district voted to overturn the assault weapons ban, she changed parties to Democrat and ran against him, making gun control the centerpiece of her successful campaign. Her story was the basis for the TV movie *The Long Island Incident.*

Tanya Metaksa, executive director of the National Rifle Association's lobbying unit, the Institute for Legislative Action. Articulate, intense, and energetic, Metaksa is often found on the front lines of the pundit circuit when gun control legislation is being debated in Congress. Metaksa's prominent role in the NRA leadership may also reflect the organization's conscious effort in recent years to appeal to women.

Michael Moore, acclaimed but controversial documentary filmmaker. Moore's activism started early when, as an Eagle Scout in 1972 he won a merit badge for creating a slide show featuring environmental abuses by businesses in his hometown of Flint, Michigan. Having barely reached the voting age of 18, Moore promptly won a seat on the local school board. After writing for *Mother Jones* and other liberal and alternative publications, Moore became interested in filmmaking. His first film, *Roger & Me*, was released in 1989. It featured what was to become his trademark approach of juxtaposing ordinary people and the powerful—in this case, laid-off workers and General Motors chairman Roger Smith, who is caught on film fleeing Moore's attempts at an interview. This financially and critically successful film was followed by a series of other projects including three best-selling books, *Downsize This!* (1996), *Stupid White Men* (2001), and *Dude, Where's My Country?* (2003). Turning his attention to the gun issue, Moore made the film *Bowling for Columbine* in 2002. It argued that there was a troubling connection between violence, guns and popular American culture. The first documentary shown in competition at the Cannes Film Festival in 46 years, it won an Oscar in 2003. Critics charged Moore with caricaturing opponents (film footage of weeping children outside Columbine High School juxtaposed with Charlton Heston holding aloft a musket at an NRA meeting) and with being selective in his recounting of facts. Moore went on in 2004 to release *Fahrenheit 9/11*, a highly controversial scathing indictment of the Bush administration's response to the terrorist attacks and of the subsequent war effort in Iraq.

Lawrence Pratt, head of the Gun Owners of America and a vigorous advocate for the right to keep and bear arms on philosophical as well as constitutional grounds. Pratt has aroused controversy because of alleged connections, which he denies, with white separatist groups.

Ronald Reagan, president of the United States, 1981–1989, former movie actor and former governor of California. Reagan began his political life espousing a generally conservative, pro–gun rights position. However on March 30, 1981, he (along with press secretary James Brady and two law enforcement officers) was wounded in an attempted assassination by John W. Hinckley, Jr. Reagan quickly recovered from his wounds, but Brady's recovery would be far more difficult. When the Bradys became involved with Handgun Control, Inc., and promoted legislation that would require background checks for gun purchasers (the Brady Bill), Reagan, along with former presidents Nixon, Ford, and Carter, endorsed the bill.

Janet Reno, attorney general of the United States, 1993–2000. A strong supporter of gun control, including registration of all guns and a licensing system similar to that used for motor vehicles, Reno has been criticized as being ultimately responsible for the FBI siege and assault on the Branch Davidian compound in Waco, Texas, that led to the death of sect members and their children. Although the question of whether the ultimate fire was set by Davidians or was a consequence of the FBI attack continues to be disputed, the Waco confrontation did have a strong effect in galvanizing the organization of militia groups to resist what they see as ongoing federal intrusions on civil rights. Revelations in 1999 of possible army involvement in the siege and attack on the compound, as well as the use of pyrotechnics (munitions capable of causing fires) complicated the question of Reno's knowledge and possible culpability. Investigations by Congress and independent investigators proved inconclusive.

J. Neil Schulman, science fiction writer, libertarian, and gun rights activist. He is active in the Libertarian Futurist Society, which gave him the Prometheus Award for *The Rainbow Cadenza*, an exploration of the meaning of individual autonomy and its relation to creativity in a collectivist society. Schulman has written several popular defenses of gun rights, including *Stopping Power: Why 70 Million Americans Own Guns.*

Charles Schumer, Democratic senator from New York, former representative from the Ninth District of New York and veteran on the House Judiciary Committee, where he chaired the subcommittee on Crime and Criminal Justice. Schumer is a strong advocate for gun control who helped pass the Brady Bill; he also advocates bans on armor-piercing ammunition and a limit on the number of guns a person may purchase or own without a special "arsenal license."

L. Neil Smith, science fiction writer, libertarian, and gun rights activist. Smith has written many pro-gun articles and opinion pieces that feature a crisp, hard-hitting style. His fiction emphasizes the moral dimensions of arms bearing and self-defense: For example, in *The Probability Broach*, virtually all people (even children) carry weapons, viewing it as a symbol of autonomy, responsibility, and moral health.

CHAPTER 5

GLOSSARY

AK-47 Also known as Kalashnikov, named for its orginator, it is an originally Soviet-built automatic rifle that is used widely throughout the world in insurgencies and other conflicts. An AK-47 is regulated (and often banned) as an assault weapon.

ammunition Collectively, the components expended by a gun, such as primer, gunpowder, and bullet(s) usually put together in the form of cartridges.

antique firearms By most regulatory standards, firearms manufactured before 1899. They often require handmade ammunition. Generally, antique firearms are excepted from regulation.

armor-piercing ammunition Bullets designed to penetrate armor, such as a bullet-proof vest. Its effectiveness comes from a metal core (such as tungsten or depleted uranium). Civilian ownership of such ammunition has been banned in most cases.

assault weapon Technically, an automatic or select-fire rifle or handgun designed for military use. In the gun control debate, however, this term is usually applied to semiautomatic rifles, shotguns, or handguns that have a high-capacity magazine and certain military-type features such as a pistol grip or bayonet mount. Laws banning assault weapons may specify certain models (and their clones), general characteristics of banned weapons, or both.

automatic weapon A type of rifle (such as the military versions of the AK-47 or M-16 submachine gun or machine pistol) that fires bullets continuously as long as the trigger is pulled. Automatic weapons have been regulated by the federal government since 1934, with extensive background checks required for purchasers, taxes for buyers and sellers, and other regulations.

background check A determination that a would-be firearms purchaser does not have a criminal or mental health record that would bar him or her from owning a gun. Today, this is usually done by an online system known as NICS.

ballistic fingerprinting   A system in which all new guns would be test-fired and the characteristics imparted by their barrels recorded. Bullets found at crime scenes could then be compared to identify the gun that fired them. The practice has been used only on a small scale and has been opposed by gun rights advocates, who believe it is unreliable and amounts to a form of gun registration.

bolt-action   A firing mechanism on some rifles. The shooter turns a bolt to insert a cartridge and load the weapon.

Bureau of Alcohol, Tobacco, and Firearms (BATF, also referred to as ATF)   Federal agency whose primary purpose is to enforce federal firearms laws by overseeing transactions and tracing or otherwise investigating guns used in crimes.

burst fire   A setting on some military rifles that fires a set number of bullets (often three) each time the trigger is pulled. The ability to select fully automatic or burst fire is one characteristic of true assault rifles.

caliber   The diameter of a bullet (and thus of the barrel of the gun that accommodates it). In the United States, the measurement is usually given in hundredths of an inch (thus, .45 caliber revolver); in many other countries it is given in millimeters (thus, 9-millimeter semiautomatic pistol).

carbine   A rifle with a short barrel (often used by cavalry in earlier times). Under federal regulations, rifles with a barrel shorter than 16 inches must be registered.

cartridge   A round of ammunition consisting of primer, propellant (powder), and bullet in one container. The cartridge replaced the use of separately poured powder and ball in the 19th century.

chamber   The part of the gun barrel that holds the cartridge for firing. Rifles and pistols normally have a single chamber into which cartridges are fed; revolvers have multiple chambers that rotate into the barrel for firing. Also, the word can be used in verb form, meaning to load a round of ammunition into firing position.

clip   A mechanism that holds a number of cartridges ("a 10-round clip"). The cartridges are fed singly (semiautomatic) or continuously (automatic) into the firing chamber as the trigger is pulled. Banning of high-capacity clips (which is usually defined as having more than 10 rounds) is a common goal of gun control advocates.

collective rights interpretation   An interpretation of the Second Amendment that sees it as guaranteeing only a general right of the people to bear arms, through an official militia organization.

concealed carry   The carrying of a firearm (usually a handgun) so that it is not visible, such as in a holster beneath clothing or in a pack or other portable container. Nearly all states require a permit for concealed carry.

Their policies range from the permissive (all law-abiding adults) to the highly restrictive (must show a definite need).

cop-killer bullet Term for armor-piercing ammunition popularized by gun control advocates. The term gets its name on the basis that it especially endangers police wearing bullet-proof vests.

curios and relics Firearms that are at least 50 years old or that are considered (because of their scarcity, historical value, or unusual nature) to be collector's items. A federal firearms license (FFL) is required for interstate purchase of such firearms.

defensive gun use An instance where a person uses a gun to prevent a crime such as assault or burglary. In most cases the gun is not actually fired. Gun rights and gun control advocates often differ concerning the number of defensive gun uses that take place annually in the United States, with estimates ranging from 100,000 to 2.5 million.

double-action A firing mechanism where the same pull of the trigger both retracts and releases the hammer or firing pin, discharging the weapon.

Federal Firearms License (FFL) A license issued by the National Licensing Center of the Bureau of Alcohol, Tobacco, and Firearms (BATF), allowing a person to manufacture, import, or deal in firearms. An FFL is also required for collectors of curio or relic firearms.

felony A serious crime such as murder, rape, or robbery that is generally punishable by a sentence in a state or federal prison. Convicted felons are generally not allowed legally to own firearms.

firearm Any portable gun-type weapon that shoots a bullet through the explosive force generated by the burning of gunpowder or a similar propellant.

flash hider (or suppressor) A device attached to the muzzle of a gun to reduce the flash caused by the exploding powder, thus making it harder to locate the shooter. It is often included in regulations as a characteristic of banned assault weapons.

Fourteenth Amendment This amendment was passed following the Civil War; it guarantees that all citizens will be treated equally under state laws and will be given their basic rights. During the 19th century the courts did not interpret it to require that states be bound by the rights given in the First, Second, and other amendments. In the 20th century many parts of the Bill of Rights have been "incorporated" in the Fourteenth Amendment guarantees, but thus far the Second Amendment has not been so incorporated.

Glock A 9-millimeter semiautomatic pistol that holds 17 shots. Typically, this type of high-capacity semiautomatic pistol has replaced the revolver as the handgun of choice for many criminals and police.

gun control   A general term for regulations affecting the ownership or use of firearms. This can include bans on certain weapons or accessories, background checks, waiting periods, and licensing for gun owners and laws regulating the storage or concealed carrying of firearms.

gun culture   A term used by both gun opponents and supporters to describe the way in which firearms ownership is viewed and promoted. Generally, control advocates see gun culture as an obsessive if not pathological preoccupation with firearms. Gun rights advocates, on the other hand, see gun culture as an expression of traditional American virtues such as self-reliance.

gun permit   A license or document that authorizes an individual to have a gun at home or to carry it on one's person.

gun show loophole   Term used by gun control advocates for the fact that federal law does not require background checks for gun transactions between private individuals, such as at gun shows. Some states do require background checks for such purchases, however.

handgun   A small firearm such as a pistol or revolver that can be held in the hand for firing and can be easily concealed.

Handgun Control, Inc.   Founded in 1974 and later led by Sarah and James Brady, it is probably the largest and most effective gun control advocacy group. It played a key role in passing the Brady Bill and the Assault Weapons Ban and supports litigation against gun manufacturers. In 2001 the organization's name was changed to the Brady Campaign to End Gun Violence.

homicide   The killing of one human being by another. An unlawful homicide may be viewed as murder or manslaughter depending on circumstances. A killing in self-defense may be considered a "justifiable homicide."

individual rights interpretation   A view of the Second Amendment that sees it as guaranteeing an individual right to keep and bear arms, independent of any collective responsibility to the organized militia.

instant background check   A background check for firearms purchasers that involves the presenting of valid identification and verification by phone or computer to check if the purchaser has a criminal or mental health record that would preclude firearms ownership. In 1998 the Brady Bill's waiting period for most gun purchases was phased out and replaced by a national instant background check.

junk guns   Poorly made, unreliable handguns; similar to **Saturday night special.**

lever action   A mechanism used in some rifles that loads a round into the chamber when the shooter pulls a lever.

licensing laws   Laws that specify the requirements and procedures for the purchase, sale, possession, or carrying of guns. In addition to basic federal requirements, states and localities often have their own licensing laws. Such laws can vary from being minimal to highly restrictive (such as the total ban on handguns in Washington, D.C.).

loaded indicator   A tab or other visual indication that a gun has a round in the chamber. Because many semiautomatic pistols can remain loaded even when the magazine has been removed, this has been advocated as a safety device.

long gun   A firearm with a long barrel such as a rifle and most shotguns. It is generally fired from the shoulder. Many jurisdictions that have restrictive regulations for handguns have fewer restrictions on long guns because they are usually not concealable and are used in only a small proportion of crimes.

M-16 rifle   A fully automatic military assault rifle, similar to a machine gun. This version is generally banned for civilian use. Similar rifles configured for semiautomatic firing are subject to assault weapons regulations.

machine gun   General term for an automatic weapon that fires moderately high-caliber ammunition. Machine guns have been heavily regulated since 1934 under federal law.

machine pistol   Also called "submachine gun"; an automatic pistol (such as the Uzi) that is generally smaller than a machine gun and fires lighter pistol ammunition.

magazine   A container (which can be box-shaped, tubular, or drum-shaped) that holds cartridges and includes a spring-loading mechanism for semiautomatic or automatic fire. It can be built into the gun itself or be detachable. Banning high capacity (more than ten rounds) magazines is a major goal of gun control advocates.

mandatory sentence   A minimum or add-on sentence for persons convicted of certain crimes or circumstances, such as committing a robbery while carrying a firearm. Gun rights advocates such as the NRA often promote mandatory sentences as an alternative to further restrictions on law-abiding gun owners.

"may issue"   A policy where a local jurisdiction can issue a concealed weapons carry at its discretion. This generally occurs only when the applicant can demonstrate a severe need for self-protection. Because the requirements are so strict, this policy can in practice amount to a ban on concealed-carry for the general public.

militia   An organized military force consisting of nonprofessional citizen-soldiers; also, persons potentially eligible for militia service. Official state militias have been incorporated into the National Guard. In recent years unofficial militias have been organized primarily by people concerned about government threats to rights, particularly gun rights.

muzzle   The opening in a gun barrel out of which the bullet emerges.

muzzle brake   A device that diverts some of the expanding gas from a gun's firing, reducing recoil. It is often considered to be a military or "assault weapon" feature.

National Crime Surveys   Reports of crime statistics from the U.S. Bureau of Justice Statistics. These include numbers of various types of crimes such as homicides, assaults, and burglaries and statistics on incarcerated persons.

National Firearms Act (NFA) weapons   Weapons regulated under Title 2 of the National Firearms Act, generally consisting of machine guns, fully automatic weapons, short-barreled shotguns, and certain accessories such as silencers. There are complex regulations regarding the transfer or modification of such weapons.

National Instant Check System (NICS)   A nationwide database of criminal and certain mental health records, used to allow gun dealers to verify that a purchaser can legally obtain a firearm.

National Rifle Association (NRA)   The United States's oldest and largest gun rights organization with more than 2 million members. As a "gun lobby" to Congress and state legislatures, it has been extraordinarily effective, at least until recent years, in blocking new federal and many state gun control proposals.

negligence   A basic component of tort liability. Gun dealers have been sued for negligence in selling firearms to intoxicated people, and gun makers have been sued for negligence in marketing guns in a way that makes them easily accessible to the criminal black market.

NFA weapon   A device (such as a machine gun) that requires registration under the National Firearms Act.

open carry   Carrying a handgun in plain sight, such as in a visible holster or on a car seat. States that allow open carry usually require a gun permit and place other restrictions, such as allowing it only while traveling. Even where allowed, the practice is likely to provoke consternation from the public and attention from law enforcers.

pistol   A general term for a handgun (a gun that can be held and fired using the shooter's hands). The two main types in modern use are those with a single firing chamber, into which bullets are loaded from a clip or magazine, and revolvers, which have multiple firing chambers that rotate into place.

police power   In general, the right of a jurisdiction to make regulations to promote public security and safety. Many court decisions have held that states and cities can exercise their police power in banning handguns or assault weapons.

product liability   The field of tort law that considers whether the manufacturer or seller of a product can be held liable for defects in or misuse of the product. Gun manufacturers have been sued for defective product design and, more recently, for reckless marketing and distribution practices.

public nuisance   A condition or situation that causes an ongoing impairment to the health, welfare, or safety of the community. A number of lawsuits have claimed with varying degrees of success that negligent marketing or distribution of firearms creates a public nuisance that endangers the community.

pump action   A mechanism by which a shell is loaded into a shotgun by the working of a "pump" or slide. This action makes a distinctive sound that is often a significant deterrent to criminal activity.

registration   The process by which identifying information about a gun purchaser and the firearm itself is recorded and filed. Under the Gun Control Act of 1968, such records are kept by gun dealers subject to examination by law enforcement officials. Many gun control advocates favor that such records be kept in a central registry by the government to make it easy to trace illegal guns. Gun rights advocates strongly oppose such a system, fearing it would make it easy for the government to confiscate all firearms at some later date.

revolver   A handgun with a revolving cylinder that contains separate chambers (usually five to nine chambers), each containing a cartridge. Each time the trigger is pulled, the cylinder revolves, bringing the next cartridge into the barrel for firing.

rifle   A long gun that has a spiral-grooved barrel. This causes the bullet to spin, improving accuracy. Rifles can have a variety of loading mechanisms such as manual (bolt or lever) or semiautomatic or automatic (magazine).

right to keep and bear arms   A right guaranteed in the Second Amendment, though there is much dispute over whether the right is absolute or limited and whether it pertains to individuals or only to the people collectively. Gun rights advocates support this right on philosophical grounds as well as believe it to be guaranteed in the Constitution as an individual right.

round   A cartridge containing everything necessary for shooting—the primer, propellant (powder), and bullet. Clips and magazines are generally rated as to the number of rounds or cartridges they hold.

safety training   A course or program intended to teach gun owners the safe handling of their weapon, such as loading, unloading, determining whether the gun is loaded, and the use of safety mechanisms. This training sometimes includes instruction in the laws pertaining to firearms and their use in self-defense.

Saturday night special   A term that probably originated in a slur against African-American neighborhoods, it has been popularized by gun control advocates in referring to cheap, low-caliber handguns that are often poorly made. A number of communities have passed laws banning such guns. Gun rights advocates oppose such laws as discriminating against the poor and depriving them of the means of self-defense.

sawed-off shotgun   A shotgun whose barrel has been shortened to less than 18 inches (or, for a rifle, 16 inches). The shortness makes it possible to conceal the weapon. Such weapons are restricted under federal law in much the same way as are machine guns.

Second Amendment   This amendment states that "A well-regulated militia, being necessary to the security of a free state, the right to keep and bear arms, shall not be infringed." Gun rights advocates interpret this as guaranteeing an essentially unlimited individual right to bear arms. Gun control advocates claim that only the right of the states to have a militia is guaranteed and that the amendment has no application to the control of private weapons ownership or use. Although scholars are divided, the courts have generally (but not conclusively) followed the latter view.

selective fire   A mechanism found in some military-type rifles that allows the shooter to set the gun to be fired automatically or semiautomatically as either a single shot or a "burst" of several rounds.

self-defense   The right to take violent action to protect oneself, others, or one's property from violent attack. Gun rights advocates often cite self-defense as a fundamental extension of the right to life and liberty and gun ownership as a right that makes self-defense truly effective. Gun control advocates emphasize self-defense as a collective function to be handled by the police. Legally, certain standards (which vary somewhat among jurisdiction) must be met for an action to be considered legitimate self-defense, such as it being necessary to prevent imminent harm to a person, it being proportional to the threat, and there being no way to safely retreat.

sentence enhancement laws   Laws that provide for an additional term of imprisonment for certain specified actions, such as being in possession of a firearm while committing a felony.

"shall issue"   A policy under which a sheriff or other official must give a gun-carrying permit to any adult applicant who doesn't have a criminal or mental health record. Gun rights advocates have been trying to enact such policies because they believe that armed citizens can significantly deter crime.

shotgun   A long gun that is fired from the shoulder like a rifle but that has one or two barrels that are smooth rather than rifled. It fires a shell, which is a container full of shot (small balls).

silencer   A device that is attached to the muzzle of a gun to reduce the sound made when the gun is fired. Silencers are strictly regulated by federal law.

Glossary

smart gun   General term for guns that use devices (such as thumbprint sensors) to verify that the user of the weapon is authorized. The gun will therefore not fire if stolen by a criminal or picked up by a child, for example. Smart gun technology has not been implemented commercially as of 2004.

snub-nose   A handgun with a short barrel (3 inches or shorter); it is easy to conceal in a pocket or purse but is rather inaccurate in aim.

straw buyer   A legally qualified purchaser who obtains guns for sale or transfer to persons (such as criminals) who would not be able to buy guns legally.

Street Sweeper   A semiautomatic 12-gauge shotgun that holds 12 rounds and can be fired quickly; a devastating weapon for close combat that was banned as an assault weapon as part of the 1994 federal Assault Weapons Ban.

submachine gun   An automatic weapon that fires pistol-caliber ammunition, such as the Uzi; also called a machine pistol. Submachine guns are generally tightly regulated under federal law, as are machine guns.

substitution theory   A hypothesis that suggests that if handguns are restricted or banned, criminals will substitute more dangerous weapons such as sawed-off shotguns or rifles.

TEC-9   A semiautomatic pistol that holds 36 shots and can be fired at a rate of one shot per second. It and similar pistols have been banned as assault weapons.

transfer of guns   The sale, exchange, or other form of conveying of a gun from one private individual to another. Recent gun control proposals would require that all transfers be done indirectly through a federally licensed dealer.

trigger lock   A lock that fits into a gun trigger so that the gun cannot be fired until the lock is unlocked. Proposals in the late 1990s in Congress called for a requirement that trigger locks be either mandatory or be made available with each new handgun sold.

undetectable firearms   Handguns made primarily of plastic, making them hard to detect through conventional metal or X-ray detectors such as those used in airports. Banning such guns is a goal of many gun control advocates. Some gun rights advocates question whether truly undetectable guns exist or constitute a real threat.

Uniform Crime Reports   An annual FBI report titled "Crime in the United States." It summarizes statistics provided by state and local law enforcement agencies.

Uzi   A machine pistol originally invented by Uzi Gal, an Israeli army officer. Uzis are regulated as a fully automatic weapon.

vigilantism   Law enforcement organized by private citizens without official sanction, often when police protection is not available, such as in

131

newly organized territories or during civil unrest. Depending on circumstances, it has ranged from unconscionable lynching to a necessary and restrained exercise of collective self-defense.

waiting period   A period that must elapse before a gun that has been purchased can be turned over to the buyer. In some cases a waiting period is necessary to allow for conducting a full background check, but the arrival of instant-check systems has removed this justification. Gun control advocates now promote waiting periods as a cooling-off mechanism to reduce impulse killings, although gun rights advocates warn that a waiting period may prevent a victim from being able to defend her- or himself from a stalker or abusive spouse.

weapon's-effect hypothesis   The idea that mere exposure to a weapon may trigger aggressive behavior in susceptible individuals.

PART II

GUIDE TO FURTHER RESEARCH

CHAPTER 6

HOW TO RESEARCH
GUN CONTROL ISSUES

As with other controversial issues, activists on both sides of the gun issue have created many useful web sites. Because they offer overviews and links to news and source materials, such sites provide a good jumping-off place for research. Of course, as you explore the web, you will encounter many references to books and other printed materials that are not available online. It will then be time to use the library and its catalog and other bibliographical tools. This chapter describes some of the most important and useful research tools, both online and traditional.

GUN CONTROL ON THE WEB

The Brady Campaign to Prevent Gun Violence (formerly Handgun Control, Inc.) and its research affiliate the Brady Center to Prevent Gun Violence) is the largest gun control advocacy group. Its web site (http://www.bradycampaign.org) provides many resources, including information about current state and federal gun laws, news about lawsuits against gun makers, fact sheets on gun use, a variety of research studies supporting gun control efforts, and links to other gun control and gun violence prevention groups.

The Coalition to Stop Gun Violence (and its associated Educational Fund to End Gun Violence) is the other large national gun control group. Its site is located at http://www.gunfree.org and has generally the same kind of offerings as the Brady Campaign's site but has its own research and reports, so you should explore both sites thoroughly.

The Violence Policy Center, at http://www.vpc.org, also provides news and links from a strong antigun point of view. The organization is currently focused on renewing the ban on assault weapons and going beyond it to ban a variety of similar weapons that are currently legal.

A number of medically oriented groups have become involved in gun control issues. The HELP (Handgun Epidemic Lowering Plan) network site at http://www.helpnetwork.org has programs and publications. The group Physicians for Social Responsibility also has part of its site devoted to violence issues (including gun control), at http://www.psr.org. The Johns Hopkins Center for Gun Policy and Research at http://www.jhsph.edu/gunpolicy/ also offers links and resources (including bibliographies). Another site to check is the Trauma Foundation's Pacific Center for Violence Prevention, which devotes part of its site at http://www.tf.org/tf/violence/violcontent.shtml to firearms-related research and issues.

Many researchers in recent years have focused on a public health approach to firearms injuries and gun safety. The Americans for Gun Safety at http://ww2.americansforgunsafety.com claims to be pursuing a moderate approach that recognizes gun owners' rights while strengthening the background check system and enforcing gun laws. It provides updates on its national and state initiatives. The Firearms Injury Center at the Medical College of Wisconsin at http://www.mcw.edu/fic/ provides comprehensive background and resources on firearms injuries for students and researchers seeking to produce safer guns and to reduce the frequency and severity of firearms injuries.

GUN RIGHTS ON THE WEB

Gun rights groups have also been very active on the Web. The largest gun rights site is, of course, the National Rifle Association at http://www.nra.org. Its site includes three major parts: the headquarters (for membership and other business queries), "NRA live," and the "NRA ILA" (Institute for Legislative Action). The "live" service provides interesting multimedia content, but the ILA site is best for in-depth access to research materials. Like the Brady Campaign site, it provides information about current gun laws and news about legislative battles, but approaches it from a gun rights point of view. The NRA also has its own collection of studies and papers that challenge those supporting gun control and argue the case for armed self-defense and crime deterrence.

There are a variety of other gun rights groups, many more militant than the NRA. The largest is probably Gun Owners of America (http://www.gunowners.com), which is oriented toward lobbying and direct political action. The Second Amendment Foundation at http://www.saf.org is an important source of litigation and legal information on gun rights. It provides news reports and policy statements on current cases and issues. One of the most extensive resource sites for gun rights advocates is found at http://

www.guncite.com. It includes extensive historical background on the Second Amendment, statistics on defensive gun use, and background to current gun issues.

See Chapter 8 for many other national gun-related groups. Most of them have web sites. Many sites have lists of links to like-minded groups so, as with all web research, exploration can become an ever-widening spiral.

GOVERNMENT AGENCIES AND STATISTICS

Not surprisingly, there are important government sites that have useful information for gun issues research. The Treasury's Bureau of Alcohol, Tobacco, and Firearms (http://www.atf.treas.gov) is the source for official federal gun regulations and their interpretation. The FBI (http://www.fbi.gov) is responsible for tracing guns involved in crime, and it gathers many statistics about gun use. And because the gun issue is so closely connected with crime trends, the Department of Justice's Bureau of Justice Statistics home page at http://www.ojp.usdoj.gov/bjs/ is another very important resource, as is its annual compilation "Sourcebook of Criminal Justice Statistics" (available at http://www.albany.edu/ sourcebook/). Note that the bureau site also has a set of links to other crime-statistics sites.

Because public opinion is very important to the future of the gun issue, it's also useful to periodically check groups such as the Gallup Organization (http://www.gallup.com/poll/) for polling data. Another source of polling information compiled from many sources is PollingReport.com at http://www.pollingreport.com.

BIBLIOGRAPHIC RESOURCES

Bibliographic resources is a general term for catalogs, indexes, bibliographies, and other guides that identify the books, periodical articles, and other printed resources that deal with a particular subject. They are essential tools for the researcher.

LIBRARY CATALOGS

Access to the largest library catalog, that of the Library of Congress, is available at http://catalog.loc.gov. This page explains the different kinds of catalogs and searching techniques available.

Gun Control

Yahoo! offers a categorized listing of libraries at http://dir.yahoo.com/Reference/Libraries/. Of course, for materials available at one's local public or university library, that institution will be the most convenient source.

Online catalogs can be searched not only by the traditional author, title, and subject headings, but also by matching keywords in the title. Thus a title search for *gun control* will retrieve all books that have the word somewhere in their title. (A book about gun control may not have that phrase in the title, so it is still necessary to use subject headings to get the most comprehensive results.)

The most important LC subject heading is, not surprisingly, *gun control*. This heading can be subdivided by place (United States, an individual state, or a foreign country). The following primary subheads are also important:

bibliography
government policy
juvenile literature
law and legislation
political aspects

Many of these subheads can also be divided by place, for example, *Gun Control—Government Policy—United States*. Naturally, *United States* is the most frequently used geographical subhead, and like others, it can be further divided using subheads such as:

Citizen participation
Evaluation
Handbooks, manuals
History
Public Opinion
Societies, etc.
Statistics

The broader topic *firearms* will also be of interest. Its subdivisions include:

government policy
history
law and legislation

This will generally overlap with *gun control*. Other firearms-related headings include:

firearm accidents
firearm ownership

firearms industry
firearms owners
firearms theft

And, of course, particular types of firearms:

machine guns
pistols
rifles

Once the record for a book or other item is found, it is a good idea to see that additional subject headings and name headings have been assigned. These in turn can be used for further searching.

BIBLIOGRAPHIES, INDEXES, AND DATABASES

Bibliographies in various forms provide a convenient way to find books, periodical articles, and other materials. Most book-length bibliographies published before the 1990s are not very useful because there has been an explosion of materials published on this topic during the past decade.

Abstracts are brief summaries of articles or papers. They are usually compiled and indexed—originally in bound volumes but increasingly available online. Some examples of indexes where you might retrieve literature related to gun control include:

Criminal Justice Abstracts (1977–)
Criminal Justice Periodical Index (1978–)
GPO (1976–) (index to government publications)
Index Medicus (1960–)
Index to Legal Periodicals & Books (1981–)
National Criminal Justice Reference Service Abstracts Database (early
    1970s to present) (NCJRS)
Social Sciences Citation Index (1956–)
Social Sciences Index (1974–)
Sociological Abstracts (1952–)

Generally these indexes are available only through a library where you hold a card and cannot be accessed over the Internet (unless you are on a college campus).

However, UnCover Web (http://www.ingenta.com) is generally available for searching and contains brief descriptions of about 13 million documents from about 26,000 journals in just about every subject area. Copies of complete documents can be ordered with a credit card, or may be obtainable for free at a local library.

There's also the National Criminal Justice Reference Service's Justice Information Center web page at http://www.ncjrs.org. It offers a searchable abstract database containing 150,000 criminal justice publications, and it can be a real gold mine for the more advanced researcher.

FREE PERIODICAL INDEXES

Most public libraries subscribe to database services such as InfoTrac or EBSCO that index articles from hundreds of general-interest periodicals (and some moderately specialized ones). The database can be searched by author or by words in the title, subject headings, and sometimes words found anywhere in the article text. Depending on the database used, "hits" in the database can result in just a bibliographical description (author, title, pages, periodical name, issue date), a description plus an abstract (a paragraph summarizing the contents of the article), or the full text of the article itself.

Many libraries provide dial-in, Internet, or telnet access to their periodical databases as an option in their catalog menu. However, licensing restrictions usually mean that only researchers who have a library card for that particular library can access the database (by typing in their name and card number). Check with local public or school libraries to see which databases are available.

For periodicals not indexed by an online service (or for which only abstracts rather than complete text is available), check to see whether the publication has its own web site (many now do). Some scholarly publications are putting all or most of their articles online. Popular publications tend to offer only a limited selection. Some publications of both types offer archives of several years' back issues that can be searched by author or by keyword.

BOOKSTORE CATALOGS

Many people have discovered that online bookstores such as Amazon.com at (http://www.amazon.com) and Barnesandnoble.com (http://www.barnesandnoble.com) are convenient ways to shop for books. A less-known benefit of online bookstore catalogs is that they often include publisher's information, book reviews, and reader's comments about a given title. They can thus serve as a form of annotated bibliography.

On the other hand, a visit to one's local bookstore also has its benefits. Although the available selection of titles is likely to be smaller than that of an online bookstore, the ability to browse through books physically before buying them can be very useful.

NEWS RESOURCES

When breaking news such as a vote in Congress, a court decision, or a major federal policy announcement occurs, the Web is a good place to go for coverage that is more detailed than that available on TV and timelier than that found in magazines. The major broadcast and cable networks, news (wire) services, most newspapers, and many magazines have web sites that include news stories and links to additional information. For breaking news the following sites are also useful:

> Associated Press (AP) wire: http://wire.ap.org/public_pages/WirePortal.
> pcgi/us_portal.html
> Cable News Network (CNN): http://www.cnn.com
> *New York Times:* http://www.nytimes.com
> Reuters: http://www.reuters.com
> *Time* magazine: http://www.time.com
> *Wall Street Journal:* http://online.wsj.com/public/us/
> *Washington Post:* http://www.washingtonpost.com

Yahoo! maintains a large set of links to many newspapers that have web sites or online editions at http://dir.yahoo.com/News_and_Media/Newspapers/Web_Directories/.

Another useful site for tracking down recent news stories is Google News at http://news.google.com. The site describes itself as "highly unusual in that it offers a news service compiled solely by computer algorithms without human intervention. While the sources of the news stories vary in perspective and editorial approach, their selection for inclusion is done without regard to political viewpoint or ideology. While this may lead to some occasionally unusual and contradictory groupings, it is exactly this variety that makes Google News a valuable source of information on the important issues of the day."

Net News is a decentralized system of thousands of "newsgroups," or forums organized by topic. Most web browsers have an option for subscribing to, reading, and posting messages in newsgroups. The Google Groups site (http://groups.google.com) also provides free access and an easy-to-use interface to newsgroups. The general newsgroup for gun matters is *"rec.guns"*. Some other possibilities are *"info.firearms," "info.firearms.politics,"* and *"talk. politics.gun."*

SEARCHING THE WEB

A researcher can explore an ever-expanding web of information by starting with a few web sites and following the links they offer to other sites, which in turn have links to still other sites. But because this is something of a hit-and-miss proposition, some important sites may be missed if the researcher only "web surfs" in this fashion. There are two more focused techniques that can fill in the information gaps.

WEB INDEXES

A web index is a site that offers what amounts to a structured, hierarchical outline of subject areas. This enables the researcher to zero in on a particular aspect of a subject and find links to web sites for further exploration.

The best known (and largest) web index is Yahoo! (http://www.yahoo.com). The home page gives the top-level list of topics, and one can follow them down to more specific areas. The area for gun issues can be reached by clicking on *"Society and Culture"* and then on *"Firearms"*. There are then the following topics: *"Gun Control," "Gun Rights,"* and *"Smart Guns"*. (Of course, there may well be others by the time you read this.) Clicking on one of these categories yields subcategories and/or specific Web sites, many of which are associated with organizations.

In addition to following Yahoo!'s outlinelike structure, there is also a search box into which the researcher can type one or more keywords and receive a list of matching categories and sites.

Web indexes such as Yahoo! have two major advantages over undirected surfing. First, the structured hierarchy of topics makes it easy to find a particular topic or subtopic and then explore its links. Second, Yahoo! does not make an attempt to compile every possible link on the Internet (a task that is virtually impossible, given the size of the Web); rather, sites are evaluated for usefulness and quality by Yahoo!'s indexers. This means that the researcher has a better chance of finding more substantial and accurate information (this advantage is also provided by sites like those of the Brady Campaign and the NRA, of course). The disadvantage of Web indexes is the flip side of their selectivity: The researcher is dependent on the indexer's judgment for determining which sites are worth exploring.

Two other web indexes are LookSmart (http://www.looksmart.com) and About.com (http://www.about.com). These work much in the same way as Yahoo!. For example, to get to gun issues on About.com, one clicks on *"News & Issues,"* then *"Crime/Punishment,"* and then on the *"Subjects,"* section on that page, click on *"Guns."*

There are also an increasing number of specialized online research guides that are like traditional bibliographical essays with the added bonus of having many of the materials discussed already linked so that they are just a click away. The Boston University Library has a research guide to gun control at http://www2.bu.edu/library/guides/gun.html.

SEARCH ENGINES

Search engines take a very different approach to finding materials on the web. Instead of organizing topically in a "top-down" fashion, search engines work their way "from the bottom up," scanning through web documents and indexing them. There are hundreds of search engines, but some of the most widely used include:

- Alta Vista (http://www.altavista.com)
- Excite (http://www.excite.com)
- Google (http://www.google.com)
- Hotbot (http://www.hotbot.com)
- Lycos (http://www.lycos.com)
- Northern Light (http://www.northernlight.com)
- WebCrawler (http://www.WebCrawler.com)

Search engines are generally easy to use by employing the same sorts of keywords that work in library catalogs. There are a variety of web search tutorials available online [try *web search tutorial* in a search engine]. One good one is published by the Web Tools Company at http://thewebtools.com/searchgoodies/tutorial.htm.

Here are a few basic rules for using search engines:

- When looking for something specific, use the most specific term or phrase. For example, when looking for information about laws concerning carrying concealed weapons, use the specific term *"concealed carry,"* because this is the standard term.
- When looking for a more general topic, such as the relationship between guns and crime, use several descriptive words (nouns are more reliable than verbs), for example, *"gun crime statistics."* Most engines will automatically put pages that match all three terms first on the results list. This search will likely get you a list that starts with statistics and then includes more general discussions of guns and crime.

- Use "wild cards" when a desired word may have more than one ending; for example, *semiauto** matches both *semiautomatic* and the more slangy *semiauto*.
- Most search engines support Boolean (*and, or, not*) operators that can be used to broaden or narrow a search:
  - Use AND to narrow a search: *"youth AND violence"* will match only pages that have both terms.
  - Use OR to broaden a search: *"gun OR firearm"* will match any page that has *either* term.
  - Use NOT to exclude unwanted results: *"gun NOT handgun"* finds articles about guns but not handguns (of course *gun* is also used as a general term for any sort of firearm, so the filtering effect will not be complete).

Because each search engine indexes somewhat differently and offers somewhat different ways of searching, it is a good idea to use several different search engines, especially for a general query. Several "metasearch" programs automate the process of submitting a query to multiple search engines. These include Metacrawler (http://www.metacrawler.com) and SurfWax (http://www.surfwax.com). There are also search utilities that can be run from a researcher's PC rather than through a web site. A good example is Copernic available for download at http://www.copernic.com.

FINDING ORGANIZATIONS AND PEOPLE

Lists of gun control or gun rights organizations can be found on major sites such as those of the Brady Campaign or the NRA and index sites such as Yahoo!. If such sites do not yield the name of a specific organization, the name can be given to a search engine. Generally, the best approach is to put the name of the organization in quotation marks such as "Mothers for Gun Control."

Another approach is to take a guess at the organization's likely Web address. For example, the National Rifle Association is commonly known by the acronym NRA, so it is not a surprise that the organization's web site is at www.nra.org. (Note that noncommercial organization sites normally use the *.org* suffix, government agencies use *.gov*, educational institutions have *.edu*, and businesses use *.com*.) This technique can save time but does not always work.

There are several ways to find a person on the Internet:

- Put the person's name (in quotation marks) in a search engine and possibly find that person's home page on the Internet.

- Contact the person's employer (such as a university for an academic, or a corporation for a technical professional). Most such organizations have web pages that include a searchable faculty or employee directory.
- Try one of the people-finder services such as Yahoo! People Search (http://people.yahoo.com) or BigFoot (http://www.bigfoot.com). This may yield contact information such as e-mail address, regular address, and/or phone number.

LEGAL RESEARCH

Gun issues inevitably become legal issues because the use (and misuse) of guns is a subject of both criminal and civil law. Because of the specialized terminology of the law, legal research can be more difficult to master than bibliographical or general research tools. Fortunately, the Internet has also come to the rescue in this area, offering a variety of ways to look up laws and court cases without having to pore through huge bound volumes in law libraries (which may not be accessible to the general public, anyway).

FINDING LAWS

When federal legislation passes, it eventually becomes part of the U.S. Code, a massive legal compendium. Laws can be referred to either by their popular name or by a formal citation. For example, the Gun Free Schools Act is cited as 18 USC §921, meaning title 18 of the U.S. Code, section 921 (actually the law amended certain subsections of section 921).

The U.S. Code can be searched online in several locations, but the easiest site to use is probably the U.S. Code database at http://uscode.house. gov. The U.S. Code may also be found at Cornell Law School (a major provider of free online legal reference material) at http://www4.law. cornell.edu/ uscode/. The fastest way to retrieve a law is by its title and section citation, but phrases and keywords can also be used.

Legislation is not immediately compiled into the U.S. Code (this is done every five years). Instead of U.S. Code numbers, one can use Public Law numbers in many databases. For example the Brady Handgun Violence Control Act is Public Law 103–159 (sometimes abbreviated P.L. 103–159).

Federal laws are generally implemented by a designated agency that writes detailed rules, which become part of the Code of Federal Regulations (C.F.R.). A regulatory citation looks like a U.S. Code citation, and takes the form *vol.* C.F.R. sec. *number.*

Regulations can be found at the web site for the relevant government agency (such as the Bureau of Alcohol, Tobacco, and Firearms, or BATF).

Many states also have their codes of laws online. The Cornell University Legal Information Institute at http://www.law.cornell.edu is an "all-in-one" site that has both federal and state laws.

KEEPING UP WITH LEGISLATIVE DEVELOPMENTS

Pending legislation is often tracked by advocacy groups. For example, the Brady Campaign has a legislative page at http://www.bradycampaign.org/legislation/ and the NRA has a similar service at http://www.nraila.org.

There continues to be considerable activity in Congress relating to gun control. The Library of Congress Thomas web site (http://thomas.loc.gov) includes files summarizing legislation by the number of the Congress. Each two-year session of Congress has a consecutive number: for example, the 108th Congress was in session in 2003 and 2004. Legislation can be searched for by the name of its sponsor(s), the bill number, or by topical keywords. Laws that have been passed can be looked up under their Public Law number. For example, selecting the 108th Congress and typing in the phrase "gun show loophole" into the search box will retrieve a number of bills pertaining to that subject, beginning with those that contain the words exactly as entered. In this case bills retrieved include the Gun Show Loophole Closing Act of 2004 from the House (and its 2003 predecessor from the Senate). Clicking on the highlighted bill number brings up a display that includes the bill's status and text as well as further details including sponsors, committee action, and amendments.

FINDING COURT DECISIONS

Like laws, legal decisions are organized using a system of citations. The general form is: *Party1 v. Party2 volume reporter* [optional start page] *(court, year)*.

Here are some examples from Chapter 2:

Presser v. Illinois, 116 U.S. 252 (1886): Here the parties are Presser and the State of Illinois. The case is in volume 116 of the *U.S. Supreme Court Reports*, and the case was decided in 1886. (For the Supreme Court, the name of the court is omitted.)

U.S. v. Warin, 530 F.2d 130 (6th Cir.): The parties are the United States and Warin, and the case is in volume 530 of the U.S. F.2d reporter, in the 6th U.S. Circuit.

City of Salina v. Blaksley, 72 Kan. 230 (1905): This is a Kansas State Supreme Court case (vol. 72 of the Kansas reporter).

To find a federal court decision, first ascertain the level of court involved: district (the lowest level, where trials are normally held), circuit (the main court of appeals), or the Supreme Court. The researcher can then go to a number of places on the Internet to find cases by citation and, often, the names of the parties. Some of the most useful sites are:

- The Legal Information Institute (http://supct.law.cornell.edu/supct/) has all Supreme Court decisions since 1990 plus 610 of "the most important historic" decisions. There are also links to other online case archives.
- Washlaw Web (http://www.washlaw.edu) has a variety of court decisions (including states) and legal topics listed, making it a good jumping-off place for many sorts of legal research.
- The site "NFA and other gun law related info and cares" has handily compiled a large collection of gun-related federal and state cases, criminal and civil, as well as a lot of other material on gun laws: including NFA (National Firearms Act) dealer registration: http://www.cs.cmu.edu/afs/cs/usr/wbardwel/public/nfalist.

LEXIS AND WESTLAW

Lexis and Westlaw are commercial legal databases that have extensive information including an elaborate system of notes, legal subject headings, and ways to show relationships between cases. Unfortunately, these services are too expensive for use by most individual researchers unless they are available through a university or corporate library.

MORE HELP ON LEGAL RESEARCH

For more information on conducting legal research, see the "Legal Research FAQ" at http://www.cis.ohio-state.edu/hypertext/faq/usenet/law/research/top.html. This also explains more advanced techniques such as "Shepardizing" (referring to *Shepard's Case Citations*, which is used to find how a decision has been cited in subsequent cases and whether the decision was later overturned).

Finally, a word of caution about the Internet: It is important to critically evaluate all materials found on the Internet. Many sites have been established by well-known, reputable organizations or individuals. Others may come from unknown individuals or groups. Their material may be equally valuable, but it should be checked against reliable sources.

CHAPTER 7

ANNOTATED BIBLIOGRAPHY

This chapter provides an extensive annotated bibliography on gun control and gun rights issues. The bibliography is divided into the following 12 categories:

- Reference Works
- Introductions, Overviews, and Anthologies
- Guns in American Society and Culture
- Gun Control Advocacy (General)
- Gun Rights Advocacy (General)
- Guns, Crime, and Violence
- Youth and Guns
- Gun Safety
- Constitutional Issues
- Laws, Legislation, and Politics
- Gun Liability
- International Perspectives

Each category is further divided into books, articles, and Web documents. Note that many print articles are also available online, either through specific Web addresses or via online periodical databases.

REFERENCE WORKS

This section lists general reference works, including encyclopedias and bibliographies.

BOOKS

Bijlefeld, Marjolijn. *People for and against Gun Control: A Biographical Reference.* Westport, Conn.: Greenwood Press, 1999. Fifty biographical profiles provide a look at the important people behind the debate over gun control. Includes appendixes summarizing gun laws, categorizing the profiles, and providing further resources.

Carter, Gregg Lee. *Guns in American Society: An Encyclopedia.* 2 vols. Santa Barbara, Calif.: ABC-CLIO, 2002. The extensive set of A–Z articles includes such topics as the development of firearms, gun control policy, legal cases, gun-related organizations, and biographies of relevant persons. The articles include brief listings for further reading. Appendixes cover state laws and constitutional provisions, organizations, and a general bibliography.

Johns Hopkins Center for Gun Policy and Research. *Firearm Violence: An Annotated Bibliography.* Baltimore, Md.: Johns Hopkins Center, 1996. Covers resources dealing with firearms ownership and use, legal and legislative issues, the gun industry, gun control supporters and opponents, and strategies for reducing gun violence.

Schultz, David. *Encyclopedia of American Law.* New York: Facts On File, 2002. Provides important background for understanding the legal issues and implications in gun-related cases.

Sifakis, Carl. *Encyclopedia of American Crime.* 2d ed. 2 vols. New York: Facts On File, 2000. Since the connection between guns and crime is a key component of the gun control debate, this comprehensive encyclopedia is a useful resource. It provides more than 2,000 entries covering events, biographies, and terminology relating to crime in the United States.

WEB DOCUMENTS

"Gun Violence & Gun Safety: National & State Resource Guide." Central Maine Medical Center. Available online. URL: http://www.cmmc.org/gunsafety.htm. Downloaded on July 7, 2004. Provides contact information and links to numerous national organizations related to gun safety and gun violence, plus state organizations in Maine.

"Uniform Crime Reports, 2002." Federal Bureau of Investigation. Available online. URL: http://www.fbi.gov/ucr/02cius.htm. Posted in 2002. Provides access to the most comprehensive and authoritative compilation of crime-related statistics, including those relating to firearms. Statistics are issued annually.

INTRODUCTIONS, OVERVIEWS, AND ANTHOLOGIES

This section covers introductory or comprehensive works on the issue of gun control/gun rights (generally presenting both sides of the issue) as well as collections of papers or articles.

Gun Control

BOOKS

Bijlefeld, Marjolijn, ed. *The Gun Control Debate: A Documentary History.* Westport, Conn.: Greenwood Press, 1997. A collection of more than 200 primary source documents relating to gun control issues. Includes historical, constitutional, legal, and legislative aspects of gun regulation.

Crooker, Constance Emerson. *Gun Control and Gun Rights.* Westport, Conn.: Greenwood Press, 2003. Designed for students but generally useful to all readers, this introduction and overview covers the key subjects relating to gun rights and gun control, with an emphasis on legal issues. Topics discussed include the meaning of the Second Amendment, gun regulations and federalism, and the history of gun control laws. There is also a survey of gun control and gun rights organizations and a bibliography.

Currie-McGhee, Leanne K. *Gun Control.* San Diego, Calif.: Lucent Books, 2003. An accessible overview of gun control for young adult readers. Issues covered include gun violence, defensive gun use, legal issues, and the effectiveness of gun laws.

Dizard, Jan E., Robert Merrill Muth, and Stephen P. Andrews, Jr. *Guns in America: A Reader.* New York: New York University Press, 1999. Provides more than 40 selections covering topics such as the origin of the gun control movement, the pros and cons of gun ownership, minorities and guns, the militia movement, and possible compromises between gun control and gun rights advocates.

Edel, Wilbur. *Gun Control: Threat to Liberty or Defense Against Anarchy?.* Westport, Conn.: Praeger Publishers, 1995. A history of the development of gun control laws in the United States and of changing attitudes toward gun regulation from colonial times to the tumultuous 1960s and beyond.

Egendorf, Laura K. *How Can Gun Violence Be Reduced?* San Diego, Calif.: Greenhaven Press, 2002. This "At Issue" book for junior high school and older readers offers pro and con analyses of existing gun control laws and policies (such as the Brady Law) and proposals such as requiring "personalized" guns that will operate only for their owner.

Exploring Gun Use in America. 4 vols. New York: Greenwood Publishing, 2004. Written for junior high school students, this comprehensive reference is useful for all readers. The four volumes explore the Second Amendment and the debate over its interpretation, the practices of the firearms industry and the movement for safer guns, children as gun users and gun victims, and the development of gun legislation and expressions of public opinion.

Gun Control: Restricting Rights or Protecting People? Detroit: Thomson/Gale, 2003. A concise but complete guide to gun issues, including historical origins, gun use today, gun laws and court decisions, firearms and crime, gun injuries, guns and youth, and public attitudes toward gun control. The book concludes with a debate and a resource list.

Kates, Don B., John K. Lattimer, and James R. Bowen. *The Great American Gun Debate*. San Francisco: Pacific Research Institute for Public Policy, 1997. Discusses all aspects of the gun debate, including defensive gun use, guns as a public health problem, media bias in coverage of gun issues, and the Second Amendment and the philosophy of self-defense. Generally, the book has a pro–gun rights perspective.

McClurg, Andrew J., David B. Kopel, and Brannon P. Denning, eds. *Gun Control & Gun Rights: A Reader & Guide*. New York: New York University Press, 2002. This is a rich collection of readings from a great variety of sources ranging from ancient philosophers to contemporary criminologists and legal experts. Readings are organized into topics such as the benefits of guns for defense and crime deterrence, the effects and social costs of guns, the philosophical debate over the right to bear arms, cases and commentary on the Second Amendment, guns and identity (race and gender), and civil liability for the misuse of firearms.

Nisbet, Lee, ed. *The Gun Control Debate: You Decide*. 2d ed. Amherst, N.Y.: Prometheus Books, 2001. The editor, a professor of philosophy and co-founder of CSICOP (Committee for the Scientific Investigation of Claims of the Paranormal), applies finely honed critical thinking skills to this more mundane issue. Contributors include many of the top researchers in firearms-related issues and policy, including Don B. Kates, Jr., Gary Kleck, David Kopel, John Lott, and Franklin E. Zimring. Both specific issues (such as the relation between guns and violence) and characteristics of the debate itself (including rhetorical techniques and possible media bias) are explored; gun rights advocacy seems to predominate, however.

O'Sullivan, Carol. *Gun Control: Distinguishing between Fact and Opinion*. Teacher's Guide Edition. San Diego, Calif.: Greenhaven Press, 1990. Although the facts cited are now outdated, this work can still be useful for leading class discussions and sharpening critical thinking skills in sorting out facts, anecdotes, opinions, and scientific conclusions.

Pontonne, S., ed. *Gun Control Issues*. Commack, N.Y.: Nova Science Publishing, 1997. Introduces the key facts and issues in the gun control debate, including the Brady Law, assault weapons, and statistics on gun use.

Torr, James D. *Gun Violence: Opposing Viewpoints*. San Diego, Calif.: Greenhaven Press, 2001. Aimed at junior high and high school students but useful for all readers, this anthology pairs pro and con articles on a variety of topics relating to guns. Areas covered include the extent of gun violence, guns and crime, the effectiveness of guns for self-defense, and whether gun ownership is protected by the Constitution. Contributors include advocates from the Violence Policy Center, the Children's Defense Fund, and the National Rifle Association.

Vizzard, William J. *Shots in the Dark*. Lanham, Md.: Rowman & Littlefield, 2000. A former agent for the U.S. Bureau of Alcohol, Tobacco, and Firearms examines the background for gun control issues and surveys the key developments in gun control legislation starting with New York's Sullivan Law in 1911. He concludes with modest proposals for strengthening gun laws, believing that more radical measures would not be politically feasible.

ARTICLES

Rosenberg, Merri, Sarah Brady, and Tanya Metaksa. "Up in Arms." *Scholastic Update*, vol. 131, November 2, 1998, pp. 10ff. Presents a panel discussion/debate between Handgun Control, Inc.'s Sarah Brady and the NRA's Tanya Metaksa. Brady argues for a variety of measures to restrict access to guns and make them safer. Metaksa says that gun owners should be held responsible for their actions, not deprived of their rights.

Witkin, Gordon. "Should You Own a Gun?" *U.S. News & World Report*, vol. 117, August 15, 1994, pp. 24ff. Uses the question of gun ownership to introduce the overall debate about gun control. The article features a debate between Gary Kleck, whose research shows that gun owners use their guns for defense up to 2.5 million times a year (seldom shooting them) and that criminals are deterred by their fear of armed citizens, and Arthur Kellermann, whose equally provocative study found that guns in the home were 43 times more likely to kill a resident or friend than an armed intruder.

Worsnop, Richard L. "Gun Control: Will It Help Reduce Violent Crime in the U.S.?" *CQ Researcher*, vol. 4, June 10, 1994, pp. 507ff. Introduces the debate over gun control as it focuses on the assault weapons ban debated in Congress in 1994. The article also includes discussion of political, social, and criminological aspects, as well as sidebars on specific gun topics.

WEB DOCUMENTS

Purtilo, James M. "Rec.guns on the Web." [Personally sponsored web site.] Available online. URL: http://www.recguns.com. Updated on November 10, 2003. Provides the FAQ file for the newsgroup rec.guns, which includes information on gun laws, gun use, and other issues involving firearms.

Annotated Bibliography

GUNS IN AMERICAN SOCIETY AND CULTURE

This section provides a home for works dealing with social, cultural, or philosophical aspects of firearms use; surveys of public opinion; and other topics that do not fit in one of the more specific categories.

BOOKS

Bellesiles, Michael. *Arming America: The Origins of a National Gun Culture.* New York: Knopf, 2000. This book touched off a firestorm: the author argued largely on the basis of probate records that prior to the Civil War not only did most Americans not own guns, they seemed to have little interest in them, indirectly undercutting the argument for the individual rights interpretation of the Second Amendment. He went on to argue that "gun culture" is primarily the creation of the development of mass-produced firearms in the later 19th century as well as myth and fiction about the Old West. However, other scholars promptly challenged Bellesisles's research (particularly his reliance on probate records), and when he was unable to substantiate his sources his prestigious Bancroft Prize was retracted.

Brown, Richard Maxwell. *No Duty to Retreat: Violence and Values in American History and Culture.* Norman: University of Oklahoma Press, 1994. A study of the social values involving the appropriate use of violence from frontier days to the present. Brown emphasizes the history of the American West. He also provides an important historical context for the development of gun regulations.

DeConde, Alexander. *Gun Violence in America: The Struggle for Control.* Boston: Northeastern University Press, 2001. While many gun rights advocates see deep historical roots for gun ownership in the United States, the author explores the less well known roots of gun control. He finds that even in the 19th century individuals and local governments sought to restrict access to firearms that they saw as contributing to violence and disorder in an increasingly urbanized America. However, he sees them as being overwhelmed by a gun culture and a powerful political lobby led by the NRA.

Homsher, Deborah. *Women and Guns: Politics and the Culture of Firearms in America.* Armonk, N.Y.: M.E. Sharpe, 2002. Extensively interviewing women who hunt, target shoot, or obtain guns for self-defense, the author suggests that there is a need to break through slogans and gender stereotypes to understand the variety of reasons women have for owning firearms. Only then can important issues (such as the relative importance of defense against strangers and against domestic abusers) be teased out.

Kennett, Lee B., and James L. Anderson. *The Gun in America: The Origins of a National Dilemma*. Westport, Conn.: Greenwood Press, 1975. Describes the many roles that firearms have played in U.S. culture and how the United States can indeed be said to be the "arsenal of democracy" with both positive and negative consequences.

McGrath, Roger D. *Gunfighters, Highwaymen, and Vigilantes: Violence on the Frontier*. Berkeley: University of California Press, 1997. Discusses the violent culture of the American West and the interaction between roles such as robber, professional gunfighter, and vigilante. Because this period created many gun-related images in U.S. culture, exploring it is useful background for the gun issue.

Smith, Tom W. *2001 National Gun Policy Survey of the National Opinion Research Center: Research Findings*. Chicago: National Opinion Research Center, University of Chicago, 2001. Also available online. URL: http://www.norc.uchicago.edu/online/guns01.pdf. The latest version of this comprehensive survey (as of early 2000) continues to show strong public support for most measures to regulate firearms, promote firearm safety, and to keep criminals from acquiring guns. About half the public now supports limiting handgun possession to law enforcement officers. However, the public is virtually evenly divided on whether concealed handguns in the possession of citizens makes the public safer or less safe.

Stange, Mary Zeiss, and Carol K. Oyster. *Gun Women: Firearms and Feminism in Contemporary America*. New York: New York University Press, 2000. Feminists are generally associated with left-liberal causes—such as gun control. However, a growing number of women are using firearms on the job as part of the police or military, obtaining guns for self-protection, or shooting for recreation. The authors attempt to offer a balanced portrayal of female firearms users and to suggest ways in which gun ownership may be compatible with feminist beliefs.

Tonso, William R., ed., and the Second Amendment Foundation. *The Gun Culture and Its Enemies*. Bellevue, Wash.: Merril Press, 1990. Presents two collections of essays. The first part deals with the gun culture that has developed around the use of guns in many parts of the United States. The second part deals with persons and groups that are determined to destroy, or at least marginalize, gun culture.

Weir, William. *A Well-Regulated Militia: The Battle over Gun Control*. North Haven, Conn.: Archon, 1997. For young adults, this book tackles both gun control and gun rights advocates. Weir criticizes their statistics and arguments and concludes that both sides are ignoring more fundamental social issues that must be addressed if violence is to be reduced.

Annotated Bibliography

Wilson, R. A. *Silk and Steel: Women at Arms*. New York: Random House, 2003. Although gun use is often associated with men, the author presents a history of prominent women (including Queen Elizabeth I of England and Russia's Catherine the Great) who were enthusiastic shooters. Women often used guns in pioneer America, and since World War II a growing number of women have taken to hunting and shooting sports.

Zimring, Franklin E., and Gordon Hawkins. *Crime Is Not the Problem: Lethal Violence in America*. New York: Oxford University Press, 1997. Argues that it is violent, often lethal, crime that is the United States's distinctive problem. (Rates of nonviolent property crimes are comparable to those of other nations.) Authors argue that it is necessary to focus on what facilitates this violence, including the availability of guns.

ARTICLES

Blendon, Robert J., John T. Young, and David Hemenway. "The American Public and the Gun Control Debate." *JAMA, The Journal of the American Medical Association*, vol. 275, June 12, 1996, pp. 1719ff. Breaks down public opinion in a detailed analysis of attitudes toward guns, nature of gun ownership, and responses to a variety of specific proposals. Although some of the data is becoming stale, the approach and organization are instructive.

Casey, Kathryn. "Up in Arms." *Ladies Home Journal*, vol. 112, August 1995, pp. 89ff. Discusses whether women should arm themselves for self-defense. Casey includes facts, anecdotes, advertising campaigns, and women's opinions on both sides of the issue.

Dowler, Kenneth. "Media Influence on Attitude toward Guns and Gun Control." *American Journal of Criminal Justice*, vol. 26, Spring 2002, pp. 235–247. Analyzes a 1995 survey on attitudes toward gun control with respect to respondents' media consumption. Concludes that most of the public's knowledge about crime comes from the mass media (particularly television news and crime dramas). Viewers are more likely to oppose gun control and support the defensive use of guns.

"Gender Gap on Gun Control: Women Want Tougher Laws." *San Francisco Chronicle*, September 8, 1999, p. A6. Reports on an Associated Press poll that shows that 52 percent of women but only 33 percent of men believe that tougher gun laws are more likely to decrease gun violence than better enforcement of existing laws.

Glaeser, Edwin L., and Spencer Glendon. "Who Owns Guns? Criminals, Victims, and the Culture of Violence." *American Economic Review*, vol. 88, May 1998, pp. 458ff. Analyzes the distribution of gun ownership and suggests that guns are concentrated in groups whose values and experiences make gun ownership a normal thing. The authors also correlate gun ownership with income, ethnicity, and other factors.

Huemer, Michael. "Is There a Right to Own a Gun?" *Social Theory and Practice*, vol. 29, April 2003, p. 297ff. In this lengthy and rigorous philosophical essay the author argues from fundamental theories of rights and actions to the conclusion that there is a right to own a gun, and that it is substantive, not trivial. Reviewing the common arguments and statistics about guns and self-defense, he suggests that even a utilitarian analysis probably leads to the value of guns outweighing their costs.

Lacayo, Richard, and Zed Nelson. "Still under the Gun." *Time*, vol. 151, July 6, 1998, pp. 34ff. Revisits a cover story *Time* ran 30 years ago. The authors find that the United States is still struggling to control the eruption of violence, this time in the schools. Prospects for passing more effective gun control legislation are dim because many Americans fiercely cling to the idea of gun ownership.

Lowell, Piper. "A .38-caliber Plowshare." *Christianity Today*, vol. 39, October 2, 1995, pp. 38ff. Describes sculptor Esther Augsberger's sculpture of a plowshare (as in the biblical "swords into plowshares") made from 3,000 guns turned in during a Washington, D.C., amnesty. The guns are melted and twisted but still recognizable in what Augsberger describes as "a symbol of hope."

Malcolm, Joyce Lee. "Concealed Weapons." *Reason*, vol. 32, January 2001, p. 47. The author critiques fellow historian Michael Bellesiles's controversial book *Arming America*. She suggests that he ignores important factors in coming to his conclusion that guns were scarce and relatively unimportant in early America. Guns were available to many parts of the British population, and in America hunting was more prevalent than Bellesiles suggests. Bellesiles's conclusions drawn from writings about the militia and from probate lists are unsupported by his sources.

McClurg, Andrew J. "The Rhetoric of Gun Control." *American University Law Review*, vol. 42, Fall 1992, n.p. Discusses the use (and abuse) of rhetorical techniques in the gun control debate, including fallacies in reasoning, emotional appeals, and disreputable argument techniques such as ad hominem, "straw man," and "slippery slope."

McConnell, Joe. "Firearms: No Right Is an Island." *Whole Earth Review*, no. 77, Winter 1992, pp. 40ff. Suggests that the problem with gun control is not so much the need for guns but the need to prevent the unraveling of constitutional protections, which are interdependent. The same kinds of emotional appeals used to promote gun control could be used to promote censorship, harsher drug laws, or many other attempts to address social problems by limiting rights. McConnell explains the technicalities of assault weapons and Saturday night specials and suggests that gun education and training requirements for gun ownership are a better approach than gun bans.

"Ready, Aim, Fire: A Census of Guns." *U.S. News & World Report*, vol. 122, May 19, 1997, p. 32. Briefly reports a study by the Police Association that reports on the distribution of gun ownership in the United States. It is rather concentrated, with 10 percent of adults owning 77 percent of the nation's guns. Other statistics are included.

Smith, Tom W. "Public Opinion About Gun Policies." *Future of Children*, vol. 12, Summer/Fall 2002, pp. 155–163. Using 1996–99 survey data from the National Opinion Research Center (NORC), this article generally supports common supposition (women, residents of large cities, liberals, and Democrats are most likely to support gun regulation, while men, rural residents, conservatives, and Republicans are least likely to do so). However, most people regardless of ideology want to keep guns out of the hands of criminals and to severely punish gun crimes. Most respondents also support measures to keep guns away from children, but a majority did not support banning families with children from having guns. A large majority also opposed an outright ban on handguns.

Smith, Tom W., and Robert J. Smith. "Changes in Firearms Ownership among Women, 1980–1994." *Journal of Criminal Law and Criminology*, vol. 86, Fall 1995, pp. 133–149. Criticizes polls and surveys by progun groups that have reported a great increase in the number of female gun owners or prospective gun owners. Proponents of these surveys have generally not made their methodology clear. The authors cite the General Social Surveys by the National Opinion Research Center to suggest that there has been no statistically significant trend in the ownership of firearms by females.

Stark, Cynthia A. "Fundamental Rights and the Right to Bear Arms." *Criminal Justice Ethics*, vol. 20, Winter–Spring 2001, pp. 25ff. Argues that it isn't coherent to consider the right to bear arms to be itself a fundamental right even though in some circumstances it may be the only way to secure the fundamental right to self-defense. However, making arms-bearing a derivative right does not mean that there aren't important interests in protecting it—although the author suggests that a utilitarian approach would therefore be justified.

Stell, Lance K. "Gun Control and the Regulation of Fundamental Rights." *Criminal Justice Ethics*, vol. 20, Winter–Spring 2001, pp. 28ff. In addition to arguing that there is a fundamental right to bear arms and discussing the relationship between citizenship and arms-bearing in works by Greek philosopher Aristotle and elsewhere, the author makes an interesting argument for equality. If people naturally have different physical abilities to protect themselves and yet people should have equal rights, the state ought not deprive less physically well-equipped persons of weapons that might put them on an equal basis with attackers.

WEB DOCUMENTS

Cramer, Clayton E. "The Racist Roots of Gun Control." Firearms and Liberty.com. Available online. URL: http://www.firearmsandliberty.com/cramer.racism.html. Posted in 1993. Argues that gun control has been used since colonial times as a tool to subdue African Americans. Many gun laws were passed in the Reconstruction era to prevent newly freed black citizens from having access to arms. Modern laws that give police "discretion" about issuing gun permits can result in discrimination against minorities.

Laughlin, Mark A. "The Philosophy in Defense of Firearms." Available online for purchase. URL: http://www.eoffshore.com/root/pofad.html. Updated on August 5, 1999. A systematic philosophical and historical argument in defense of gun rights that is based on Ayn Rand's philosophy of objectivism, which includes concepts of individual self-ownership and thus an absolute right of self-defense.

GUN CONTROL ADVOCACY (GENERAL)

Works in this section advocate the control or prohibition of firearms based on a variety of arguments. Note that most pro–gun control books deal more specifically with gun crime and gun safety and thus will be found in those categories.

BOOKS

Jacobs, James B. *Can Gun Control Work?* New York: Oxford University Press, 2002. This careful consideration of approaches to gun control eschews strident advocacy in favor of evaluation of existing laws (notably the Brady Law) and their shortcomings (such as the "gun-show loophole"). The author then evaluates a variety of possible further approaches, including comprehensive licensing and registration or a complete prohibition on guns and disarmament of gun owners—a strategy that he admits would run into serious if not fatal problems.

Sugarmann, Josh. *Every Handgun Is Aimed at You: The Case for Banning Handguns.* New York: New Press, 2001. The author, executive director of the Violence Policy Center, takes an uncompromising stance in favor of gun control, targeting handguns in particular. He asserts that handguns are of little use for self-defense and contribute greatly to the suicide rate. He also excoriates gun manufacturers for marketing to women and minorities in their greed to expand their market. His conclusion is that such half measures as trigger locks, "smart guns," and enhanced registration avoid the real issue, which is that Americans are virtually the only people in the industrialized world who have millions of handguns.

ARTICLES

Bogus, Carl T. "The Strong Case for Gun Control." *The American Prospect*, no. 10, Summer 1992, pp. 19–28. Reviews studies and concludes that gun laws work, guns in the hands of citizens do not deter crime, guns are seldom used for self-defense, and people would not substitute other deadly weapons if guns were not available.

Drinan, Robert F. "America Needs Gun Control If It Is to Call Itself a 'Civilized Society.'" *National Catholic Reporter*, vol. 27, May 24, 1991, p. 11. A passionate moral argument for gun control from noted liberal Catholic priest and social commentator Robert Drinan.

Keller, Barbara L. "Frontiersmen Are History." *Newsweek*, August 16, 1993, p. 10. Recounts a break-in at the author's home and her decision not to buy a gun for self-defense. Keller argues that Americans need to abandon the frontier mentality and accept a ban on assault weapons and strict controls on other firearms.

GUN RIGHTS ADVOCACY (GENERAL)

Works in this section defend the right to keep and bear arms and/or oppose gun control for a variety of reasons.

BOOKS

Gottlieb, Alan M. *Politically Correct Guns: Please Don't Rob or Kill Me*. Bellevue, Wash.: Merril Press, 1996. Takes on the gun control advocates by deploying humor and sarcasm but also provides a useful (though one-sided) overview. Gottlieb is chairman of the Citizens Committee for the Right to Keep and Bear Arms.

Hornberger, Jacob G., and Richard M. Ebeling, ed. *The Tyranny of Gun Control*. Fairfax, Va.: Future of Freedom Foundation, 1997. A collection of essays opposing gun control; includes philosophical discussion of the right to armed self-defense from a libertarian standpoint.

LaPierre, Wayne R. *Guns, Crime, and Freedom*. Washington, D.C.: Regnery Publishing, 1994. A vigorous defense of gun rights by the CEO of the National Rifle Association; emphasizes the constitutional right to bear arms, on the one hand, and the ineffectiveness of gun control against criminals, on the other.

———. *Guns, Freedom, and Terrorism*. Nashville, Tenn.: WND Books, 2003. LaPierre's latest advocacy of gun rights takes place in the context of the post–September 11, 2001 world. Along with a defense of the historical meaning of the Second Amendment and assertions about bias and venal politics on the part of gun control advocates, the author argues for arming airline pilots and suggests that armed, prepared citizens are a vital part of the defense against terrorism.

———. *Shooting Straight: Telling the Truth About Guns in America*. Washington, D.C.: Regnery Publishing, 2002. LaPierre provides a systematic presentation of the major arguments for gun rights (including the individual rights interpretation of the Second Amendment), refutes pro–gun control arguments, and argues that approaches to gun control have failed.

Lott, John R. *The Bias Against Guns: Why Almost Everything You've Heard About Gun Control Is Wrong*. Washington, D.C.: Regnery Publishing, 2003. A noted critic of gun control charges the media and celebrity anti-gun activists with bias and distortion. He also shows that statistics cited by gun control proponents are often "cooked" or skewed in various ways, including distortion of risks. Citing his earlier work, Lott argues that more guns in the hands of law-abiding citizens means less crime, and that many types of gun laws (including those regulating gun storage and transactions at gun shows) are counterproductive.

Poe, Richard. *The Seven Myths of Gun Control: Reclaiming the Truth About Guns, Crime, and the Second Amendment*. Roseville, Calif.: Prima Lifestyles, 2001. A popular pro–gun rights exposition that identifies and refutes seven major arguments for gun control, drawing on the findings of legal and criminal justice experts.

Schulman, J. Neil. *Self Control, Not Gun Control*. Santa Monica, Calif.: Synapse-Centurion, 1995. Presents a forceful progun viewpoint based on both philosophical arguments for self-defense rights and practical arguments against the effectiveness of proposed gun control measures.

———. *Stopping Power: Why 70 Million Americans Own Guns*. Santa Monica, Calif.: Synapse-Centurion, 1994. Similar to the preceding book; a gun advocacy book that attempts to confront the gun control advocates head on.

Smith, L. Neil. *Lever Action: Essays on Liberty*. Las Vegas, Nev.: Mountain Media, 2001. A collection of 20 years' worth of essays by an uncompromising libertarian polemicist and science fiction author. A number of these wide-ranging essays deal with gun control (which Smith calls "victim disarmament") and the politics of gun rights.

ARTICLES

Hornberger, Jacob G. "Gun Control, Patriotism, and Civil Disobedience." *Freedom Daily*, 1991, n.p. in Hornberger, Jacob G., ed. *The Tyranny of Gun Control.* Fairfax, Va.: Future of Freedom Foundation, 1997. Also available online. URL: http://www.fff.org/freedom/0591a.asp. Posted in May 1991. Asserts that resistance to gun control is an aspect of civil disobedience that is often needed to preserve liberty against government encroachment.

"An Outrage That Will Last: The Public Has Had Its Fill of Politicians Who Won't Touch the Gun Problem." *Time*, vol. 153, May 10, 1999, p. 35. Argues that the Littleton shootings have led to a new resolve for gun control that can be seized by Democratic candidates. The article argues for age limits for gun ownership, registration, a ban on semiautomatic weapons, and requirements for trigger locks.

Polsby, Daniel D. "The False Promise of Gun Control." *Atlantic Monthly*, March 1994, pp. 57ff. Argues that gun control laws do not work and actually increase the disadvantage between law-abiding citizens and criminals. Social problems, such as poor education, lack of jobs, and broken families, rather than guns, are the root cause of crime that must be addressed.

Snyder, Jeff. "An Argument for Assault Weapons." *Insight on the News*, vol. 10, October 3, 1994, pp. 34ff. Argues against the Clinton administration's claim that assault weapons should not be allowed to citizens because they have become the "weapon of choice for criminals." The actions of criminals should not constrain the rights of citizens, and the very fact that police also use such weapons belies the argument that they are of no use for self-defense.

Sullum, Jacob. "Voodoo Social Policy: Exorcising the Twin Demons, Guns and Drugs." *Reason*, vol. 26, October 1994, pp. 26ff. Argues that the gun control movement, like the war on drugs, is tainted by racism, elitism, and the demonization of offenders. Both policies have badly eroded fundamental civil liberties.

WEB DOCUMENTS

Botsford, David. "The Case against Gun Control." [Personal Web page.] Available online. URL: http://www.logicsouth.com/ lcoble/2ndamend/control.txt. Posted on April 17, 1997. A historical and philosophical essay on individuals, weapons ownership, and the history of gun regulation from a strongly pro–gun rights viewpoint.

Hornberger, Jacob G. "Gun Control Would Make Us Less Safe." Future of Freedom Foundation. Available online. URL: http://www.fff.org/comment/ed1298g.asp. Posted in December 1998. Argues that gun control, like other government efforts, would achieve results opposite to its intentions. Instead of a more peaceful and secure society, gun control would bring about a society that was less secure (because criminals would remain armed) and in which people would be less able to deter encroachments on their democratic rights.

Morgan, O. Reynolds, and W. W. Caruth III. "Myths About Gun Control." National Center for Policy Analysis. Available online. URL: http://www.ncpa.org/ea/eama93/eama93g.html. Posted December 1992. Succinctly rebuts various common assertions supporting gun control, such as the connection between guns and crime, defensive gun use, and the role of Saturday night specials.

"Off Target with Gun Controls." National Center for Policy Analysis. Available online. URL: http://www.ncpa.org/ba/ba294.html. Posted June 11, 1999. Gives reasons to not adopt various types of new gun legislation following the Columbine killings. These include mandatory gun locks/smart guns, new gun show regulations, and waiting periods.

Polsby, Daniel D., and Dennis Brennen. "Taking Aim at Gun Control." Heartland Institute. Available online. URL: http://www.heartland.org/pdf/polsby-ps.pdf. Posted on October 30, 1995. Analyzes gun-related issues such as whether gun owners are more violent than the general population, the true relationship between perpetrators and victims of homicide, and the utility of waiting periods and laws targeting drive-by shootings. The site presents what it calls 10 "myths" favored by gun control advocates, reviews the effects of existing gun control laws, and challenges studies supporting gun control.

"The War against Handguns." National Rifle Association Institute for Legal Action. Available online. URL: http://www.nraila.org/Issues/FactSheets/Read.aspx?ID=17. Posted on February 15, 2001. Summarizes history, statistics, and arguments against handgun control and discusses legal cases and attacks strategies of handgun control groups.

GUNS, CRIME, AND VIOLENCE

This section focuses on topics such as the relationship between the presence of guns and crime and the utility of firearms for defending against or preventing crime or terrorism and the question of whether concealed-carry gun laws should be liberalized. There are also works assessing the social, economic, or public health impacts of gun violence. Works dealing specifically with the impact of gun violence on youth are found in the section on Youth and Guns.

BOOKS

Berger, Loren, and Dennis Henigan. *Guns and Terror.* Washington, D.C.: Brady Center to Prevent Gun Violence, 2001. Also available online. URL: http://www.bradycampaign.org/pdf/facts/reports/gandt.pdf. Describes how terrorists such as al-Qaeda, the IRA, and white supremacists have used gun shows and corrupt dealers to obtain large quantities of guns and ammunition. The authors recommend requiring background checks for all sales at gun shows, renewing the assault weapon ban, and banning high-volume purchases.

Clarke, R. V. G., and David Lester. *Suicide: Closing the Exits.* New York: Springer Verlag, 1989. Advocates gun control (among other measures) as a way to reduce suicide by removing the means for easy, impulsive suicide.

Coalition to Stop Handgun Violence. *The Unspoken Tragedy: Firearm Suicide in the United States.* Washington, D.C.: Educational Fund to End Handgun Violence and Coalition to Stop Gun Violence, 1995. Reports that firearms are being increasingly used in suicides by females, a group that had previously preferred poison. Because firearms are more often lethal than other means, the fatality rate for female suicide attempts has increased.

Cook, Philip J., and Jens Ludwig. *Gun Violence: The Real Costs.* New York: Oxford University Press, 2000. The authors, both public policy experts, painstakingly calculate the total economic impact of gun violence. They consider it to be a major public health problem that costs Americans about $100 billion a year, including both the direct costs of injury and the cost of increased security at airports and schools. However, the authors take a moderate stance on gun control, advocating registration of handguns and stricter enforcement and increased sentencing for gun-related crimes.

Harcourt, Bernard E., ed. *Guns, Crime, and Punishment in America.* New York: New York University Press, 2003. A collection of reprinted articles by legal experts and criminologists. The first part deals with the "talk" about guns—in academia, on the street, and in American culture, as well as recent developments in the Second Amendment debate, suggesting new approaches that might break the dichotomy between the collective and individual rights interpretations. The second, longer, part deals with more practical issues—firearms tracing, community antiviolence programs, the use of criminal profiling, the effects of the Brady Law, and criminal and civil approaches to gun violence.

Hemenway, David. *Private Guns, Public Health*. Ann Arbor: University of Michigan Press, 2004. The author, a leader in the movement to treat gun violence as a public health and consumer safety problem, argues for a comprehensive policy to reduce gun injuries based on earlier campaigns involving tobacco, infectious disease, automobiles, and other risks. He also examines and refutes claims by gun rights advocates concerning the defensive and deterrent use of guns.

Izumi, Michael T. *In Self Defense: The Legal, Ethical and Tactical Use of Deadly Force*. Concord, N.H.: Police Bookshelf, 1995. Although designed as a practical handbook for persons who want to be able to defend themselves with a firearm, this book also shows the potential complexity of such situations including possible legal consequences.

Kessler, Jim, and Lisa Kimbrough. "Stolen Firearms: Arming the Enemy." Washington, D.C.: Americans for Gun Safety Foundation, 2002. The studies featured here tallied 1.7 million firearms stolen from January 1993 to August 2002. States with safe gun storage laws had dramatically lower firearms theft rates. The authors' recommendations include more vigorous prosecution of offenses, more effective locking or storage devices to make stolen guns unusable or unobtainable, and public education about the problem.

Kessler, Jim, Michael Harrington, and Ed Hill. *Enforcement Gap: Federal Gun Laws Ignored*. Washington, D.C.: Americans for Gun Safety Foundation, 2003. A survey of federal gun prosecutions for 2000–02 found that only 25,002 prosecutions were filed, even though more than 330,000 guns used in violent crimes may have been received illicitly, more than 420,000 guns were stolen, and 450,000 persons did not fill out the federal background check truthfully. One of the few things the NRA and the Americans for Gun Safety agree on is that much more prosecution of gun offenses is necessary.

Kleck, Gary. *Point Blank: Guns and Violence in America*. New York: Aldine de Gruyter, 1991. Describes gun owners as a remarkably normal group, socially and psychologically, with only a small percentage of inappropriately violent individuals. Kleck suggests that the value of guns for self-defense outweighs the dangers, as well as providing an important deterrent effect. He develops a methodology for understanding the interaction between aggressor and victim and the role played by the presence of a weapon.

———. *Targeting Guns: Firearms and their Control*. New York: Aldine de Gruyter, 1997. Reviews and critiques studies of gun violence, from a generally pro–gun rights viewpoint. This book also acts as an update to Kleck's previous book, *Point Blank*.

Kleck, Gary, and Don B. Kates. *Armed: New Perspectives on Gun Control*. Amherst, N.Y.: Prometheus Books, 2001. A noted criminologist and a legal expert join forces to argue that studies show that the risks of gun accidents have been mischaracterized or overstated and that guns are an effective deterrent to crime. They also argue that reasonable gun regulation has been hampered by an agenda dedicated to banning gun ownership and biased coverage of the issue in the media, which in turn have provoked an extreme reaction by progun activists in the NRA and elsewhere.

———. *The Great American Gun Debate: Essays on Firearms and Violence.* San Francisco: Pacific Research Institute for Public Policy, 1997. Essays exploring criminological issues, the social utility of firearms, and the biased role of the media in covering the gun debate.

Kopel, David B., ed. *Guns: Who Should Have Them?* Amherst, N.Y.: Prometheus Books, 1995. Presents opinions by experts in law, criminology, medicine, psychiatry, and feminist studies; suggests that the emphasis on gun control is misplaced and that the real causes of crime lie in social factors such as the breakdown of the family.

Ludwig, Jens, and Philip J. Cook, eds. *Evaluating Gun Policy: Effects on Crime and Violence.* Washington, D.C.: Brookings Institution Press, 2003. Because the relationship between the prevalence of guns and rates of crime and violence is at the heart of the gun control debate, this collection of studies is a valuable resource for developing what the authors consider to be a "pragmatic gun policy." Topics covered include the prevalence of guns in suicide and burglary, the effects of gun buyback policies, restricting firearms ownership by domestic batterers, restrictions on gun carrying versus concealed carry laws, and data and analysis for policymakers. Each article is followed by one or more critical commentaries.

Quigley, Paxton. *Armed and Female.* New York: E. P. Dutton, 1989. A combination of gun advocacy and a "how to" manual for women who want to obtain a gun for self-defense. Quigley covers both practical and legal considerations for gun use and includes real-life accounts of crime incidents to illustrate tactical problems.

Torr, James D., ed. *Guns and Crime.* San Diego: Greenhaven Press, 2003. For young adult or older readers, this "At Issue" book explores many facets of the relationship between guns and crime, including the debate over the defensive value of firearms held by private citizens.

Violence Policy Center. *Bullet Hoses: Semiautomatic Assault Weapons. What Are They? What's So Bad About Them?* Washington, D.C.: Violence Policy Center, 2003. Also available online. URL: http://www.vpc.org/studies/hosecont.htm. Posted in May 2003. Defines semiautomatic weapons and distinguishes them from fully automatic ones (machine guns), but argues that there is no effective difference in killing power—indeed, semiautomatic weapons may be more deadly than machine guns because they are more accurate. The large magazine and high rate of fire are the most important features. The report refutes arguments by the gun industry that such weapons are not particularly deadly.

————. *Credit Card Armies: Firearms and Training for Terror in the United States.* Washington, D.C.: Violence Policy Center, 2003. Also available online. URL: http://www.vpc.org/graphics/creditcardarmies.pdf. Posted in November 2002. Argues that because the United States has lax gun regulations compared to most other countries as well as a plentiful supply of guns and shooting ranges, terrorist groups have found America an attractive location for training. Specific groups and training opportunities for terrorists are described.

————. *"Just Like Bird Hunting": The Threat to Civil Aviation from 50 Caliber Sniper Rifles.* Washington, D.C.: Violence Policy Center, 2003. Also available online. URL: http://www.vpc.org/graphics/birdhuntingstudy. PDF. Posted in January 2003. Argues that these powerful, long-range rifles (such as the Barrett anti-armor rifle) could disable (and ultimately destroy) a commercial jet airliner or a helicopter in flight, using readily available armor-piercing or incendiary ammunition. Thus, these weapons and related ammunition should be banned from civilian use.

————. *License to Kill IV: More Guns, More Crime.* Washington, D.C.: Violence Policy Center, 2002. Also available online. URL: http://www.vpc. org/studies/ltk4cont.htm. Posted in June 2002. Gun rights advocates such as John Lott *(More Guns, Less Crime)* have argued not only that allowing citizens to carry concealed firearms reduces the crime rate, but that very few gun permit holders are arrested for gun-related crimes. This report attempts to refute that argument by compiling the numbers of offenses charged to concealed carry permit holders (CCWs) in Texas—5,314 offenses between January 1, 1996, and August 31, 2001. However, it should be noted that many individuals were charged with multiple offenses, and that only about 2,200 of the offenses were actually weapon-related.

————. *Officer Down: Assault Weapons and the War on Law Enforcement.* Washington, D.C.: Violence Policy Center, 2003. Also available online. URL: http://www.vpc.org/studies/officecont.htm. Posted in May 2003. This report compiles incidents in which criminals used assault weapons to kill police, and argues that, contrary to assertions by gun rights advocates, assault weapons represent a significant, continuing threat to law enforcement.

————. *The Threat to the Chemical and Refinery Industry from 50 Caliber Sniper Rifles.* Washington, D.C.: Violence Policy Center, 2002. Also available online. URL: http://www.vpc.org/studies/duckcont.htm. Posted in August 2002. Warns that .50 caliber sniper rifles could be used by terrorists to cause a disaster in a chemical plant or refinery.

———. *Unintended Consequences: Pro-Handgun Experts Prove That Handguns Are a Dangerous Choice for Self-Defense.* Washington, D.C.: Violence Policy Center, 2001. Also available online. URL: http://www.vpc.org/studies/uninsum.htm. Posted in November 2001. This lengthy report refutes arguments made by gun advocates concerning the effectiveness of the handgun as a weapon for self-defense. The report often attempts to turn the words of caution (and emphasis on the need for training and safe handling) of such experts as Massad Ayoob against them. The conclusion is that handguns are a poor, risky choice for self-defense for all but a relatively few highly trained individuals.

Waters, Robert A. *The Best Defense: True Stories of Intended Victims Who Defended Themselves with a Firearm.* Nashville, Tenn.: Cumberland House, 1998. A collection of vivid accounts of ordinary people who used guns to defend themselves against attackers. Waters explores both their thoughts and feelings and the response of police and society in general; the book leans to strong gun rights advocacy.

Webster, Daniel. *Myths About Defensive Gun Use and Permissive Gun Carry Laws.* Berkeley, Calif.: Berkeley Media Studies Group, 2000. Also available online. URL: http://www.bmsg.org/content/myths.pdf. Offers refutation of studies by John Lott and David Mustard (recounted in the book *More Guns, Less Crime*) and studies by criminologists Gary Kleck and Marc Gerz at the University of Florida. The objections are primarily methodological, but also assert that any correlation has not been shown to imply causation. The author suggests that no reexamination of the view that gun regulations can reduce lethal crimes is necessary at this time.

Wellford, Charles F., John V. Pepper, and Carol V. Pertrie, eds. *Firearms and Violence: What Do We Know?* Washington, D.C.: National Academies Press, 2004. Members of the National Research Council's Committee to Improve Research and Data on Firearms attempt to scientifically assess the quality of the existing data, believing this to be essential to doing good science in a field often distorted by advocacy.

Wintermute, Garen, et al. *Effectiveness of Denial of Handgun Purchase by Violent Misdemeanants, Final Report.* Sacramento: University of California, Davis. Violence Prevention Research Program, available through Rockville, Md.: National Institute of Justice, 2002. This report compares persons convicted of at least one violent misdemeanor who were denied purchase of a gun from a licensed dealer to similar persons who were able to purchase a gun prior to enactment of the California law. The study concludes that the successful purchasers are more likely to be arrested for new gun and/or violent crimes; thus the law has a crime-reducing effect.

Wright, James D. *Armed and Considered Dangerous: A Survey of Felons and Their Firearms.* New York: Aldine de Gruyter, 1994. Revision of a classic study that looked at the attitude of hardened criminals toward their use of guns—and the possibility of their victims being armed.

ARTICLES

Adler, Karl P., et al. "Firearm Violence and Public Health: Limiting the Availability of Guns." *JAMA, The Journal of the American Medical Association*, vol. 271, April 27, 1994, pp. 1281ff. Cites statistics that indicate that firearm violence has reached "epidemic proportions." Urges tough federal gun control laws to bring the epidemic under control, including requiring that prospective gun owners be tightly screened, undergo training, and have to "rigorously" show they have a good reason to have a gun. An expansion of the assault weapons ban and higher taxes to discourage gun purchases are also recommended.

Alter, Jonathan. "Curb Violence by Targeting Bullets." *Washington Monthly*, vol. 26, January–February 1994, p. 45. Argues that although gun control can and should be strengthened, the huge number of existing guns will limit its effectiveness. Therefore, the author suggests imposing strict control on the sales of bullets, as well as marking bullets for identification, perhaps with embedded microchips; making bullets both more expensive and easier to trace should cut down on gun-related crimes. He also suggests that conservatives may be willing to accept more methods of gun control in exchange for more certain and effective punishment for criminals.

———. "On the Cusp of a Crusade." *Newsweek*, May 10, 1999, p. 59. Suggests a range of reasonable responses to the Littleton tragedy, including requiring "smart guns" that can only be fired by their owner, along with economic boycotts to force media moguls to act more responsibly concerning violent content in movies and video games.

———. "Pull the Trigger on Fingerprints." *Newsweek*, October 28, 2002, p. 41. Argues that taking ballistic fingerprints (in which a gun is fired and its characteristics recorded before sale for matching with crime bullets later) is reliable and useful, objections from the gun lobby notwithstanding. Although the database is currently small, as more states adopt the practice the system will gradually start to catch more criminals.

Anderson, George M. "Gun Control: New Approaches." *America*, vol. 172, March 11, 1995, pp. 26ff. Describes emerging groups such as the Violence Policy Center and the HELP (Handgun Epidemic Lowering Plan) Network that are recasting gun control as a public health, child safety, or suicide prevention issue. The groups hope to counter gun advertising targeted at women and other groups as being deceptive in its claims about the utility of guns for self-protection.

Annotated Bibliography

Becker, Gary S. "Stiffer Jail Terms Will Make Gunmen More Gun-Shy." *Business Week*, no. 3360, February 28, 1994, p. 18. Argues that high taxes on guns and ammunition will prevent only law-abiding citizens from purchasing guns, while criminals buy most of their guns on the illegal market and pay no tax. However, a study by James Q. Wilson and Richard H. Herrnstein suggests that "add-on" sentences for using a gun in a crime do deter criminals from choosing to carry a gun.

Blackman, Paul H., et al. "Firearms and Fatalities." *JAMA, The Journal of the American Medical Association*, vol. 275, June 12, 1996, pp. 1723ff. Criticizes epidemiological approaches to firearms violence, focusing on a study by Stephen W. Hargarten on characteristics of firearms involved in fatalities. Argues that analogies between intentional gun injuries and unintentional injuries (such as auto accidents) may be flawed and that small-caliber handguns focused on by the Hargarten study are actually declining as a factor in crime. Another letter defends the importance of addressing firearms violence.

Bronars, Stephen G., and John R. Lott, Jr. "Criminal Deterrence, Geographic Spillovers, and the Right to Carry Concealed Handguns." *American Economic Review*, vol. 88, May 1998, pp. 475ff. Argues that when communities adopt laws that allow more citizens to carry guns, criminals tend to migrate to neighboring areas where stricter laws make it less likely that citizens have guns to defend themselves or their property.

Calhoun, John A. "Project Safe Neighborhoods: America's Network against Gun Violence Facilitating the Work of Outreach." *USA Bulletin*, vol. 50, January 2002, pp. 26–28. Describes a program that combines stronger enforcement of gun laws with community outreach and education. (The same issue has a related article with 10 case studies.)

Callahan, Charles M., Frederic P. Rivara, and Thomas D. Koepsell. "Money for Guns: Evaluation of the Seattle Gun Buy-Back Program." *Public Health Reports*, vol. 109, July–August 1994, pp. 472ff. Evaluates a Seattle gun buyback program. The mean age of people turning in guns was 51 years, and about 25 percent were women, suggesting that the people most likely to use guns for crime (young adult males) responded only minimally. There were no statistically significant changes in firearms-related crimes and deaths in the months before and after the program.

"Can Hidden Guns Cut Crime? Concealed Weapons Laws." *The Economist*, vol. 347, May 30, 1998, pp. 24ff. Summarizes John Lott's studies that claim to show crime reduction as a consequence of liberalization of concealed-carry laws, and recounts opposing views of critics such as Franklin Zimring. The latter claims that Lott does not account for other possible causes of lower crime, nor for intermediate causality (such as whether the

169

change in law actually led to more people carrying concealed guns). Lott in turn replies to his critics in his new book *More Guns, Less Crime.*

Caplan, David L. "Firearms Registration and Waiting Periods: New York City's Lesson." *American Rifleman,* vol. 141, October 1993, p. 67A. Studies the effects of gun legislation passed in New York City in 1967 and claims that it has been ineffective in reducing crime.

Carlson, Tucker. "Handgun Control, M.D." *Weekly Standard,* April 15, 1996, n.p. Argues that the characterization of gun violence as a public health problem is based on flawed reasoning. Guns are passive and do not infect people the way germs do, and crime, rather than being of epidemic proportions, has actually been declining. Carlson also criticizes the *New England Journal of Medicine*'s 1986 study on guns in the home.

Chauvin, McKay. "Project Backfire: The Beginning of the End of Gun Crime in Kentucky." *USA Bulletin,* vol. 50, January 2002, pp. 36–39. Describes an ambitious program that has county, state, and federal attorneys cooperating to prevent gun offenses from "slipping through the cracks" or being pled down. The message is being sent that committing a gun crime means more certainty of more jail time.

Cheng, Vicki. "Firearms Injure 3 for Every 1 They Kill, New Research Finds." *The New York Times,* June 14, 1995, p. A15. Reports on Centers for Disease Control research that highlights the underemphasized extent to which firearms injure as well as kill people.

Cole, Thomas. "Extending Brady Background Checks Opposed." *JAMA, The Journal of the American Medical Association,* vol. 280, December 23, 1998, p. 2065. Reports on a conference held by a group called Academics for the Second Amendment. Speakers at the conference argued that gun control laws have been shown to have no significant effect on homicide rates. New, tougher laws are likely to discourage law-abiding citizens from acquiring the means to defend themselves, while having little or no effect on criminals who do not bother with paperwork in their gun transactions. Researchers Don B. Kates, Chester L. Britt, David B. Mustard, and others present their conclusions.

Cole, Thomas B., and Franklin E. Zimring. "On Law and Firearms." *JAMA, The Journal of the American Medical Association,* vol. 275, June 12, 1996, p. 1709. Cole interviews legal scholar Franklin E. Zimring, who explains that the new emphasis on firearms as a public health issue is encouraging legal scholars to reexamine the role of firearms and approaches to risk reduction.

Comey, Jim, and Stephen Miller. "Project Exile." *USA Bulletin,* vol. 50, January 2002, pp. 11–15. Describes Project Exile, an anti–gun crime program first tried out in Richmond, Virginia, which had been suffering from one of the highest per capita murder rates in the country. The premise is that any criminal found with a gun will be "exiled" from the community by a mandatory federal prison sentence, usually 5–10 years.

Cook, Philip J., Stephanie Molliconi, and Thomas B. Cole. "Regulating Gun Markets." *Journal of Criminal Law and Criminology*, vol. 86, Fall 1995, pp. 59–92. Suggests that regulators and policy makers must pay more attention to the complicated role that guns play in the criminal "economy" and that the ease with which guns are stolen and transported tends to make regulations centered on legitimate dealers less effective. The authors urge a police focus on stolen guns and the regulation or abolition of gun transactions that do not involve a licensed dealer.

Daughtry, Sylvester, Jr., and John M. Snyder. "Will Gun Control Laws Help Reduce Crime in America?" *CQ Researcher*, vol. 4, June 10, 1994, p. 521. Debates philosophically and practically whether gun control laws will actually reduce the crime rate.

Donohue, John J., III, and Stephen D. Levitt. "Guns, Violence and the Efficiency of Illegal Markets." *American Economic Review*, vol. 88, May 1998, pp. 463ff. Analyzes the role of guns in economic planning by criminals such as drug gangsters. The authors conclude that their decisions are based more on who is likely to win a confrontation than on the lethality of the weapons used.

"Don't Withhold Treatment on This Epidemic." *U.S. Catholic*, vol. 63, September 1998, p. 25. Points out that homicide is the second leading cause of death for youths aged 15–24, and that the U.S. homicide rate is far higher than that of other countries. The article reports on efforts of the Centers for Disease Control and others to treat gun violence as an epidemic and ponders whether other social problems might be better dealt with if people treated them as seriously as physical diseases.

Fenoglo, Gia. "You've Got to Have a Way of Defending Yourself." *National Journal*, vol. 32, July 22, 2000, p. 2372. Presents the case for armed self-defense against criminals. The article begins with the story of a woman who only reluctantly agreed to have a gun in the house and to learn how to use it. She then used the gun to save her family from two armed intruders. She concludes that she is in favor of making guns safer, but that people need them for self-defense.

Golden, Frederic. "Drop Your Guns!" *Time*, vol. 150, Fall 1997, pp. 56ff. Reports on Dr. Garen Wintermute's efforts to treat the "epidemic" of gun violence by establishing the Violence Prevention Research Program in 1991. His studies show that gun violence is far more likely to cause fatal or serious injuries than is other forms of attack. Golden reports on Wintermute's 1994 "Ring of Fire" study that identified a small group of California gun makers as being responsible for the spread of Saturday night specials.

"Gun Ownership Tied to Higher Risk for Women's Murder, Suicide." *American Medical News*, vol. 40, April 21, 1997, p. 18. Reports a study that identified risk factors for death of women by murder or suicide. Guns are the most common cause of death, and mental illness, substance abuse, and domestic violence are all important factors. The article recommends encouraging people to store guns safely or to remove them from the household and supports laws that forbid gun purchase by convicted batterers.

Hahn, Robert A., et al. "First Reports Evaluating the Effectiveness of Strategies for Preventing Violence: Firearms Laws: Findings from the Task Force on Community Preventative Services." *Mortality and Morbidity Weekly Report*, October 3, 2003, pp. 11–20. Also available online. URL: http://www.cdc.gov/mmwr/preview/mmwrhtml/rr5214a2.htm. Evaluates the current scientific evidence for the effectiveness of various types of firearms laws including gun bans, restrictions on firearms acquisition, waiting periods, and "will issue" concealed weapon carry laws. The report concludes that there was insufficient evidence to determine the effectiveness of any of the types of laws studied.

Hargarten, Stephen W. "Characteristics of Firearms Involved in Fatalities." *JAMA, The Journal of the American Medical Association*, vol. 275, January 3, 1996, pp. 42–45. Study breaks down firearm fatalities by type of gun. Eighty-nine percent of firearm homicides were caused by handguns. Guns are categorized further by caliber and model.

Headden, Susan. "Guns, Money and Medicine: The Proliferation of Powerful New Weapons Has Sent the Cost of Crime Spiraling. Here's Why You Pay." *U.S. News & World Report*, vol. 121, July 1, 1996, pp. 30ff. Analyzes the health costs caused by gun crime, using a variety of example cases. The costs are increasing due to the proliferation of more powerful weapons. All consumers end up paying more for these health costs because tax money must be used to care for the majority of victims, who are uninsured.

Hemenway, David, Sara J. Solnick, and Deborah R. Azrael. "Firearms and Community Feelings of Safety." *Journal of Criminal Law and Criminology*, vol. 86, 1995, pp. 121–132. Reports a survey that finds that about 85 percent of non–gun owners would feel less safe if more people in their community owned guns, while for gun owners, about 50 percent would feel safer, and 50 percent less safe.

Hewitt, Bill. "A Separate Peace: Dismayed by Violence on the Streets, a New York Businessman Offers to Swap Toys for Guns and Starts a Disarmament Crusade Across the Country." *People Weekly*, vol. 41, January 17, 1994, pp. 84ff. Tells the story of carpet store owner Fernando Mateo, Sr. Dismayed by media reports of violent deaths just before Christmas in 1993, Mateo hit upon the idea of organizing a program to swap toys for guns. He believes the program provides some Christmas cheer for poor families while making homes and streets a little safer.

Kates, Don B., et al. "Guns and Public Health: Epidemic of Violence or Pandemic of Propaganda?" *Tennessee Law Review*, vol. 62, Spring 1995, pp. 513ff. Argues that studies purporting to show an "epidemic" of gun violence are heavily propagandistic and filled with errors of fact and reasoning. Suggests that many such studies fail to differentiate among firearms users by not employing well-established criminological and sociological factors.

Kellermann, Arthur L., and Donald T. Reay. "Protection or Peril?" *New England Journal of Medicine*, vol. 314, June 12, 1986, pp. 1557–1560. Highly influential but controversial study of the risks of keeping firearms in the home. The authors conclude that there are 43 suicides, criminal homicides, or accidental gunshot deaths for every case of homicide for self-protection.

Kellermann, Arthur L., et al. "Weapon Involvement in Home Invasion Crimes." *JAMA, The Journal of the American Medical Association*, vol. 273, June 14, 1995, pp. 1759ff. Analyzes home invasion crimes. The authors found that homeowners seldom used guns against intruders. Persons who resisted in some way were less likely to lose property but more likely to be injured. Security measures such as locks are likely to be more useful than firearms for deterring such invasions.

Kleck, Gary, and Marc Gertz. "Armed Resistance to Crime: The Prevalence and Nature of Self-Defense with a Gun." *Journal of Criminal Law and Criminology*, vol. 86, no. 1, 1995, n.p. Argues that use of guns for self-defense is underreported in surveys by government agencies because of fear of prosecution. Kleck's own survey finds an estimated 2.2 to 2.5 defensive gun uses per year.

Kopel, David B. "The Federal Government Should Set a Better Example: Militias and Gun Control." *Vital Speeches*, vol. 62, March 1, 1996, pp. 315ff. Suggests that the right-wing militia activities of recent years should be seen in the historical context of violent dissent and government overreaction, citing such examples as the repression of abolitionists and labor organizers. Policy makers should try to avoid hysteria and distortion when assessing the real nature of threats. Local rather than federal action is usually better at providing precisely tailored responses.

———. "The Untold Triumph of Concealed-Carry Permits." *Policy Review: The Journal of American Citizenship*, no. 78, July–August 1996, n.p. Argues that liberalization of concealed-carry laws did not substantially affect homicide rates and that the previous study by David McDowall, Colin Loftin, and Brian Wiersema suffers from methodological flaws. Kopel reiterates that the rate of crime by permit holders is very low.

Kovandzic, Tomislav V., and Thomas B. Marvell. "Right-to-Carry Concealed Handguns and Violent Crime: Crime Control through Gun Decontrol?" *Criminology and Public Policy*, vol. 2, July 2003, pp. 363–396. The authors were unable to find a statistically significant correlation in 58 Florida counties from 1980 to 2000 between the number of concealed carry permits issued and a reduction in violent crime.

Krug, E. G. "Firearm-Related Deaths in the United States and 35 Other High- and Upper-Middle-Income Countries." *JAMA, The Journal of the American Medical Association*, vol. 280, August 5, 1998, p. 401. Reports that the 49th World Health Assembly has declared violence a worldwide public health problem. Using data provided by health officials, a study concludes that firearms death rates are much higher in the United States and that types of death (murder or suicide) as well as rates vary with national income.

Kuhn, E. M., et al. "Missing the Target: A Comparison of Buyback and Fatality Related Guns." *Injury Prevention*, vol. 8, June 2002, pp. 143ff. This study concludes that the guns typically turned in to gun buyback programs are not the types most commonly associated with murder or suicide. Therefore, although gun buyback programs may increase the public's awareness of the dangers of guns, their effectiveness in reducing injuries is likely to be minimal.

LaPierre, Wayne. "Standing Guard." *American Rifleman*, vol. 146, November–December, 1998 p. 10. Describes Project Exile, the NRA-promoted program first adopted in Richmond, Virginia, to strictly enforce gun laws against felons. LaPierre claims this approach has deterred many criminals from obtaining guns.

Lewis, Bobbie. "Preventing Firearm Violence: A Public Health Imperative." *Annals of Internal Medicine*, vol. 122, February 15, 1995, pp. 311ff. Points out that the United States has the world's highest rates of firearms-related injury and death. Strong action is needed to address this public health problem, including gun owner training, safety, and storage requirements.

Lott, John R. "Gun Show." *National Review*, vol. 51, May 31, 1999, p. 32. Argues that new gun laws proposed in the wake of the Littleton shootings would have little effect on preventing such shootings in the future. Although the media seldom mentions it, armed adults in schools have been more successful in stopping some shootings, such as the one in Pearl, Mississippi, in 1997. Lott's studies conclude that of all proposed policies, only giving law-abiding citizens (and school officials) the right to carry guns has any actual effect on reducing the number and severity of mass shootings.

————. "Guns, Crime, and Health." *World and I*, vol. 18, October 2003, p. 32. The author argues that the public health–based justifications for gun control are misguided. The risks of guns to children are overstated (juvenile gun deaths are only one-third as frequent as drownings of children in bathtubs). The costs of guns must be balanced by their effectiveness in deterring crime and saving lives. The author also asserts that studies properly controlled for economic and demographic factors show that countries with strict gun control laws actually have higher homicide rates than the United States.

————. "Half Cocked: Why Most of What You See in the Media About Guns Is Wrong." *The American Enterprise*, vol. 14, July–August 2003, pp. 28ff. The noted pro–gun rights scholar cites a number of cases of successful armed self-defense (involving only brandishing a gun) that were virtually ignored by the media. Since it is not news when "nothing happens," the result is a distortion of the nature and extent of gun violence. In shootings at the Appalachian Law School, the fact that two students used their guns to halt the attack was ignored by most national media. Lott argues that such bias both distorts the debate about the risks and benefits of guns, it can also endanger people by making them think that an unarmed approach is best when dealing with criminals.

————. "How to Stop Mass Public Shootings." *Los Angeles Times*, May 25, 1998, p. B5. Asserts that studies show that allowing qualified citizens to carry concealed weapons is the best way to prevent multiple-victim shootings.

————. "Trigger Happy." *National Review*, vol. 50, June 22, 1998, p. 49. Recounts author's personal experience dealing with gun control advocates who responded to his studies linking concealed weapons to lower crime by unleashing a barrage of distortions and attacks on his professional integrity. When accusations were shown to be false, the media was generally not interested in running corrections.

Lott, John R., and David B. Mustard. "Crime, Deterrence, and the Right-to-Carry Concealed Handguns." *Journal of Legal Studies*, vol. 26, January 1997, pp. 1–68. Also available online. URL: http://teapot.usask.ca/cdn-firearms/Lott/lott.pdf. The now-famous study finding a correlation between the enacting of liberalized concealed carry laws and reduction in the crime rate.

MacDonald, Sam. "Gun Control's New Language: How Anti-Terror Rhetoric Is Being Used against the Second Amendment." *Reason*, vol. 33, March 2002, pp. 16ff. Analyzes the use by gun control advocates of concern about terrorism in the aftermath of the September 11, 2001, attacks. As a libertarian the author views this as a threat to liberty comparable to (and simultaneous with) the pushing through of the USA PATRIOT Act. A major component of the agenda is the use of the NICS (National Instant

Criminal Background Check System) for criminal and antiterrorist prosecutions in addition to its intended use for checking gun buyers. U.S. Attorney General John Ashcroft opposes such measures, however.

Marwick, Charles. "A Public Health Approach to Making Guns Safer." *JAMA, The Journal of the American Medical Association*, vol. 273, June 14, 1995, pp. 1743ff. Reports on a conference titled "Guns—A Public Health Approach: Making Changes in Making Guns," sponsored by the Association of Trial Lawyers of America and the Johns Hopkins Center for Gun Policy and Research. Participants said their goal was not banning guns but making them safer by applying commonly accepted product regulatory standards to firearms, just as medicines now come with childproof safety caps.

———. "Help Network Says Firearms Data Gap Makes Reducing Gun Injuries More Difficult." *JAMA, The Journal of the American Medical Association*, vol. 218, March 3, 1999, p. 784. Reports surveys conducted by the Handgun Epidemic Lowering Plan (HELP) that tried to measure accuracy and completeness in the reporting of gun-related deaths and injuries. The study found that the reporting of nonfatal injuries was "spotty" and that reports often lacked needed information about the type of firearm involved and the circumstances of the injury.

McDowall, David, Colin Loftin, and Brian Wiersema. "Easing Concealed Firearms Laws: Effects on Homicide in Three States." *Journal of Criminal Law and Criminology*, vol. 86, Fall 1995, pp. 193–206. Studies the effects of the liberalization of concealed-carry gun permit laws in Florida, Mississippi, and Oregon. The authors point out that firearm homicides increased in four out of the five areas studied. The authors conclude that liberalized concealed-carry does not reduce gun crime and may increase it.

"Medical Costs for Gunshot Victims Estimated at $2.3 Billion Annually." *San Francisco Chronicle*, August 4, 1999, p. A2. Reports on a study by researchers at the Sanford Institute of Public Policy at Duke University, based on 1994 data gathered from hospitals. The average cost per injury was $17,000.

Murray, Frank J. "Despite Risks, Americans Use Guns in Self-Defense." *Insight on the News*, vol. 15, June 14, 1999, p. 42. Argues that despite the uproar over guns in the United States, thousands of Americans continue quietly to arm themselves and use their guns to drive away criminals. Because actual shootings are rare, the media tends to ignore this phenomenon as not being newsworthy. Accurate numbers about defensive gun use are hard to come by, however. Includes anecdotes, such as a citizen successfully taking on cop-killing drug traffickers.

Orr, Daniel L., II, et al. "Regulating Firearm Advertisements." *JAMA, The Journal of the American Medical Association*, vol. 278, September 3, 1997, pp. 701ff. Includes responses to a paper arguing that firearms ads that tout guns for self-protection should be banned as deceptive. Critics argue that the evidence of the prevalence of successful defensive gun use is strong and that the paper mischaracterizes accepted interpretation of the Second Amendment and the language of the advertisements in question. The paper's authors offer rebuttals, critiquing the gun defense studies of Gary Kleck and others, and pointing out that the courts have had the last word on the Second Amendment.

Polsby, Daniel D. "The False Promise of Gun Control." *Atlantic Monthly*, vol. 273, March 1994, pp. 57ff. Argues that new gun laws designed to make guns more expensive and harder to get can have unintended consequences, feeding the illegal market. It is necessary to understand the "rational" motives of criminals and others who seek guns to maximize their chance of achieving their goals. To reduce gun violence, one should try to change the social conditions that make criminal choices attractive.

Pratt, Larry. "Health Care and Firearms." *Journal of the Medical Association of Georgia*, vol. 83, March 1994, pp. 149–152. The executive director of Gun Owners of America argues that any study of the health costs of firearms must take into account the deaths and injuries prevented by defensive uses of firearms, including many incidents during which the gun is never fired.

Ragavan, Chitra. "Ready, Aim, Misfire." *U.S. News & World Report*, vol. 130, May 21, 2001, p. 16. Project Exile is a program that intended to get tough on gun offenders and hopefully get more of them (and their guns) off the streets. But while the federal version of the program had some initial success, state efforts such as that in Virginia seem to have had disappointing results. Some causes may be a slackening of effort to convict offenders and judicial resistance to long sentences for relatively mild gun offenses.

Ratnesar, Romesh. "Should You Carry a Gun? A New Study Argues for Concealed Weapons." *Time*, vol. 151, July 6, 1998, p. 48. Reports on John Lott's book *More Guns, Less Crime*. The most extensive study on concealed-carry laws and crime rates yet undertaken, it concludes that areas with more liberal gun-carry laws have lower crime rates. The book has touched off fierce controversy, and gun control advocates dispute some of Lott's statistical methods.

Rosenberg, Joel. "Protecting Home and Hearth with Guns." *Minneapolis-St. Paul Star-Tribune*, January 23, 1994, n.p. Gives anecdotes about how people used firearms to defend themselves and their families successfully from burglars.

Rubin, Paul H., and Hashem Dezhbakhsh. "Lives Saved or Lives Lost? The Effects of Concealed-Handgun Laws on Crime." *American Economic Review*, vol. 88, May 1998, pp. 468ff. Suggests that any crime reductions due to concealed-carry laws are much smaller than suggested by John Lott and David Mustard's work. Some crime rates may even increase. Lawmakers should take these patterns into account.

"Rusty Got His Gun." *The New Republic*, vol. 219, August 17, 1998, p. 8. Agrees with the NRA that more gun laws would not have stopped gunman Rusty Weston from stealing his parents' revolver and using it in a shooting spree in the U.S. Capitol. However, the answer is to get serious about drying up the huge supply of guns that is available to criminals and the insane.

Sack, Kevin. "Gunman Slays 9 at Brokerages in Atlanta." *The New York Times*, July 30, 1999, p. A1. Reports on a killing rampage by failed Atlanta securities day-trader Mark O. Barton who killed nine people, wounded 12, and finally killed himself when cornered by police.

Sowell, Thomas. "Gun-Control Crowd Misuses Fear Factor to Distort the Truth." *Insight on the News*, vol. 18, November 12, 2002, pp. 50ff. The author, a well-known conservative/libertarian commentator, argues that gun control advocates are drawing all the wrong conclusions from the Washington, D.C., sniper killings. Mass murderers would not follow gun laws; so-called ballistic fingerprints are unreliable; and the presence of armed citizens could have quickly brought the killing spree to a stop. Gun control might save a few children's lives, but the unavailability of defensive weapons might take many more.

Suter, Edgar A. "'Assault Weapons' Revisited—An Analysis of the AMA Report." *Journal of the Medical Association of Georgia*, vol. 85, May 1994, n.p. Criticizes the American Medical Association report "Assault Weapons as a Public Health Hazard in the United States." Suter argues that the high ammunition capacity of such weapons is usually irrelevant because only a few shots are fired in most incidents other than well-publicized mass shootings. Suter also accuses the report for relying only on unsubstantiated anecdotal data.

———. "Guns in the Medical Literature—A Failure of Peer Review." *Journal of the Medical Association of Georgia*, vol. 83, March 1994, pp. 133–147. Also available online. URL: http://www.cely.com/firearms/medlit.html. Criticizes the new wave of studies of gun violence by medical researchers. Suter suggests that political biases and ignorance of basic principles of criminology and social science are leading to flawed results.

Suter, Edgar A., James J. Fotis, and Arthur L. Kellermann. "Weapons for Protection in Home Invasion Crimes." *JAMA, The Journal of the American Medical Association*, vol. 275, January 24, 1996, pp. 280ff. Suter argues that Kellermann's study of home invasions was skewed by being based only on police reports and trauma admissions and that what it really looked at was stealth crimes (burglaries), not true home invasions. Homeowner use of firearms is often not reported to police. Even under such circumstances, however, guns proved to be the safest method of resistance. Kellermann defends his data sources and questions the objectivity of his critics.

Thurman, James N. "Disconnect between Gun Crime and Gun-Control Laws." *The Christian Science Monitor*, May 19, 1999, p. 2. Suggests that the most popular proposals among gun control activists bear little relationship to the actual problem of gun-related crime. Neither foreign-made assault weapons nor high-capacity clips play much role in crime, which generally involves ordinary U.S.-made revolvers and pistols. Some gun control advocates believe systematic product regulation for all firearms would be a more effective approach.

Van Derbeken, Jaxon, and Erin Hallisy. "L.A. Gunman Wounds 5—Suspect Named." *San Francisco Chronicle*, August 11, 1999, pp. A1, A13. Reports on the wounding of five people at a Jewish community center in Los Angeles with the suspect identified as Buford Furrow. The shootings sent a tremor of fear through other Jewish organizations. The article includes a chronology of mass shootings during 1999.

Vernick, Jon S., Stephen P. Teret, and Daniel W. Web. "Regulating Firearm Advertisements That Promise Home Protection: A Public Health Intervention." *JAMA, The Journal of the American Medical Association*, vol. 277, May 7, 1997, pp. 1391ff. Reports that the American Academy of Pediatrics has joined other organizations in petitioning the Federal Trade Commission to regulate firearms advertisements. Such ads often tout the benefits of guns for self-protection, but studies show that guns have more risks than benefits for their owners. The advertising is therefore deceptive.

Voelker, Rebecca. "Taking Aim at Handgun Violence." *JAMA, The Journal of the American Medical Association*, vol. 273, June 14, 1995, pp. 1739ff. Interviews Dr. John P. May, who suggests that doctors recognize risks for firearms injury (including the very presence of any gun in the home) and talk to their patients about risky behaviors and conditions such as depression.

Webster, Daniel W., et al. "Flawed Gun Policy Research Could Endanger Public Safety." *The American Journal of Public Health*, vol. 87, June 1997, pp. 918ff. Attacks the methodology of John Lott and David Mustard's recent study that claims that liberalizing gun-carry laws reduces the crime rate. Among other things, the authors argue that Lott and Mustard mishandled variables and did not take into account the cyclical nature of crime trends.

Weil, Douglas S. "Effects of Limiting Handgun Purchases on Interstate Transfer of Firearms." *JAMA, The Journal of the American Medical Association*. vol. 275, June 12, 1996, pp. 1759–1761. Study suggests that Virginia's law restricting firearms purchases to one gun per month reduced the number of firearms purchased in Virginia recovered by law enforcement officers from 27 percent to 19 percent.

Wildes, Kevin W. M. "Medicalization and Social Ills." *America*, vol. 180, April 3, 1999, p. 16. Argues that treating firearms misuse as a disease (akin to alcoholism) will fail. Such an approach treats people as passive victims of a condition beyond their control, requiring medical intervention. People are then unlikely to take responsibility for their actions or develop a robust ability to cope with life's challenges.

Yurk, Robin, et al. "Educating the Community About Violence through a Gun Turn-In Program." *Journal of Community Health*, vol. 26, October 2001, p. 331. Describes the Ceasefire Oregon gun turn-in program. The program combines a voluntary gun turn-in with educational efforts about violence, including school and media programs. Between 1994 and 1999, 4,345 guns were turned in. About half of the people who turned in guns did so because of incentives (such as gift certificates); about a quarter said it was because they did not want guns any more. The program is described as being effective educationally and as providing resources to the community, but there was no attempt to measure the actual impact on crime.

WEB DOCUMENTS

"Armed Citizens and Police Officers." National Rifle Association, Institute for Legislative Action. Available online. URL: http://www.nraila.org/Issues/Articles/Read.aspx?ID=30. Posted on July 16, 1999. Compilation of incidents where armed citizens helped police officers subdue criminals.

Blackman, Paul H. "Criminology's Astrology: An Evaluation of Public Health Research on Firearms and Violence." [Personal web site.] Available online. URL: http://teapot.usask.ca/pub/cdn-firearms/Blackman/medbash1.txt. Posted on January 31, 1995. Takes on the "gun violence epidemic" researchers, arguing that their studies are simplistic, focus only on the "bottom line" of deaths and injuries without understanding context, ignore sound principles of criminology, and are driven by a policy agenda.

"Concealed Truth: Concealed Weapons Laws and Trends in Violent Crime in the United States." Brady Campaign to Prevent Gun Violence. Available online. URL: http://www2.bradycampaign.org/facts/research/?page=conctruth&menu=gvr. Posted on October 22, 1999. Attacks John Lott's research that suggests that allowing more citizens to carry concealed weapons reduces crime. The center's own study concludes that in states with liberalized gun-carry laws, crime either increased or decreased to a smaller extent than the national trends. The article includes charts.

Annotated Bibliography

"Criminal Use of the 50 Caliber Sniper Rifle." Violence Policy Center. Available online. URL: http://www.vpc.org/snipercrime.htm. Posted in 2001. Recounts incidence of the use of the .50 caliber sniper rifle in criminal activity. Some gun control opponents have said this heavy gun has never been used in crimes. While it apparently has, the number of incidents appears to be very small.

Douglass, Linda. "Where Criminals Get Their Guns: So Few Dealers Supply So Many Weapons Used in Crimes." ABC News.com. Available online. URL: http://abcnews.go.com/sections/wnt/CloserLook/gun_sales040112.html. Downloaded on July 7, 2004. A surprising fact is that more than half of the firearms traced in crimes come from about 1 percent of the nation's gun stores. A new study by Americans for Gun Safety found that federal agents seldom audit, let alone prosecute, these gun stores.

"Fact Sheet: Assault Weapons." Johns Hopkins Center for Gun Policy and Research. Available online. URL: http://www.jhsph.edu/gunpolicy/assaultweapons_fs_rev2.pdf. Updated in October 2003. Gives the definition, legal status, and statistics about the use of assault weapons.

"Fact Sheet: Firearm Injury and Death in the United States." Johns Hopkins Center for Gun Policy and Research. Available online. URL: http://www.jhsph.edu/gunpolicy/US_factsheet_2004.pdf. Updated in January 2004. Gives statistics and trends relating to gun violence in the United States. Overall gun-related deaths have declined by 25 percent between 1993 and 2001. Other topics summarized include effects on youth, public health effects and cost of gun ownership, summary of the effects of different types of gun laws, legal issues, regulation and litigation, and public opinion.

"Fact Sheet: Firearms and Intimate Partner Violence." Johns Hopkins Center for Gun Policy and Research. Available online. URL: http://www.jhsph.edu/gunpolicy/IPV_firearms2.pdf. Updated in October 2003. Gives statistics on the prevalence of firearms in domestic homicides and the associated risks: The presence of a gun in the home is associated with a three-times-higher homicide risk, which becomes eight times higher when the offender is an intimate partner of the victim and becomes 20 times higher when previous domestic violence exists. The suggested legal policy is to prohibit firearms purchase or ownership by perpetrators of domestic violence or persons under restraining orders.

"Fact Sheet: Guns in the Home." Johns Hopkins Center for Gun Policy and Research. Available online. URL: http://www.jhsph.edu/gunpolicy/Guns_in_Home.pdf. Posted in May 2002. Describes the prevalence and characteristics of guns in the home. About 35 percent of U.S. households have at least one firearm and about 25 percent have a handgun. Handguns are responsible for about 88 percent of firearms homicides in which the type of gun used is known.

Kistner, William. "Firearm Injuries: The Gun Battle Over Science." Frontline, PBS Online. Available online. URL: http://www.pbs.org/wgbh/pages/frontline/shows/guns/procon/injuries.html. Posted in May 1997. Describes the science and politics of research into gun violence, including the NRA's attempt to remove funding for the Centers for Disease Control's research, claiming that it is biased "junk science." This article accompanies a PBS *Frontline* episode called "Ring of Fire."

Kopel, David. "Anti-Gun, Anti-Science: The Real Enemy Is Shoddy Research." National Review Online. Available online. URL: http://www.nationalreview.com/kopel/kopel022701.shtml. Posted on February 27, 2001. Kopel, a criminologist and research director for the Independence Institute, imagines what it would be like if diseases were treated as crimes. The results would be as absurd and the research as shoddy as in the real world where some advocates want to treat gun violence as a health rather than criminal issue. An example of such "junk science" are studies that show higher risks of murder for people who have guns do not show causation and do not control for numerous related variables.

LaRosa, Benedict D. "Can Gun Control Reduce Crime?" Future of Freedom Foundation. Available online. Part 1, URL: http://www.fff.org/freedom/fd0210e.asp. Posted in October 2002. Part 2, URL: http://www.fff.org/freedom/fd0211f.asp. Posted in November 2002. Argues that gun control advocates have wrongly taken credit for the overall decrease in crime since the mid-1990s, which had little to do with the Brady Law and other gun control measures. Guns deter crime, and a variety of examples from around the world are cited to show that gun control has led to crime, victimization, and even genocide.

"Liberalized Concealed Carry Laws." Guncite.com. Available online. URL: http://www.guncite.com/gun_control_gcdgcon.html. Updated on December 13, 2003. Explains the movement to change gun carry permits from discretionary (and often restricted) to available to all qualifying persons. Discusses the Lott-Mustard hypothesis (more guns means less crime), providing pro and con links as well as other links.

"Man Charged in Supremacist Gun Sale." *New York Times*, July 7, 1999. Available online. URL: http://www.nytimes.com/aponline/a/AP-Chicago-Shootings.html. Reports that an unlicensed gun dealer sold several guns to Benjamin Nathaniel Smith, a white supremacist gunman who went on a racist killing spree. Such revelations are likely to heighten concern about the illegal gun market that is not directly affected by laws such as the Brady Law.

Morgan, Eric, and David Kopel. "The Assault Weapon Panic: 'Political Correctness' Takes Aim at the Constitution." Independence Institute. Available online. URL:. http://www.firearmsandliberty.com/assault. weapon.html. Posted on October 10, 1991. Analyzes the rhetoric of the campaign against assault weapons as a species of political correctness. The authors provide background on the nature and characteristics of so-called assault weapons. They then argue that the campaign's goals are ill-defined and deceptive and would result in diminishing freedom without having a beneficial effect on public safety. The authors believe that action directed at actual criminals is the answer.

Webster, Daniel W. "Comprehensive Ballistic Fingerprinting of New Guns: A Tool for Solving and Preventing Violent Crime." Johns Hopkins Center for Gun Policy and Research. Available online. URL: http://www.jhsph.edu/gunpolicy/ballistic_fingerprinting.pdf. Updated on November 21, 2002. Reports that the efficiency of ballistic fingerprinting (the matching of bullets to records made from guns at the time of manufacture) has greatly increased because of advances in computer technology. Making ballistic fingerprinting of new guns mandatory would reduce the supply of guns available to criminals and youth and deter criminal use of guns. The report also refutes common objections to the adoption of ballistic fingerprinting.

YOUTH AND GUNS

This section includes works that deal primarily with youth and firearms and the impact of gun violence on young people, including shootings in schools.

BOOKS

Apel, Lorelei. *Dealing with Weapons at School and at Home*. New York: PowerKids Press, 1997. Simple guide to help young people avoid danger from guns and other weapons they may encounter in their daily life.

Clise, Michele Durkson. *Stop the Violence Please*. Seattle: Allied Arts Foundation and University of Washington Press, 1994. For young readers. The book begins with a tragic gun accident and then gives facts about youths and gun violence and suggests steps young people and parents can take to reduce it. It includes a list of books, films, and organizations.

Cox, Vic. *Guns, Violence, and Teens*. Springfield, N.J.: Enslow, 1997. Written for teenagers, the book takes a teen viewpoint in looking at guns in schools, gang violence, and the positions in the public debate over gun control. Cox includes statistics and suggestions for nonviolent approaches to conflict resolution.

Moore, Mark H., et al. *Deadly Lessons: Understanding Deadly School Violence.* Washington, D.C.: National Academies Press, 2003. Because of the importance of the mass shootings in schools to the gun control debate, this set of case studies exploring the impact of these tragedies on the community is an important resource. The contributors attempt to extract lasting lessons on how to prevent such violence and how to help heal the anguish it causes.

Schulson, Rachel. *Guns—What You Should Know.* Morton Grove, Ill.: A. Whitman, 1997. For children ages four through eight. Without taking sides, this book clearly and simply describes how guns work and how dangerous they can be. The author includes a list of simple rules for a child to follow if he or she finds a gun.

Schwarz, Ted. *Kids and Guns: The History, the Present, the Dangers, and the Remedies.* New York: Franklin Watts, 1999. For young readers. Gives an overview of the history and issues involved in gun control, including recent events, facts, and statistics.

Sheley, Joseph F. *In the Line of Fire: Youths, Guns, and Violence in Urban America.* New York: A. de Gruyter, 1995. Describes an extensive study that focuses on the growing problem of gun violence among youth. Sheley points to fear rather than criminal intent as the main motivating factor for young people to get guns and suggests addressing the conditions for such fear rather than focusing on the guns themselves.

Sheley, Joseph F., and James D. Wright. *High School Youths, Weapons, and Violence: A National Survey.* Washington, D.C.: National Institute of Justice, 1998. Reports and analyzes national survey results on youth violence.

Sheley, Joseph F., Zina T. McGee, and James D. Wright. *Weapon-Related Victimization in Selected Inner-City High School Samples.* Washington, D.C.: National Institute of Justice, 1995. An analysis of the types of weapons and circumstances involved in high school violence.

Violence Policy Center. *"A .22 for Christmas": How the Gun Industry Designs and Markets Firearms for Children and Youth.* Washington, D.C.: Violence Policy Center, 2001. Also available online. URL: http://www.vpc.org/studies/22cont.htm. Posted in December 2001. Describes how the gun industry, facing a stagnated market, is increasing its marketing to young people and their parents. (Purchasers must be over 18 to legally buy a long gun, and over 21 for handguns, but younger people can legally possess a firearm in many cases.) Gun designers are now creating firearms (particularly rifles) more suited to the smaller hands and lighter frames of young people.

Annotated Bibliography

ARTICLES

Allen, Tom. "Keep Guns out of School." *Education Digest,* vol. 64, December 1998, pp. 27ff. Suggests approaches to keeping guns out of schools. Allen argues that metal detectors are no substitute for creating a social environment that rewards cooperation and discourages violence.

Ayoob, Massad. "Arm Teachers to Stop School Shootings." *The Wall Street Journal,* May 21, 1999, p. A12. Suggests that having some trained and qualified teachers with weapons in school could prevent mass killings like the Littleton High School shootings.

"Children and Guns." *Pediatrics for Parents,* vol. 16, May 1995, p. 1. Reports a study by Sara M. Naureckas, M.D., of Chicago's Children's Memorial Hospital that found that, contrary to popular belief, even very young children have the strength to fire most available handguns.

Christoffel, Katherine Kaufer. "Commentary: When Counseling Parents on Guns Doesn't Work: Why Don't They Get It?" *Journal of the American Academy of Child and Adolescent Psychiatry,* vol. 39, October 2000, p. 1226. Draws conclusions from a study of the results of counseling parents of children being treated for depression. Because of the correlation between availability of guns and suicide, doctors try to get parents to remove guns from their homes or at least secure them better. However, the number of families that follow such advice seems disappointingly small. Doctors are urged to try new ways of conveying the risk of guns to parents and to deal with fears that might be motivating them to keep firearms in the house.

Cole, Thomas B. "Authorities Address U.S. Drug-Related 'Arms Race.'" *JAMA, The Journal of the American Medical Association,* vol. 275, March 6, 1996, pp. 672ff. Reports on the 1996 Conference on Guns and Violence in America. Participants concluded that the distribution of guns among youth, initially fueled by drugs, is increasing the risk of mortality in the population as guns spread to youths who are not involved in the drug trade. Cole quotes opinions based on studies by a variety of criminologists and other researchers, with no consensus on banning all guns but with some agreement on measures to more tightly regulate the gun trade, such as through registration and banning of private sales.

Davis, James W. "More Guns and Younger Assailants: A Combined Police and Trauma Center Study." *JAMA, The Journal of the American Medical Association,* vol. 279, March 4, 1998, p. 640. Studies admissions to a regional trauma center. Davis finds that more young assailants are using guns than before and that the average age of victims is getting younger.

Fagan, Jeffrey. "Policing Guns and Youth Violence." *The Future of Children,* vol. 12, Summer–Fall 2002, pp. 133ff. Presents eight case studies showing different ways in which cities have sought to control gun crime. The measures varied from emphasizing police-citizen partnerships to aggressive enforcement aimed at suppressing delinquency and gang-type activity to softer approaches aimed at diverting offenders from the criminal justice system into settings where their behavior might be modified. While harsh enforcement can reduce the crime rate, softer approaches may lead to stronger relationships with minority communities.

Fogg, Piper. "I Regret Having It in the House." *National Journal*, vol. 32, July 22, 2000, p. 2374. Tells the story of Teavious Whatley, who carefully trained his 13-year-old son Michael the safe handling of the shotgun kept in their home. Despite this, the boy and some friends fooled with the gun while drinking, and Michael was killed. Whatley has decided to no longer keep any guns.

Fortgang, Erika. "How They Got the Guns." *Rolling Stone*, June 10, 1999, pp. 51ff. Explores the question of where young mass shooters, such as the Columbine High School students Dylan Klebold and Eric Harris, obtain their guns. The main sources are gun shows (where no background check is required) and unlicensed dealers, though guns are also stolen from parents or others.

Gibbs, Nancy. "*Time* Special Report; Guns in America; Troubled Kids." *Time*, vol. 153, May 31, 1999, p. 32. Reflects on the feeling of helplessness as people in the media, who love to provide answers, can find no answers to the violence erupting in the schools.

Hardy, Marjorie S. "Behavior-Oriented Approaches to Reducing Youth Gun Violence." *Future of Children*, vol. 12, Summer/Fall 2002, pp. 101–117. Various programs, laws, and policies have sought to encourage parents to store guns safely and to teach children to avoid playing with guns and to resolve disputes without violence. However, while such programs are beneficial in dealing with violence as a whole, they have not had much effect on youth use of or access to guns. Adolescent psychology may limit their effectiveness as it does that of "Just Say No" drug programs or "abstinence-oriented" sex education.

Heim, David. "American Mayhem: School Shootings." *The Christian Century*, vol. 115, June 3, 1998, pp. 563ff. Explores the disturbing increase in the number and severity of school shootings (prior to the Littleton, Colorado, incident). Heim suggests that although poverty, family breakdown, and the availability of guns all play a role, the responsibility of the media cannot be ignored. Media creators cannot at the same time tout the power of imagination and refuse to take some responsibility for its effects.

"High-School Violence in Decline." *Los Angeles Times*, August 4, 1999, p. A1. Reports on a study from the U.S. Centers for Disease Control and Prevention that found that the number of high school students who said they carried a weapon to school fell by 28 percent from 1993 to 1997. However, significant violence and the perception of lack of safety persists in many areas.

Kopel, David B. "Gun Play: What Kids Don't Know About Guns Can Kill Them." *Reason*, vol. 25, July 1993, pp. 18ff. Argues that new gun laws are actually endangering children by making it harder to give them proper training in safe handling of firearms. Youngsters are left to learn about guns from TV or their peers. Kopel also argues that distortion of facts and figures is making rational gun policy difficult.

Levin, Bob. "Casualties of the Right to Bear Arms: Today's Outcasts Can Grab a Handy Semiautomatic and, Taking Cool Moves from the Latest Flick, Go Kill Their Classmates." *Maclean's*, May 3, 1999, p. 27. Author provides a Canadian pro–gun control viewpoint on the Columbine High School shootings. Levin ridicules the U.S. gun culture in recounting his personal experience with aspects of it.

Noonan, Peggy. "Sins of the Fathers." *Good Housekeeping*, vol. 227, July 1998, p. 178. Suggests that although the right to keep and bear arms is important, gun owners must personally exercise more "gun control" by handling and storing their guns safely, teaching youngsters that guns are not toys, and combating the glorification of violence in the media.

Page, Randy M., and Jon Hammermeister. "Weapon-Carrying and Youth Violence." *Adolescence*, vol. 32, Fall 1997, pp. 505ff. Reviews surveys and studies on the prevalence and patterns of weapons carrying among youth. The authors suggest that weapons carrying is associated more with aggressive or criminal behavior than the desire for self-defense. The authors also describe specifics involving firearms and the need for schools to develop policies and practices to keep guns out of schools, as well as specifics for promoting gun control legislation.

Pipho, Chris. "Living with Zero Tolerance." *Phi Delta Kappan*, vol. 79, June 1998, pp. 725ff. Discusses the problems of crafting weapons bans for schools to comply with federal mandates. Some states ban a broader range of weapons, including knives, which are not covered under the federal law. This has led to embarrassing incidents such as a student being suspended for having a tiny paring knife used to cut a lunchtime apple. Some states have also broadened their policy to include drugs, alcohol, and other items. Pipho gives examples of state provisions.

"Rates of Homicide, Suicide, and Firearm-Related Death among Children—26 Industrialized Countries." *Morbidity and Mortality Weekly Report*, vol. 46, February 7, 1997, pp. 101ff. Concludes that the United States has by far the highest rates of child homicide, suicide, and firearms-related deaths among the industrialized nations.

Rivo, Marc. "Counseling Parents About Firearm Safety." *American Family Physician*, vol. 53, February 1, 1996, p. 693. Reports a survey of physicians that indicates that although a majority of the doctors believe they should counsel patients about firearms safety, few actually do so.

Senturia, Yvonne D., et al. "Gun Storage Patterns in U.S. Homes with Children: A Pediatric Practice–Based Survey." *Archives of Pediatrics & Adolescent Medicine*, vol. 150, March 1996, pp. 265ff. Finds that the majority of gun owners do not lock up their guns and that persons who use guns at work or for self-protection are most likely to have them loaded at home. The authors suggest that children's doctors talk to parents about the need to store firearms safely.

Shapiro, Bruce. "The Guns of Littleton." *The Nation*, vol. 268, May 17, 1999, p. 4. Insists that whatever the complex social and psychological causes that alienated Littleton, Colorado, shooters Dylan Klebold and Eric Harris, what adds a new dimension to the threat is today's ready availability of powerful firearms. Gun makers have flooded the market, with many sales targeted to young people.

Teret, Stephen P., and Patti L. Culross. "Product-Oriented Approaches to Reducing Youth Gun Violence." *Future of Children*, vol. 12, Summer/Fall 2002, pp. 119–131. The authors suggest that design changes in guns (such as "childproofing" by making guns difficult for children to operate or by equipping them with loaded-chamber indicators or magazine-disconnect devices) are more likely to be effective than attempts to change children's behavior around guns. However, the introduction of new, safer guns in substantial numbers is likely to be a slow process.

Tyson, Anne Scott. "How to Keep Firearms Out of Children's Hands." *The Christian Science Monitor*, vol. 89, April 6, 1998, p. 3. Gives suggestions for storing firearms safely and keeping them out of the hands of children.

Walsh, Edward. "Big Drop in Kids Expelled for Guns at School." *San Francisco Chronicle*, August 11, 1999, p. A3. Reports a survey by the federal Department of Education that found that the number of students expelled from schools for gun possession during the 1997–98 school year declined sharply from previous years. Both demographics and heightened security efforts may be responsible for the decline.

Wilkinson, Todd. "At Home with Guns." *The Christian Science Monitor*, May 26, 1999, p. 11. Describes the relationship between youngsters and guns in communities where hunting is popular. Families in these communities often practice gun safety and tend to support some gun control, especially on assault weapons and Saturday night specials. But the declining number of hunters and the shock of school shootings may be eroding rural gun culture.

Witkin, Gordon. "Stopping Youth Violence by Stopping Gun Theft." *U.S. News & World Report*, vol. 123, no. 23, December 15, 1997, p. 26(1). Argues that schools can do only so much to keep guns out. The root of the problem is stolen guns—about 500,000 a year, 80 percent from private homes. Better locking and "personalization" devices may eventually keep guns from being stolen.

Wolcott, Jennifer. "Parent-to-Parent: Is the Gun Safely Stored?" *The Christian Science Monitor,* May 26, 1999, p. 15. Discusses approaches to parents talking to their neighbors about the safe storage of firearms. The recent school shootings can provide a springboard for such discussion while concern is high.

WEB DOCUMENTS

"Clarence and Guns." Brady Center to Prevent Gun Violence. Available online. URL: http://www.bradycenter.org/clarence/index_0.php. Downloaded on March 14, 2004. Interactive game that teaches children how to respond appropriately to guns in their environment.

"Clarence's Adventure." Brady Center to Prevent Gun Violence. Available online. URL: http://www.bradycenter.org/clarence. Posted on February 14, 1999. Interactive game that teaches children to avoid playing with guns they encounter in various settings.

Cullen, David. "The Depressive and the Psychopath: Assessment." Slate.com. Available online. URL: http://slate.msn.com/id/2099203. Posted on April 20, 2004. Reports on new studies by FBI psychiatrists and psychologists that cast new light on the motives on Eric Harris and Dylan Klebold, the perpetrators of the 1999 Columbine High School massacre. These experts concluded that the shootings were not simply a spontaneous striking back at bullies who had victimized the shooters. Rather, they were a grandiose attempt to win fame by a terrorist act. Indeed, if the numerous bombs the shooters had also set had gone off as planned, hundreds of people would have been killed, creating the largest terrorist death toll until September 11, 2001. The psychiatrists diagnose Harris as a psychopath with grandiose conceptions of his superiority, and argue that he was the dominant partner to the less complicated Klebold.

Kopel, David B. "Children and Guns: Sensible Solutions." Independence Institute. Available online. URL: http://rkba.org/research/kopel/kids-gun.html. Downloaded on April 25, 1993. Argues that safety education, youth development, and proper law enforcement can reduce gun accidents and violence involving children, while "gimmicky" safety devices, laws, and lawsuits are unlikely to be effective.

"Parents, Kids, & Guns: A Nationwide Survey." Brady Campaign to Prevent Gun Violence. Available online. URL: http://www.bradycampaign.org/facts/research/?page=hart98&menu=gvr. Posted in 1998. Surveys parents' attitude toward the danger of guns in the home. Most parents seem aware of the issue and concerned in the abstract. However, they tend to not see a risk to their own children and most have not thought of asking whether there are guns in the homes of their children's friends.

GUN SAFETY

Works in this section discuss devices or measures designed to make guns safer or less accessible to criminals or children, as well as educational programs aimed at teaching gun safety.

BOOKS

Karlson, Trudy Ann, and Stephen Hargarten. *Reducing Firearm Injury and Death: A Public Health SourceBook on Guns.* New Brunswick, N.J.: Rutgers University Press, 1997. Applies product design principles to guns and argues that they should be regulated for safety as with other products.

Violence Policy Center. *Poisonous Pastime: The Health Risks of Shooting Ranges and Lead to Children, Families, and the Environment.* Washington, D.C.: Violence Policy Center, 2001. Also available online. URL: http://www.vpc. org/studies/leadcont.htm. Posted in May 2001. Few people think of guns as an environmental problem (although hunting is opposed by many people). This report, however, focuses on the spread of lead (from bullets) into the environment on and around shooting ranges, as well as noise pollution and danger from wayward bullets. The practice of ammunition reloading is also described as a safety hazard, particularly to children. Policy recommendations include banning children from shooting ranges, enforcing environmental laws against the ranges, and directing a portion of firearms tax revenue to pay to clean up lead pollution.

ARTICLES

Butterfield, Fox. "Study Finds Unsafe Practices by People Trained in Firearms." *The New York Times,* January 20, 1995, p. A12. Reports that although many people on both sides of the gun debate advocate firearms safety training, a study by the Harvard School of Public Health found that people who had taken safety courses are actually more likely to keep a gun loaded and unlocked at home.

Cummings, Peter, et al. "State Gun Safe Storage Laws and Child Mortality Due to Firearms." *JAMA, The Journal of the American Medical Association,*

Annotated Bibliography

vol. 278, October 1, 1997, pp. 1084ff. Finds that unintentional deaths from firearms dropped an average of 23 percent in 12 states that had passed laws making parents liable for injuries caused by guns that were not securely stored.

D'Agnese, Joseph. "Smart Guns Don't Kill Kids." *Discover Magazine*, September 1999, pp. 90–93. Describes and illustrates advanced prototype handgun safety devices, including fingerprint sensors, electronic rings, magnetic locks, and other systems that might make it impossible for persons other than the gun owner to fire the weapon.

Easterbrook, Gregg. "Load and Lock: Making Guns Safer." *The New Republic*, May 31, 1999, p. 13. Suggests that there is no reason not to bring guns into the normal system of product safety regulations. By applying the modern engineering principles used for other products, guns can be equipped with trigger locks, loaded-round indicators, magazine safeties, and internal safeties (to prevent dropped guns from firing).

Feldman, Richard J., and Garen Wintermute. "Firearm Design and Firearm Violence." *JAMA, The Journal of the American Medical Association*, vol. 276, October 2, 1996, p. 1035. Begins with criticism by Feldman of Wintermute's approach to relating firearms design to violence and severity of injury. Feldman argues that the study ignores the likelihood that banning some types of handguns would lead to the substitution of more lethal firearms such as shotguns and rifles and that criminals prefer more expensive "quality" handguns, not cheap Saturday night specials. Wintermute replies that cheap handguns show up disproportionately in guns recovered from crimes and that lack of safety regulations make the weapons a danger even to their owners.

Frattaroli, S., D. W. Webster, and S. P. Teret. "Unintentional Gun Injuries, Firearm Design, and Prevention: What We Know, What We Need to Know, and What Can Be Done." *Journal of Urban Health*, vol. 79, 2002, pp. 49–59. After surveying the background of this field, the article presents possible explanations for the decline in unintentional (*i.e.*, accidental) firearms death and injuries. Possible interventions (including changes in firearms design) are also explored.

Hammer, Marion P. "NRA's Friendly Face Draws Hateful Fire." *American Rifleman*, vol. 146, February 1998, pp. 10ff. Complains that Josh Sugarmann's Violence Policy Center unfairly attacks the NRA's Eddie Eagle gun safety program because he does not want gun safety but rather the complete banning of firearms.

Hemenway, David, Sara J. Solnick, and Deborah R. Azrael. "Firearm Training and Storage." *JAMA, The Journal of the American Medical Association*, vol. 273, January 4, 1995, p. 46. This study found that gun owners who participated in firearms training courses were more likely to store their

191

guns in unlocked containers, as were handgun owners in general and those who stated self-defense as their main reason for having a gun.

Lucas, Robert A. "Hunting Rhinos." *National Review*, vol. 47, May 1, 1995, pp. 70ff. Suggests that public hysteria over armor-piercing "cop-killer" bullets such as the Black Rhino is misplaced. Tests reveal the bullets are not nearly as effective as advertised. The issue reveals sloppy thinking and garbled facts in Congress and the media.

"Maker of Tiny Pistol Denies It Is Deadly." *The New York Times*, May 8, 1998, p. A8. The Milex company, makers of the tiny Osa pistol (about the size of a key chain), denies that it is unusually deadly or hazardous.

Nelson, David E. "Population Estimates of Household Firearm Storage Practices and Firearm Carrying in Oregon." *JAMA, The Journal of the American Medical Association*, vol. 275, June 12, 1996, pp. 1744–1748. Gives a percentage breakdown of households with firearms stored in various ways (such as loaded and unlocked) and of firearm carrying. Nelson also gives correlation with alcohol use.

Ottaway, David B. "A Boon to Sales, or a Threat? Safety Devices Split Industry." *The Washington Post*, May 20, 1999, p. A1. Discusses the uncertainty in the gun industry about whether adding safety devices such as trigger locks will help sales by offering added security or will hobble the industry by encouraging mandatory federal standards.

Peterson, Iver. "'Smart Guns' Set Off Debate: Just How 'Smart' Are They?" *The New York Times*, October 22, 1998, p. A1. Discusses development of "smart gun" features by Colt and other companies and debates the effectiveness of devices that would make guns usable only by their owner. Although the idea is attractive, the devices still have technical problems.

Suter, Edgar A., et al. "Firearm Training and Storage." *JAMA, The Journal of the American Medical Association*, vol. 273, June 14, 1995, pp. 1733ff. Criticizes a previous study on this topic for focusing only on how a gun is stored and not on the specific circumstances and for not considering that in some households the risk of criminal attack may outweigh the risk of accident. The authors point out that despite the new focus on the topic, gun accidents in the United States are at an all-time low. The authors of the study rebut, saying that they did consider relevant variables and that keeping loaded guns is risky even when safety rules are followed.

"Talk to Your Patients About Gun Safety." *American Medical News*, November 9, 1998, p. 19(1). Urges doctors to discuss gun safety issues with their patients. The AMA has a new publication, "Physician Firearm Safety Guide," which can be helpful.

Teret, Stephen P., et al. "Making Guns Safer." *Issues in Science and Technology*, vol. 14, Summer 1998, pp. 37ff. Describes various technologies that can make guns "personalized" and able to be fired only by their owner.

Besides reducing accidents involving children, such guns would be virtually useless to thieves.

————. "Support for New Policies to Regulate Firearms: Results of Two National Surveys." *New England Journal of Medicine*, vol. 339, 1998, pp. 813–818. Reports surveys showing high public support for requiring various gun safety devices including support for childproofing (88 percent), personalization (71 percent), magazine safeties (82 percent), and loaded chamber indicators (73 percent).

Teret, S. P., and N. L. Lewin. "Policy and Technology for Safer Guns: An Update." *Annals of Emergency Medicine*, vol. 41, 2003, pp. 32–34. Summarizes the current state of "safe gun" technology. Some handguns now include built-in locking devices. Gun personalization (such as fingerprint readers) have been developed as prototypes but are not yet widely available commercially in firearms.

Vernick, J. S., et al. "Unintentional and Undetermined Firearm-Related Deaths: A Preventable Death Analysis for Three Safety Devices." *Injury Prevention*, vol. 9, 2003, pp. 307–11. Concludes that 44 percent of the deaths studied could have been prevented if the gun in question had at least one of the following safety devices: personalization, loaded-chamber indicator, or magazine safety.

Wade, Beth. "Aiming to Reduce Gun Violence." *American City & County*, vol. 115, August 2000, p. 38. Describes efforts by local governments to mandate or encourage gun safety such as through distributing trigger locks in Montgomery County, Maryland. A number of cities now require the use of trigger locks or locked storage boxes. Other efforts include surveying gun owners to determine their gun-handling practices and initiating gun buyback programs.

Wintermute, Garen J. "The Relationship between Firearm Design and Firearm Violence, Handguns in the 1990s." *Journal of the American Medical Association*, vol. 275, June 12, 1996, n.p. Identifies disturbing trends in firearm manufacturing in recent years, including more semiautomatic pistols, higher-capacity and higher-powered handguns, and guns that are easier to conceal and to operate. Many of these factors may result in higher rates of gun fatalities.

WEB DOCUMENTS

"Joe Camel with Feathers: How the NRA with Gun and Tobacco Industry Dollars Uses Its Eddie Eagle Program to Market Guns to Kids." Violence Policy Center. Available online. URL: http://www.vpc.org/fact_sht/eddiekey.htm. Posted in 1998. Argues that the NRA's real agenda with its Eddie Eagle program in the schools is not to teach gun safety but to make guns more acceptable to children and youth and to create future customers for its products. Funds for the program come through the NRA Foundation, which has retrieved contributions from tobacco companies as well as firearms manufacturers. The report suggests that firearms companies are facing the same sort of public relations problem faced by tobacco, and has adopted similar strategies.

"A Model Handgun Safety Standard Act." Johns Hopkins Center for Gun Policy and Research. Available online. URL: http://www.jhsph.edu/gunpolicy/Model_Law_2ed.pdf. Posted in May 2000. Presents and describes a model state law enacting gun safety standards; features include the formation of a State Handgun Standard Commission, the required incorporation of "personalization" technology in all new handguns, and designation of one or more laboratories for testing compliance.

CONSTITUTIONAL ISSUES

Most works in this section deal with the meaning or purpose of the Second Amendment to the U.S. Constitution. Other constitutional issues involving gun control are also included, such as federalism/state's rights and the regulation of interstate commerce.

BOOKS

Bogus, Carl T., ed. *The Second Amendment in Law and History: Historians and Constitutional Scholars on the Right to Bear Arms.* New York: New Press, 2001. Contributors such as legal scholars Bogus and Robert Spitzer and historian Michael Bellesiles buttress the collective rights interpretation of the Second Amendment—that is, that its purpose and effect is only to guarantee the right of states to have armed militias that remain independent of federal control. Much of the discussion also involves critiques of the historical and legal scholarship employed by supporters of the individual right interpretation. (It should be noted that Bellesiles's own historical methodology also came under severe criticism following the publication of his book *Arming America*.)

Carmer, Clayton E. *For the Defense of Themselves and the State: The Original Intent and Judicial Interpretation of the Right to Keep and Bear Arms.* Westport, Conn.: Praeger Publishers, 1994. Explores the conflict between the original intent of the Second Amendment, well established by scholarship as conferring an individual right to keep and bear arms, and the judicial interpretation of the Supreme Court and most other courts that have preferred a collectivist interpretation and that have avoided a direct confrontation with the language of the Constitution.

Cottrol, Robert J., ed. *Gun Control and the Constitution: Sources and Explorations on the Second Amendment.* New York: Garland Publishing, 1994. Collects historical and legal material that illuminates many facets of the gun control debate in terms of the intent and interpretation of the Constitution, original intent versus broad interpretation, and the political philosophy of republicanism.

Gottlieb, Alan M. *Gun Rights Affirmed: The Emerson Case.* Bellevue, Wash.: Merril Press, 2001. Recounts the arguments and ruling in a federal district court that for the first time affirmed that the Second Amendment guaranteed an individual right to keep and bear arms. (Note that an appeals court subsequently found against the defendant but left the Second Amendment interpretation intact.)

Halbrook, Stephen P. *Freedmen: The Fourteenth Amendment and the Right to Bear Arms, 1866–1876.* Westport, Conn.: Greenwood Publishing, 1998. A little-known episode in the history of the gun control/gun rights debate is the importance of the right to keep and bear arms as seen by both proponents and opponents of Southern Reconstruction. Halbrook traces the intent behind the Fourteenth Amendment and asserts that its framers had a particularly strong interest in ensuring that the newly freed slaves could have weapons. He observes that it is ironic that of all the major provisions in the Bill of Rights, only the Second Amendment has not been incorporated by federal courts into the Fourteenth Amendment protections against state action.

———. *That Every Man Be Armed: The Evolution of a Constitutional Right.* Albuquerque: University of New Mexico Press, 1984. Traces the right to bear arms through common law, the colonial experience, and the framers of the U.S. Constitution. Halbrook continues with survey of cases and interpretations in the post–Civil War period and later, as well as Supreme Court decisions.

Kates, Don B. *Handgun Prohibition and the Original Meaning of the Second Amendment.* Bellevue, Wash.: Second Amendment Foundation, 1984. Discusses whether the prohibition of handguns (as opposed to rifles and other weapons of a more military application) is compatible with the original understanding of the Second Amendment.

Kopel, David B., Stephen P. Halbrook, and Alan Korwin. *Supreme Court Gun Cases.* Phoenix, Ariz.: Bloomfield Press, 2003. Although the Supreme Court has had few modern cases touching on the Second Amendment, dozens of cases have dealt with other aspects of gun laws. This compendium includes summaries and excerpts from 92 cases (including full text of the decisions in 42 of them). There are also introductory essays on the background of gun rights and on court strategies for gun rights advocates.

Kruschke, Earl R. *The Right to Keep and Bear Arms: A Continuing American Dilemma.* Springfield, Ill.: Thomas, 1985. Explores the legal history of firearms law and cases in the United States.

Malcolm, Joyce Lee. *To Keep and Bear Arms: The Origins of an Anglo-American Right.* Cambridge, Mass.: Harvard University Press, 1994. Explores the evolution of the right to keep and bear arms in the English common law and colonial experience. Malcolm concludes that the Second Amendment, arising out of that tradition, was intended to guarantee an individual right.

Violence Policy Center. *Shot Full of Holes: Deconstructing John Ashcroft's Second Amendment.* Washington, D.C.: Violence Policy Center, 2001. Also available online. URL: http://www.vpc.org/studies/ashcont.htm. Posted in July 2001. Takes issue with Attorney General John Ashcroft's adoption of the individual rights theory of the Second Amendment. The report in a point-by-point "deconstruction" of Ashcroft's letter to the Justice Department disputes his interpretation and use of early quotations about the militia and the right to bear arms, and reiterates standard arguments in favor of the collective or militia-centered interpretation of the Second Amendment. The text of Ashcroft's letter and one by U.S. Solicitor General Waxman (embodying the Department of Justice's previous position) are also included.

ARTICLES

Amar, Akhil Reed. "Second Thoughts." *Law and Contemporary Problems*, vol. 65, Spring 2002, pp. 103ff. Also available online. URL: http://www.law.duke.edu/journals/65LCPAmar. This interesting take on the Second Amendment suggests that both the NRA and gun control advocates have it partly right and partly wrong. He rejects both the collective (statist) interpretation and the solely individualist one in favor of a "communitarian" approach. He suggests that there is an individual right to own guns, but it is inextricably bound up with people acting together to defend the community. By implication, guns that could give individuals the ability to kill masses of people could be banned and licenses and training be required for other guns.

Barnett, Randy E. "Guns, Militias, and Oklahoma City." *Tennessee Law Review*, vol. 62, Spring 1995, pp. 443ff. Explores the emergence of the militia movement and its social and cultural roots. Suggests that one source of the movement is frustration with the refusal of the courts to enforce the Second Amendment.

Annotated Bibliography

Batey, Robert. "Techniques of Strict Construction: The Supreme Court and the Gun Control Act of 1968." *American Journal of Criminal Law*, vol. 13, Winter 1986, n.p. Discusses Supreme Court cases involving the Gun Control Act of 1968, pointing out ways that a case for reasonable doubt can be construed from the language, intent, or history of the law.

Bogus, Carl T. "Race, Riots, and Guns." *Southern California Law Review*, vol. 66, May 1993, n.p. Counters arguments by gun rights advocates that the history of gun control is bound up with the use of gun laws to suppress minorities. Bogus suggests that the Second Amendment and other gun rights statements might be themselves construed as a means for controlling minorities and that, at any rate, the connection between race and violence is very complex.

Brown, Wendy. "Guns, Cowboys, Philadelphia Mayors, and Civic Republicanism: On Sanford Levinson's 'The Embarrassing Second Amendment.'" *Yale Law Journal*, vol. 99, December 1989, pp. 661–667. A rebuttal to Levinson's influential article that suggested that the Second Amendment needs to be taken seriously as a guarantee of an individual right to keep and bear arms. Brown criticizes Levinson's appeal to "republicanism" in the arming of the individual against the state. She also criticizes the image of the armed citizen, noting that it is, from the feminist viewpoint, an armed male.

Burger, Warren E. "The Right to Bear Arms." *Parade Magazine*, January 14, 1990, n.p. Recounts the history of the militia in America and argues that the Second Amendment, although a valid expression of the framers' concerns, is no longer relevant. Burger (the renowned retired Supreme Court justice) thus believes that the keeping and bearing of arms should be subject to the same sorts of regulations as, for example, the owning and driving of automobiles. Thus he considers the screening, licensing, and identification of gun owners and their firearms to be appropriate.

Carney, Dan. "Brady Decision Reflects Effort to Curb Congress' Authority." *Congressional Quarterly Weekly Report*, vol. 55, June 28, 1997, p. 1524. Explains the U.S. Supreme Court decision in *Printz v. U.S.*, where the Court struck down the part of the Brady Bill that required local sheriffs to perform background checks on gun purchasers. The justices ruled that the provision extended beyond Congress's power to regulate interstate commerce.

Cottrol, Robert J., and Raymond T. Diamond. "The Second Amendment: Toward an Afro-Americanist Reconsideration." *Georgetown Law Journal*, vol. 809, December 1991, pp. 309–361. Suggests that while African-American intellectuals have generally followed the pro–gun control stance of modern liberals, the authors suggest that in the light of the historical failure of the government to protect African Americans, the Second Amendment's concept of an armed citizenry may still be valid.

Gun Control

"Does the Brady Bill Violate States' Rights?" *CQ Researcher*, vol. 6, September 13, 1996, p. 809. Gives pro and con arguments on whether the Brady Bill violates states' rights in imposing an unfunded mandate to perform background checks. (The Supreme Court later overturned this provision.)

Dowlut, Robert. "Federal and State Guarantees to Arms." *Dayton Law Review*, vol. 15, 1989, pp. 59–89. Suggests that the right to keep and bear arms be treated in a way similar to other fundamental rights such as freedom of speech. This would mean that there can be narrowly tailored restrictions, such as prohibiting the bringing of arms into public buildings, but not the peaceful bearing of arms at home or in the street. Dowlut criticizes the courts' ignorance of the Second Amendment and argues that an armed populace is still important to a free society.

Ehrman, Keith A., and Dennis A. Henigan. "The Second Amendment in the Twentieth Century: Have You Seen Your Militia Lately?" *University of Dayton Law Review*, vol. 15, 1989, pp. 5–58. Argues that the Second Amendment guarantees an individual right to keep and bear arms only to the extent it is necessary for the maintenance of an effective militia. Because the federally directed National Guard has replaced the old state militias, it is no longer necessary for private individuals to have firearms, and there is no obstacle to prohibiting them.

Fedarko, Kevin. "A Gun Ban Is Shot Down." *Time*, vol. 145, May 8, 1995, p. 85. Describes the Supreme Court decision *U.S. v. Lopez*, where the justices overturned the Gun Free Schools law, saying that the federal government's power to regulate interstate commerce did not extend to banning guns around schools.

Glaberson, William. "Court Says Individuals Have a Right to Firearms." *New York Times*, October 17, 2001, p. 14. Reports on the finding of a Fifth Circuit federal appeals court that the Second Amendment does confer an individual right to have firearms. In this particular case *(U.S. v. Timothy Emerson)*, the Court went on to say that the denying of firearms to persons under a domestic restraining order was a reasonable exercise of regulation.

"Gun Decision Puts a Check on Federal Authority." *Congressional Quarterly Weekly Report*, vol. 53, April 29, 1995, pp. 119ff. Gives excerpts from the *U.S. v. Lopez* decision, in which the Supreme Court rules that the Gun Free School Zones Act was an impermissible use of the power of Congress to regulate interstate commerce.

Halbrook, Stephen P. "To Keep and Bear Their Private Arms: The Adoption of the Second Amendment 1787–1791." *Northern Kentucky Law Review*, vol. 10, no. 1, 1982, n.p. Argues that for the framers of the Bill of Rights, the term *the people* as used in the Second Amendment means the same thing as it does in the First, Fourth, Ninth, and Tenth Amendments– "each and every free person."

Jost, Kenneth. "The States and Federalism; Should More Power Be Shifted to the States?" *CQ Researcher*, vol. 6, September 13, 1996, pp. 795ff. Places the challenge of local sheriffs to the Brady Bill in the context of a resurgent movement toward "federalism," or recognition of states' rights.

Kinsley, Michael. "Second Thoughts." *The New Republic*, vol. 202, February 26, 1990, p. 4. Argues that the Second Amendment remains disturbing for thoughtful liberals, despite their advocacy for gun control. Liberals would never accept for the First Amendment the narrow parsing they are willing to mete out to the Second, while conservatives who defend gun rights often disregard freedom of speech. Kinsley favorably reviews Don Kates's arguments for a right to keep and bear arms subject to certain limitations.

Levinson, Sanford. "The Embarrassing Second Amendment." *Yale Law Journal*, vol. 99, 1989, pp. 637–659. Also available online. URL: http://www.guncite.com/journals/embar.html. Signals a major shift of scholarship from the collectivist to the individualist interpretation of the Second Amendment. Levinson argues that the right to keep and bear arms should be acknowledged, even though, like many other fundamental social rights, it can have considerable costs.

Malcolm, Joyce Lee. "The Right of the People to Keep and Bear Arms: The Common Law Tradition." *Hastings Constitutional Law Quarterly*, Winter 1983, pp. 313–314. Argues that the Second Amendment must be understood in terms of how the English common law was understood by the Constitution's framers. This law saw the militia as springing from all citizens and was kept strong by maintaining their individual right to keep and bear arms.

Metaksa, Tanya K. "Constitutional Quake Rocks California Gun Ban." *American Rifleman*, vol. 146, May 1998, p. 44. Reports on a California district court decision that prevents the state attorney general from adding new firearms to the state assault weapons ban. The court said the existing procedure was arbitrary and failed to provide due process.

Metaksa, Tanya K., and Dennis A. Henigan. "At Issue: Does the Second Amendment Guarantee an Individual Right to Keep and Bear Arms?" *CQ Researcher*, vol. 7, December 19, 1997, p. 1121. A debate between the NRA's chief lobbyist and a leading pro–gun control litigator over whether the Second Amendment guarantees an individual right to bear arms, or only the right of the state to keep a militia. The authors give opposing citations from scholars of the "individualist" camp and former chief justice Warren Burger, who considered statements made by the NRA about the Second Amendment to be deceptive.

Murray, Frank J., and George Archibald. "Constitution Scholars Divided over Issues of Self-Defense." *Insight on the News*, vol. 11, May 29, 1995, p. 32. Discusses the applicability of constitutional protections to privately organized militias, such as those that came into prominence in the late 1980s and early 1990s. The Clinton administration and many scholars stated that the "well-regulated militia" of the Second Amendment refers only to official organizations such as the National Guard. However, other scholars and some court decisions support the right of individuals to keep and bear arms, and the First Amendment allows people to "peacefully assemble" for redress of grievances.

Reynolds, Glenn Harlan. "A Critical Guide to the Second Amendment." *Tennessee Law Review*, vol. 62, Spring 1995, pp. 461ff. Asserts that a "standard model" of interpreting the Second Amendment has emerged from recent scholarship. In this model, the right to keep and bear arms is an individual right but as such is subject to limitations such as the prohibition of weapons of mass destruction. Reynolds also reflects on the difference between the scholarly consensus and the views that seem to dominate the popular media.

Reynolds, Glenn Harlan, and Don B. Kates. "The Second Amendment and States' Rights: A Thought Experiment." *William & Mary Law Review*, 1995, pp. 1737–1768. Also available online. URL: http://www.sirius.com/~gilliams/second.html. Unfolds logical possible consequences of accepting the premise of many gun control advocates that the Second Amendment guarantees only the right of states to have a militia. The resulting possibilities may be surprising: independent state military forces, a different view of the National Guard, and a radically different form of federalism.

Rosen, Jeffrey. "Dual Sovereigns: Who Shall Rule—Congress or the Court?" *The New Republic*, vol. 217, July 28, 1997, p. 16. Reports on recent Supreme Court decisions (such as the *Lopez* decision), which overturned the Gun Free School Zones Act and part of the Brady Law that seem to be giving greater weight to state sovereignty. Rosen argues that the conservative majority on the Court may be applying the same sort of "judicial activism" that conservatives generally oppose when employed by liberals. The effects of any attempt to restore something like the pre–Civil War balance between federal and state powers are likely to be subtle and complex, with unintended consequences.

Safra, Seth J. "The Amended Gun-Free School Zones Act: Doubt as to Its Constitutionality Remains." *Duke Law Journal*, vol. 50, November 2000, p. 637. Following the Supreme Court's *Lopez* decision Congress amended the Gun-Free School Zones Act to make it refer only to guns that were connected to interstate commerce. The author suggests that this connection may still be too tenuous to pass constitutional muster. The alternate approach of asserting that guns threaten education (and thus the economy) would also be hard, though perhaps not impossible, to sustain.

Shulman, J. Neil. "The Text of the Second Amendment." *Journal on Firearms and Public Policy*, Summer 1992, n.p. The author asked Roy Copperud, an expert on English grammar, to interpret the language of the Second Amendment. Copperud concludes that the amendment specifies a preexisting, unconditional right of the people. The "militia clause" may describe the reason for guaranteeing the right, but the right does not depend on the existence of (or membership in) the militia.

Sprigman, Chris. "This Is Not a Well-Regulated Militia." *Open Forum*, Winter 1994, n.p. Reviews Supreme Court cases and concludes that the Court has interpreted the Second Amendment as protecting state militias, not as an individual right to bear arms. Sprigman cites *United States v. Miller* (1939) and argues that the militia concept is probably not relevant to modern America.

U.S. Congress. Committee on the Judiciary. Subcommittee on the Washington, D.C. Hearings. U.S. G.P.O., 1982. Transcript of Congressional hearings on the Second Amendment and the right to keep and bear arms. These hearings are of historical importance as they represent ascendancy of a generally conservative (or libertarian) viewpoint that supports the individual rights interpretation of the Second Amendment.

Weatherup, Roy G. "Standing Armies and Armed Citizens: An Historical Analysis of the Second Amendment." *Hastings Constitutional Law Quarterly*, Fall 1975, pp. 1000–1001. Argues that the sole effect of the Second Amendment is collective, affirming the right of the states to maintain National Guard units and conferring no individual right to keep and bear arms.

WEB DOCUMENTS

"The Intent of the Second Amendment to the Constitution of the United States of America." Kentucky Coalition to Carry Concealed. Available online. URL: http://www.kc3.com/editorial/quotes.htm. Posted on September 20, 1996. Quotes from the framers of the Constitution (and their contemporaries) on the right to keep and bear arms as an exposition of the historical intent of the Second Amendment.

Ostrowski, James. "The Growing Triumph of the Second Amendment." Future of Freedom Foundation. Available online. URL: http://www.fff.org/comment/com0301s.asp. Posted on January 22, 2003. Argues that the tide has turned in the battle over guns and the Constitution: A growing number of legal scholars and even judges are coming to acknowledge that the Second Amendment gives individuals a right to own and carry guns. The scholarship of gun-minimizer Michael Bellesiles has been discredited and people now realize the practical value of an armed citizenry in the wake of the September 11 terrorist attacks.

Polsby, Daniel B. "Treating the Second Amendment as Normal Constitutional Law." Kentucky Firearms Foundation. Available online. URL:http://www.kyfirearms.org/news/polsby.htm. Posted on December 13, 1997. Explores how the Second Amendment would be applied if it were treated like other "first class" provisions of the Bill of Rights, such as the First Amendment. Polsby suggests that, like speech, the "time, place and manner" of bearing arms could be regulated, but the right itself would have to be respected.

Shade, Gary A. "The Right to Keep and Bear Arms: The Legacy of Republicanism vs. Absolutism." Firearmsandliberty.com. Available online. URL: http://www.firearmsandliberty.com/militia_.htm. Posted on January 10, 1993. Concludes that history has shown that the right to keep and bear arms is integral to the duties of the citizens of a republic.

Volokh, Eugene. "The Commonplace Second Amendment." UCLA Law School. Available online. URL: http://www1.law.ucla.edu/~volokh/common.htm. Posted in 1998. Argues that the unusual structure of the Second Amendment (with its introductory clause about the militia) was actually a quite common construction in contemporary American constitutions. A change in the conditions used to justify a right does not imply that the right will expire.

———. "Sources on the Second Amendment and Right to Keep and Bear Arms in State Constitutions." UCLA School of Law. Available online. URL: http://www.law.ucla.edu/faculty/volokh/2amteach/sources.htm. Updated on July 7, 1999. Collection of texts, cases, and commentaries relating to the Second Amendment, including provisions in state constitutions and bills of rights. An interesting inclusion is state provisions that are grammatically similar to the Second Amendment in that they have an introductory clause, but that they also refer to such provisions as the freedoms of speech and expression.

LAWS, LEGISLATION, AND POLITICS

This section deals with the interpretation or effects of specific existing gun laws and proposed legislation. Also included are works dealing with the political process as it impacts gun legislation, including the activities of lobbying or advocacy groups.

Annotated Bibliography

BOOKS

Anderson, Jack. *Inside the NRA: Armed and Dangerous, An Exposé.* Beverly Hills, Calif.: Dove Books, 1996. Takes on the National Rifle Association, which prizewinning investigative reporter Jack Anderson believes has become an extremist group that lobbies against reasonable gun control measures.

Bird, Chris. *Concealed Handgun Manual.* 3d ed. San Antonio, Tex.: Privateer Publications, 2002. Contains the latest current state laws and regulations relating to concealed carrying of firearms, beginning and advanced shooting instruction, advice on handgun selection, and updated safety advice.

Brown, Peter, and Daniel Abel. *Outgunned: Up Against the NRA—The First Complete Insider Account of the Battle over Gun Control.* New York: Free Press, 2003. A journalist and an attorney join forces to provide detailed accounts of the attempt to make an end run around what many gun control advocates perceive to be the National Rifle Association's stranglehold over the legislative process. Much of the action focuses on the efforts of Wendell Gauthier, the Louisiana attorney who tried to apply his successful experience suing tobacco companies to municipal civil suits against gun manufacturers. The legal settlement by Smith & Wesson during the Clinton administration is also discussed, as are legislative counterattacks by gun advocates and their allies in the George W. Bush administration. A continuing theme is the power of trial lawyers who serve as a "fourth branch of government" in their impact on legislation and policy.

Bruce, John M., and Clyde Wilcox, eds. *The Changing Politics of Gun Control.* Lanham, Md.: Rowman & Littlefield, 1998. A collection of essays that explores the growing passion on both sides of the gun debate and the changes in political alignment since the wounding of James Brady gave gun control advocates a new focus for their efforts. The book also charts developments in Congress, the state legislatures, and the courts.

Buckwalter, Jane, ed. *Gun Control in the United States: A Comparative Survey of State Firearm Laws.* New York: Open Society Institute, 2000. Also available online. URL:http://www.soros.org/initiatives/justice/articles_publications/publications/gun_report_20000401/GunReport.pdf. Posted April 2000. This survey and study assesses the current gun laws of each state and rates their comparative strictness. Massachusetts and Hawaii are considered to be strictest, while Montana, Texas, Alaska, Louisiana, and Maine are at the tail end of the list. There are also international rankings that consider, among other things, licensing of gun owners, registration of firearms, percent of households with guns, and rates of gun homicide and gun suicide.

Davidson, Osha Ray. *Under Fire: The NRA and the Battle for Gun Control.* Expanded edition. Iowa City: University of Iowa Press, 1998. A balanced, detailed "report from the trenches" detailing the operation of the

National Rifle Association. Davidson describes the evolution of the NRA from an organization oriented toward promoting marksmanship to the United States's most powerful gun lobby in battles against gun control proposals in Congress.

Dees-Thomases, Donna, and Alison Hendrie. *Looking For a Few Good Moms: How One Mother Rallied a Million Others Against the Gun Lobby.* Revised ed. Emmaus, Pa.: Rodale Press, 2004. Recounts how a shooting tragedy at a day-care center impelled Dees-Thomases and others to organize the Million Mom March for gun control. There are also many vivid accounts of the experiences of gun victims. The book also includes much information and suggestions for activists for gun control and other issues.

Halbrook, Stephen P. *Firearms Law Deskbook: Federal and State Criminal Practice.* Eagan, Minn.: Thomson/West Group, 2003. The latest edition of a comprehensive guide to firearms laws and cases. Giving legal principles and prosecution and defense strategies, it is designed primarily for lawyers and law students, but could also be used as a reference by other researchers.

Korwin, Alan, and Michael P. Anthony. *Gun Laws of America: Every Federal Gun Law on the Books.* Phoenix, Ariz.: Bloomfield Press, 1999. Gives the actual text as well as "plain English" interpretation for all federal gun laws, including the assault weapons ban.

Magaw, John W., ed. *Federal Firearms Regulations Reference Guide.* Collingdale, Penn.: Diane Publications, 2000. A compilation of federal firearms laws, administrative rulings, and information from the Bureau of Alcohol, Tobacco, and Firearms.

Patrick, Brian Anse. *The National Rifle Association and the Media: The Motivating Force of Negative Coverage.* New York: Peter Lang, 2002. The author uses content analysis and other procedures to conclude that the media has a strong negative bias toward the NRA and the "gun lobby." More surprisingly, perhaps, he goes on to find that this hostile environment has actually strengthened the NRA and motivated gun supporters to work harder to get their points across. Finally, the author suggests that the role of the media in this issue shows the dangers of an unchecked, one-sided media, and he suggests that people find alternative ways to obtain and promulgate information.

Spitzer, Robert J. *The Politics of Gun Control.* 3d ed. New York: CQ Press, 2004. This updated survey and analysis covers the development of "gun culture," criminological issues, legislative and legal debates (including the Second Amendment), interest groups (including the NRA and Brady Campaign), public opinion, and the relationship of gun issues to overall political trends.

Annotated Bibliography

Thomas, Lee O., and Jeffrey Chamberlain. *Firearms and Weapons Laws: Gun Control in New York.* Flushing, N.Y.: Looseleaf Law Publications, 1998. A detailed reference to New York's complicated firearms laws.

United States Code of Federal Regulations. *Title 27: Alcohol, Tobacco Products, and Firearms.* 2 vols. Revised as of April 1, 2003. Washington, D.C.: U.S. Government Printing Office, 2003. This part of the U.S. Code embodies federal firearms legislation.

United States Congress House Committee on the Judiciary. *Gun Laws and the Need for Self-Defense: Hearing Before the Subcommittee* on Crime of the Committee on the Judiciary, House of Representatives, One Hundred Fourth Congress, first session, March 31, 1995. Washington, D.C.: Government Printing Office, 1996. Hearings on the impact of gun control laws on the ability of people to defend themselves against criminals.

United States General Accounting Office. *Gun Control: Implementation of the Brady Handgun Violence Prevention Act.* Washington, D.C.: Government Printing Office, 1996. Evaluates the effectiveness of the Brady Law and concludes that the law is of limited effectiveness because it applies only to guns sold by federally licensed dealers, not those sold by private individuals (such as at gun shows). The law also neither provides funds to help local law enforcement officers conduct background checks nor imposes penalties for their failure to do so.

Violence Policy Center. *Closing the Gun Show Loophole: Principles for Effective Legislation.* Washington, D.C.: Violence Policy Center, 2001. Also available online. URL: http://www.vpc.org/studyndx.htm. Posted in February 2001. Describes the "loophole" in federal firearms regulations resulting from the 1986 Firearms Owners Protection Act, which allows individuals to sell a considerable number of firearms at gun shows without holding federal firearms licenses, as well as the exemption of private sellers from required background checks under the Brady Law. The report argues for immediate application of Brady background checks to all sales at gun shows, noting that 95 percent of such "instant" checks are completed within two hours and that an even stricter state law has not led to the extinction of gun shows in California.

Violence Prevention Campaign. *From the Gun War to the Culture War: How the NRA Has Become the Pillar of the Right.* Washington, D.C.: Violence Prevention Campaign, 2002. Also available online. URL:http://www.vpc.org/graphics/gunwar.pdf. Posted in February 2002. This publication by the organization later renamed the Violence Policy Center argues that the National Rifle Association is far more than "the gun lobby"—it is a major part of the conservative or right-wing movement in America. As such, it has added strengths, but its extreme views on many social issues may also mean vulnerability.

Gun Control

ARTICLES

Ayoob, Massad. "Political Activism, Backwoods Style." *Backwoods Home Magazine*, May–June 2002, pp. 51ff. Recounts the Alaska gubernatorial campaign, which featured several gun-related issues. Republican candidate Wayne Anthony Ross has been a longtime director and officer in the NRA. He supports hunting and gun owners' rights; the state's voters have passed liberalized concealed carry laws over the veto of the Democratic governor, Tony Knowles.

Barone, Michael. "A Dangerous Gun Show." *U.S. News & World Report*, vol. 126, May 31, 1999, p. 30. Argues that gun control advocates, like other advocates of far-reaching reform (such as abortion and campaign finance), do not pay enough attention to the practical difficulties and consequences of any truly serious program. Millions of gun owners will not give up their rights any more easily than millions of women would give up their right to choose abortion. Defenders of the Second Amendment are as passionate as those who stand up for the First, and they have some impressive scholarship on their side.

Beachler, Donald W. "Militias and Segregationists: The Politics of Low-Turnout Elections in the United States." *Polity*, vol. 35, April 2003, pp. 441ff. The author describes the political strategy of using issues (such as fear of gun confiscation often associated with radical right-wing groups) that can intensely motivate small but potentially decisive constituencies. He argues that the Republicans are able to use such issues effectively in low-turnout elections "under the radar" without becoming associated with extremism in the national debate, even though a majority supports at least some gun control measures.

Bogus, Carl T. "NRA: Money, Firepower, and Fear." *Tikkun*, January/February 1994, pp. 79ff. Autobiographical article that tells the story of a prominent attorney who became a convert to the cause of gun control after he was shot by a disturbed client. At first he tries to mediate between gun control supporters and the NRA, but he concludes that gun supporters are intransigent and that only a massive political mobilization of gun control advocates will achieve the necessary objective of restricting guns to only a few categories of people.

Bowman, Catherine. "Alameda County Moves against Gun Shows." *San Francisco Chronicle*, July 28, 1999, pp. A1, A16. Reports that Alameda County supervisors approved an ordinance that prohibited people from possessing firearms on county property, in effect banning gun shows from the Alameda County Fairgrounds.

Bruning, Fred. "Decency, Honor and the Gun Lobby." *Maclean's*, vol. 108, June 12, 1995, p. 9. Reports with approval on former president George

H. W. Bush's resignation from the NRA after it issued a fund-raising letter that referred to federal agents as "jack-booted thugs." Bruning portrays the NRA as increasingly extreme, taking on characteristics of radical right-wing militias.

Buckley, Gail Lumet. "The Gun Cult." *America*. vol. 175, October 19, 1996, p. 8. Argues that the NRA represents a quasi-religious "gun cult" and that Catholics should reject religious arguments for gun ownership and instead support gun control efforts.

Buckley, William F., Jr. "Heston to the Rescue." *National Review*, vol. 49, June 2, 1997, pp. 62ff. Suggests that Charlton Heston, newly elected president of the NRA, may be able to improve the image of the beleaguered organization but that the NRA will also need to accept some compromises on gun rights issues.

Cannon, Angie. "Guns and the Mentally Ill." *U.S. News & World Report*, April 1, 2002, p. 22. Existing laws only criminalize gun sales to persons who had been previously committed to a mental institution or who have been legally adjudicated as mentally ill. As a result, many people who do not fit these criteria but are severely depressed or disturbed can obtain guns and kill themselves or others. Some states have become more proactive in requiring a doctor's certification of fitness for obtaining or renewing a gun license. Gun rights groups oppose this as a violation of rights, while some advocates for the mentally ill fear that tighter restrictions will contribute to stigmatization, pointing out that many forms of mental illness do not involve propensity to violence.

Chew, Sally. "Shotgun Wedding." *Lear's*, vol. 6, January 1994, pp. 30ff. Argues that the NRA is using feminist rhetoric to lure women to obtain guns for self-defense and that this is not really in the interests of women.

Coffey, Kathy. "One Year after Columbine: Reflections on the Million Mom March." *America*, vol. 182, June 17, 2000, p. 22. The author reflects on the continuing fear brought about by the Columbine shootings, and the spirit of resolve of participants in the Million Mom March. She believes that the strength of mothers just might overcome the vast resources of the NRA.

Cohn, Jonathan. "Guns 'n' Moses." *The New Republic*, vol. 218, June 22, 1998, p. 42. Reports on the efforts of Aaron Zelman, founder of Jews for the Preservation of Firearms Ownership. Although the majority of Jews tend to support gun control and other liberal positions, Zelman calls upon Jewish people to reject gun control as an invitation to genocide. He finds the right and duty of self-defense to be at the core of the Jewish tradition.

Cramer, Clayton E., and David B. Kopel. "'Shall Issue': The New Wave of Concealed Handgun Permit Laws." *Tennessee Law Review*, vol. 62, Spring

1995, pp. 679ff. Describes the movement to reform concealed handgun laws so that permits would be available to all law-abiding citizens rather than issued at the discretion of a sheriff or other official. Considering Florida as a test case, the authors point out that contrary to the prediction of opponents, only a tiny number of permit owners lost their permit later because of a gun-related crime. At the same time, crime rates were reduced considerably.

Dao, James. "Congressman's Gun Votes: Consistency or Calculation? Differing Views of a Republican's Choices." *The New York Times*, June 21, 1999, p. A15. Explores the battle over gun control in Congress, where a vote may not really mean what it seems to mean. Representative Rick A. Lazio's alleged political calculations are used as an example.

Dreyfuss, Robert. "Good Morning, Gun Lobby!" *Mother Jones*, vol. 21, July–August 1996, pp. 38ff. Describes the politics of Neal Knox, the NRA vice president, as accommodating militialike radicals internally while trying to create an outward image of the NRA as mainstream. The article recounts the increasing radicalization of the NRA since the late 1970s and claims that Knox had achieved an iron grip on the organization's governance.

"Faces of Violence: Lobbyists, Politicians and Haters, Guns Are the Tie That Binds." *Rolling Stone*, no. 710, June 15, 1995, pp. 57ff. Gives profiles of 45 people and companies active in lobbying for gun rights, generally portraying them as extremist and insensitive to social needs.

Farrell, Lawrence P., Jr. "Assault on the Small Arms Industrial Base." *National Defense*, vol. 86, February 2002, p. 4. Suggests that gun control efforts or lawsuits that directly or indirectly target small arms manufacturers threaten the supply of weapons to the military. A case in point has been recent efforts to ban the .50 caliber "sniper rifle," even though this type of weapon has not been linked to criminal activity.

Feinstein, Dianne, and Dan Gifford. "Q: Is the Federal Ban on Assault Weapons Working?" *Insight on the News*, vol. 12, February 26, 1996, pp. 26ff. A debate between Senator Feinstein (D-Calif.) and Dan Gifford, a gun rights advocate, about whether the national assault weapons ban has worked. Feinstein argues that the number of such weapons used in crime as well as the killing of police officers has been reduced. Gifford, however, argues that assault-type weapons play only a minor role in crime and that gun control advocates have cynically used factoids and scare-mongering tactics.

Gest, Ted. "Little Think Tank; Big Impact." *U.S. News & World Report*, vol. 115, December 6, 1993, p. 26. Describes the efforts of Josh Sugarmann, founder of the Violence Policy Center. The organization has issued research reports that zero in on emerging controversies such as those over assault weapons and gun dealer licensing.

Annotated Bibliography

Goode, Stephen. "A Mainstream Freedom Fighter Defends the Right to Bear Arms." *Insight on the News*, vol. 13, February 3, 1997, pp. 22ff. Interviews Wayne LaPierre, who became CEO of the National Rifle Association (NRA) in 1991. LaPierre rebuts criticisms that the NRA has become an extremist group, saying that the organization is mainstream and stands for fundamental American values of freedom and responsibility.

———. "NRA: Exposed or Demonized?" *Insight on the News*, vol. 13, February 3, 1997, pp. 8ff. Compares the "demonization" of the NRA by outspoken gun control advocates and the organization's own image of itself as being in the U.S. mainstream. Goode quotes gun control advocate Josh Sugarmann of the Violence Policy Center, the NRA's Wayne LaPierre, and progun criminologist Gary Kleck on various gun-related issues.

Harrison, Barbara Grizzuti. "Cease Fire." *Mother Jones*, vol. 22, March–April 1997, pp. 32ff. Interviews Tanya Metaksa, the NRA's chief lobbyist. Harrison paints a vivid and not entirely unsympathetic portrait as Metaksa recounts her life and the personal experiences that shaped her attitude toward the right of self-defense and gun ownership.

Hemenway, David. "Regulation of Firearms." *The New England Journal of Medicine*, v. 339, September 17, 1998, pp. 843ff. Argues that regulators should focus on imposing safety requirements and tightening controls on gun distribution to keep firearms out of the hands of criminals.

Heston, Charlton. "My Crusade to Save the Second Amendment." *American Rifleman*, vol. 145, September 1997, pp. 30ff. Heston, newly elected president of the NRA, explains why he came out of retirement to participate actively in the fight for gun rights.

Hilts, Philip J. "The New Battle Over Handguns." *Good Housekeeping*, vol. 224, June 1997, pp. 110ff. Discusses proposals to limit handgun purchases to one gun per month. Hilts argues that the only private parties who need to buy large numbers of guns are those acting as "straw purchasers" who will resell the guns to criminals who are not eligible to buy firearms. Gun control advocates point to a study showing that Virginia's gun purchase limits have taken that state off the list of sources of guns used in major crimes. Gun rights advocates such as the NRA oppose the law as being ineffective because most criminals obtain guns by stealing them or by buying them from individuals on the black market. The article includes sidebars with information about other legislative proposals and current state laws.

Jacobs, James B., and Kimberly A. Potter. "Keeping Guns out of the 'Wrong' Hands: The Brady Law and the Limits of Regulation." *Journal of Criminal Law and Criminology*, vol. 86, Fall 1995, pp. 93–120. Argues that the results of the Brady Act have fallen far short of the expectations of its proponents. An unknown but probably large number of persons denied firearms under the Brady background check were able to obtain them through illegal means. The authors suggest that gun control proponents will soon view the Brady Act only as a "small step" toward more comprehensive regulations.

"James Brady: Felled by a Bullet Intended for Ronald Reagan, He Inspired the First Federal Handgun-Control Law." *People Weekly*, March 15, 1999, p. 106. Profiles James Brady, who fought his way to recovery from severe injury at the hands of an assassin to join his wife, Sarah, in a successful campaign for federal handgun control.

King, Sue. "Now That We Have Running Water in the Kitchen . . ." *American Rifleman*, vol. 146, November–December 1998, p. 60. Argues that gun enthusiasts should reach out and help more women become involved in shooting and hunting.

Lacayo, Richard. "A Small-Bore Success." *Time*, vol. 145, February 20, 1995, pp. 47ff. Suggests that the Brady handgun control law has had only limited success in keeping criminals from buying guns. Problems include the selling of many guns through private channels, not dealers; confidentiality laws that prevent many mental problems from showing up in background checks; and a loophole that exempts guns claimed from pawnshops.

Lloyd, Jilian. "For Real Gun-Control Action, Watch the States." *The Christian Science Monitor*, May 28, 1999, p. 3. Suggests that even though gun control efforts may be stalling in Congress, the tide may have turned in favor of gun control in the state legislatures. The NRA says it will recover its power, but other observers suggest that there may be a permanent change in the balance between pro–gun control and progun groups.

MacDonald, Sam. "An Antigun Firefight." *Insight on the News*, vol. 18, April 22, 2002, pp. 12ff. In the wake of the September 11, 2001, attacks a number of gun control activists, including Representative John Conyers (D-Mich.), expressed confidence that Americans would support new gun measures (such as a bill to close the gun show "loophole.") Gun control groups such as the Brady Center to Prevent Gun Violence retooled their message to emphasize the need to keep guns out of the hands of terrorists, even as gun rights groups pointed out that none of the September 11 hijackers had used guns. Gun measures made little headway in Congress.

Maranz, Matthew. "Guns 'R' Us: So You Want to Buy a Machine Gun." *The New Republic*, vol. 200, January 23, 1989, pp. 12ff. Describes a reporter's efforts to buy a fully automatic weapon. Although the federal requirements are complicated and expensive, he finds that it is possible to do so.

Mitchell, Alison. "Politics Among Culprits in Death of Gun Control." *The New York Times*, June 19, 1999, p. A11. Analyzes Congress's failure to pass gun control legislation in spring 1999. Outrage over the Littleton,

Colorado, shootings was apparently insufficient to break the logjam caused by competing political interests.

Montgomery, Jill. "National Instant Criminal Background Checks System." *USA Bulletin*, vol. 50, January 2002, pp. 50–51. Describes the national instant check system (NICS) developed to implement the Brady Handgun Violence Prevention Act. Montgomery explains how the databases are searched and what efforts are being made to speed up the system and to deal with the fact that the databases remain incomplete. Between November 1998 and the end of 2001, NICS had processed more than 23 million transactions and denied more than 190,000 sales to felons or other ineligible persons.

Norquist, Grover G. "Have Gun, Will Travel: GOP Concealed Gun Laws Are Spreading Like Wildfire." *The American Spectator*, vol. 31, November 1998, pp. 74ff. Reports that gun rights activists, inspired by studies by John Lott and others who say that concealed weapons deter crime, are promoting laws in many states that would make it easier to carry a gun legally. (This trend reversed for awhile following the 1999 Littleton school shooting.)

"Operators Are Standing By." *U.S. News & World Report*, December 14, 1998, p. 32. Criticizes the new "instant check" system for gun purchasers because it often has technical problems that delay processing. This can lead to premature gun sales, so gun control advocates demand minimum waiting periods such as three days. Meanwhile, the NRA is criticizing the system because it may be used to surreptitiously maintain a list of gun owners.

Politano, Teresa. "One-in-a-Million Mom." *New Jersey Monthly*, vol. 26, June 2001, p. 76. Donna Dees-Thomases, the woman who led the Million Mom March for gun control, is busier than ever. Her daily life is described as she prepares to focus more on local gun issues, such as laws requiring that guns be childproof or personalized with a safety locking system.

Pollitt, Katha. "Moms to NRA: Grow Up!" *The Nation*, vol. 270, June 12, 2000, p. 10. A political and social commentator gives a mixed review to the Million Mom March. "Maternalist" politics are suspect from a feminist viewpoint but the participation of many minority women who had lost family members to gun violence was impressive. However, the gathering seemed more like a political campaign rally than the beginnings of more radical direct action.

Reibstein, Larry, and John Engen. "One Strike and You're Out." *Newsweek*, vol. 128, December 23, 1996, p. 53. Explains that a 1996 law, intended to cut down domestic violence by banning gun ownership by persons convicted of even relatively minor violent acts, may result in many law enforcement officers being no longer able to carry guns. Police unions oppose the law, and critics suggest that it may violate the constitutional ban against ex post facto laws that punish acts retroactively.

"The Same Old NRA; Its Policies Are Harmful, Even with 'Moses' as Leader." *Los Angeles Times*, vol. 117, June 9, 1998, p. B6. Suggests that the election of Charlton Heston as head of the NRA does not change the harmful activities of the organization in blocking reasonable gun control efforts.

Stolberg, Sheryl Gay. "Looking Back and Ahead After Senate's Votes on Guns." *New York Times*, March 4, 2004, p. A20. While the Democrats may have won a tactical victory in provoking the Republicans into scuttling the gun lawsuit immunity bill, some Republicans believe they can make election hay in conservative states by portraying Democrats as antigun.

———. "Senate Leaders Scuttle Gun Bill over Changes." *New York Times*, March 3, 2004, p. A1. Reports on the apparent abrupt end to gun legislation in the 108th Congress. Republicans had seemed to be on the verge of getting to President George W. Bush's desk a bill banning lawsuits against gun makers—but Democrats, seeing a political opportunity to push widely supported measures in an election year, tacked on amendments to renew the ban on assault weapons and require background checks on customers at gun shows. In reaction, Republicans withdrew their support from the overall bill.

Sugarmann, Josh. "Reverse Fire: The Brady Bill Won't Break the Sick Hold Guns Have on America. It's Time for Tougher Measures." *Mother Jones*, vol. 19, January–February 1994, pp. 36ff. Argues that halfway measures such as the Brady Bill with its background check and waiting period will not really stop violence. The government should ban the new, deadlier types of guns (especially handguns and assault weapons) that are creating a serious public health problem. This would be in keeping with the way other dangerous products are regulated.

Thurman, James N. "NRA's New Aim: To Soften Its Edges and Re-Enlist Moderates." *The Christian Science Monitor*, vol. 90, June 10, 1998, p. 5. Suggests that the NRA, in electing Charlton Heston as its head, is trying to reposition itself in the mainstream and bring back members who had left after incidents (such as the "jack-booted thugs" remark about federal agents) made the organization appear extreme.

"Time to Aim Our Outrage at the Gun Lobby." *National Catholic Reporter*, vol. 34, April 3, 1998, p. 36. Recites the sad litany of school shootings such as those at West Paducah, Kentucky, and Jonesboro, Arkansas. The article says that it is time to react as Americans would react to deaths in a senseless war or as they have reacted to the tobacco companies—and take on the gun lobby.

Annotated Bibliography

VandeHei, Jim. "On the Hill: Guns 'n' Poses." *The New Republic,* June 28, 1999, p. 15. Points out the little-recognized fact that about 50 House Democrats follow the National Rifle Association's lead and usually vote with Republicans against gun measures. The Democratic leadership often does not push hard for gun control for fear of alienating these members, who are generally Southern conservatives, or causing them to lose their seats.

Webster, D. W., J. S. Vernick, and L. M. Hepburn. "Effects of Maryland's Law Banning Saturday Night Special Handguns on Homicides." *American Journal of Epidemiology,* vol. 155, 2002, pp. 406–412. The study concludes that homicides in Maryland were 9 percent lower after the law was passed than they would have been without the law. This translates to saving an average of 40 lives per year. The correlation is shown by there not being a change in the rate of homicides committed with other types of weapons.

Whitlock, Craig. "Delays in FBI Checks Put 1,700 Guns in the Wrong Hands; System Failed to Detect Banned Buyers within Time Limit." *The Washington Post,* June 25, 1999, p. A01. Reports that technical problems prevented the FBI from completing background checks in three days as required. As a result, some applicants who were not eligible to receive guns got them. ATF agents are attempting to retrieve the guns.

"Wife-Abusing Cops?" *Off Our Backs,* vol. 27, February 1997, p. 3. Describes new regulations that will take away guns from persons convicted of domestic violence crimes—even law enforcement officers.

WEB DOCUMENTS

"Brady Campaign to Prevent Gun Violence 2003 Report Card—Detailed Grade Information." Available online. URL: http://www.bradycampaign. org/facts/reportcards/2003/details.pdf. Posted on January 9, 2004. Gives letter grades for each state on how well it is doing from a gun control point of view. Items graded include laws restricting children's access to guns, safety standards, concealed carry laws (presence of which gives a downgrade), and "extra credit or demerit."

"A Citizen's Guide to Federal Firearms Laws." National Rifle Association, Institute for Legislative Action. Available online. URL: http://www. nraila.org/GunLaws/FederalGunLaws.aspx?ID=60. Downloaded on March 14, 2004. Integrates and summarizes federal firearms laws by topic, such as a person's right to own firearms, laws relating to particular kinds of guns, transporting firearms, and carrying firearms.

"Compendium of State Firearm Laws." National Rifle Association, Institute for Legislative Action. Available online. URL: http://www.nraila.org/

213

media/misc/compendium.htm. Downloaded on March 14, 2004. Includes tables summarizing features of state firearms laws and an interactive summary of state laws accessed by clicking on a map.

Kopel, David B. "Polls: Anti-Gun Propaganda." National Rifle Association, Institute for Legislative Action. Available online. URL: http://www. nraila.org/Issues/Articles/Read.aspx?ID=40. Posted on September 13, 2000. Gives examples to argue that pollsters such as Gallup and Harris often frame their questions on gun issues in a biased way. For example, "assault rifles" are conflated with fully automatic weapons, the NRA "instant background check" is not presented as an alternative to waiting periods, and polls are sometimes "warmed up" with emotional material on gun violence.

Krafft, Bruce W. "My Day at the Mall." Firearms and Liberty.com. Available online. URL: http://www.firearmsandliberty.com (via link). Posted on July 25, 2003. Reports the author's confrontation with security guards after carrying a gun in a shopping mall in what he says was a violation of a new law that does not allow businesses to ban customers or guests from carrying guns.

"On Target: The Impact of the 1994 Federal Assault Weapons Act." Brady Center to Prevent Gun Violence. Available online. URL: http://www. bradycampaign.org/xshare/200403/on_target.pdf. Posted March 1, 2004. As Congress debates renewing the assault weapons ban, the Brady Center concludes from BATF gun trace data that the law has led to a reduction of 66 percent in gun traces involving banned assault weapons. There is a 45 percent decline even when "copycat" guns produced in an attempt to evade the law are included.

"Right to Carry 2004." National Rifle Association, Institute for Legislative Action. Available online. URL: http://www.nraila.org/Issues/FactSheets/ Read.aspx?ID=18. Posted on September 11, 2003. Lists the states that have laws allowing for concealed carrying of a gun. Thirty-four states now have permissive "shall issue" laws; Alabama and Connecticut have what the NRA calls "fair" discretionary carry laws; Alaska and Vermont respect the right to carry without a permit. Sixty-four percent of Americans now live in states that have a right to carry.

GUN LIABILITY

Works in this section deal with issues of civil liability for the manufacture, distribution, or use of firearms. These include specific cases and general issues such as product defects or negligent marketing, as well as general works about the firearms industry.

Annotated Bibliography

BOOKS

Diaz, Tom. *Making a Killing: The Business of Guns in America.* New York: New Press, 1999. Attacks the gun industry for irresponsibility in the manufacture and marketing of its products and advocates a legal strategy to attack manufacturers similar to that successfully used against the tobacco industry.

Larson, Eric. *Lethal Passage: The Story of a Gun.* New York: Vintage Books, 1995. Works backward from a 1988 murder rampage by a disturbed teenager to unravel how the weapon used was obtained by the shooter. The book exposes irresponsible practices of the gun industry, resulting in a powerful argument for gun control.

Rand, Kristen. *Lawyers, Guns, and Money: The Impact of Tort Restrictions on Firearms Safety and Gun Control.* Washington, D.C.: Violence Policy Center and Public Citizen, 1996. Discusses the effects of civil court decisions in shaping the practices of the firearms industry, including the use of safety devices, as well as the impact on the overall gun control movement.

Violence Policy Center. *Firearms Production in America.* 2002 Edition. Washington, D.C.: Violence Policy Center, 2002. Also available online. URL: http://www.vpc.org/graphics/prod2002.pdf. Posted in March 2003. A comprehensive listing of U.S. gun manufacturers who are currently active according to Bureau of Alcohol, Tobacco, and Firearms records. The list includes the weapons produced by each manufacturer by caliber, and the number of each produced.

Viscusi, W. Kip, ed. *Regulation through Litigation.* Washington, D.C.: Brookings Institution Press, 2002. Discusses an evolving modern strategy in which high-stakes litigation is used to pressure an industry into agreeing to stricter regulation, making an end run around the industry's political power. This strategy was first used successfully against tobacco companies and is being deployed against gun manufacturers with more mixed results.

ARTICLES

Allen, Mike. "Colt's to Curtail Sale of Handguns, Hoping to Limit Liability." *New York Times.* October 11, 1999, p. A1. Also available online. URL: http://www.nytimes.com/library/national/101199ct-colt.html. Reports that Colt, one of America's oldest gun manufacturers, is pulling out of the consumer gun market and will concentrate on manufacturing military weapons. A senior executive is quoted as saying that fear of future liability judgments is making it very hard for firearms manufacturers to obtain financing from lenders.

Arrow, Paul S. *"Kelley v. R.G. Industries:* California Caught in the Crossfire." *Southwestern University Law Review,* vol. 17, 1988, n.p. Argues that the court in the Kelley case should not have required that the gun in question have an actual defect in its design before determining whether it posed an excessive or unreasonable risk.

Barrett, Paul M. "Jumping the Gun? Attacks on Firearms Echo Earlier Assaults on Tobacco Industry; But Contrasts Are Big, Too; No Leaked Memos Yet, Nor Same Sums at Stake; 'Cigarettes Can Only Kill You.'" *The Wall Street Journal,* March 12, 1999, p. A1. Suggests that although comparing gun makers to tobacco companies may be good public relations strategy, there are many key differences between the two industries and the outcome of the legal assault is not certain.

Boyer, Peter J. "Big Guns." *The New Yorker,* vol. 75, May 17, 1999, pp. 54ff. Describes the efforts of Dennis Henigan and the Castano group of lawyers who, fresh from their victory over Big Tobacco, are organizing the legal assault on the firearms industry. They believe that public reaction to the Littleton, Colorado, shootings may aid their cause considerably.

Brazil, Jeff, and Steve Berry. "Federal Safety Law Targets 15,000 Items, but Not Guns." *Los Angeles Times,* vol. 117, February 1, 1998, p. A1. Points out the fact, surprising to many people, that guns are not subject to the federal regulations governing most products. The authors explain the legal and political history that led to this situation.

Butterfield, Fox. "New Data Point Blame at Gun Makers." *The New York Times,* November 28, 1998, p. A9. Reports a recent study that suggests many criminals may be getting guns through legal dealers (via "straw purchasers") rather than through theft, as had been previously assumed. This may reinforce plaintiff lawyers' claims that gun makers are deliberately distributing guns into markets that they should know are being used to supply criminals.

Chiang, Harriet, and Kevin Fagan. "Gunmakers Can Be Sued by Victims." *San Francisco Chronicle,* September 30, 1999, p. A1, A19. Reports that a California state court of appeals has, for the first time in U.S. legal history, ruled that a gun maker can be held liable for the criminal use of its products. The case arose from a 1993 mass shooting in a San Francisco office building.

Cohen, Adam. "When There's Smoke." *Time,* vol. 153, February 22, 1999, p. 65. Describes the results of a Brooklyn, New York, lawsuit that found some gun makers liable for shootings. Plaintiffs hailed the decision as a breakthrough in holding the gun manufacturers liable, although defendants pointed to the fact the jury cleared 10 of 25 defendants and found no damages against six others. Although the outcome of future cases remains uncertain, gun makers may now be themselves under the gun.

"D.C. Law Makes Innocent Pay for Crime." *American Rifleman*, vol. 140, May 1992, p. 63. Criticizes a District of Columbia ordinance that holds gun makers liable for direct and indirect damages caused by misuse of their products, without requiring that the product actually have any defects.

Elvin, John. "The Thinning Ranks of America's Gun Dealers." *Insight on the News*, vol. 13, April 7, 1997, p. 23. Reports that there are 100,000 fewer gun dealers, and argues that ever more strict gun laws are the reason. Elvin describes a number of proposals that would go beyond the Brady Bill in increasing paperwork and expense for gun dealers and that could lead to a national registration system that would facilitate gun confiscation.

Feldman, Danielle. "Making Social Policy through Courts: Gun Control Advocates Fight Firearms." *Defense Counsel Journal*, vol. 68, January 2001, p. 72. The author argues that gun manufacturers and distributors should not generally be considered liable under the standard theories of strict liability. The argument that guns lack "social utility" is contradicted by the congressional intent in the 1968 gun control act to protect legitimate gun ownership. Further, making social policy through the courts usurps the legislative function and ignores economic realities.

Henigan, Dennis, and Bob Barr. "Symposium [on Gun Lawsuits]." *Insight on the News*, vol. 15, April 26, 1999, p. 24. A debate by Dennis Henigan, director of the Legal Action Project of the Center to Prevent Handgun Violence, and progun Congressman Bob Barr. Henigan describes the pioneering suits and says they are justified by the damage guns do to society and the costs imposed on taxpayers and are in accordance with basic principles of tort law such as the obligation not to create hazardous products. Barr, who is sponsoring federal legislation to ban such suits, argues that they amount to an assault on constitutional rights that would not be tolerated if similar arguments had been raised against books that can contain harmful ideas but are protected by the First Amendment.

Hewitt, Bill. "Retribution: Not Forgiving or Forgetting, a Shooting Victim's Family Takes a Pair of Gunmakers to Court." *People Weekly*, vol. 49, March 23, 1998, pp. 81ff. Reports on the lawsuit filed by the family of gun victim Aaron Halberstam against Wayne and Sylvia Daniel, the makers of the Cobray semiautomatic pistol. The gun is sold as a mail-order kit (except for one part); the makers are accused of inflammatory advertising ("the Drug Lord's choice") and negligent marketing and distribution. (The jury later found the gun makers not to be liable.)

Horwitz, Joshua M. "*Kelley v. R.G. Industries, Inc.*: A Cause of Action for Assault Weapons." *University of Dayton Law Review*, vol. 15, 1989, pp. 125–139. Argues that the legal theory used against manufacturers of Saturday night specials (cheap, easily concealable handguns) could also be applied to makers of assault weapons. In both cases the weapons are not designed for traditional sporting uses, and their design makes them unreasonably dangerous.

"John Coale's Next Case." *The Economist,* vol. 350, February 27, 1999, p. 32. Describes the efforts of attorney John Coale to organize legal action against gun makers. Coale has won a large judgment on behalf of victims of attention deficit disorder, successfully sued Ford for defects in its school buses, and played a large part in the record-breaking state tobacco settlement. Now he has used his media contacts to help turn public attention to negligent marketing by gun companies—the main grounds for the upcoming civil trials.

Lee, Henry K. "Gunmaker Not at Fault in Slaying, Jury Says." *San Francisco Chronicle,* November 17, 1998, pp. A17, A19. Reports the finding of a Berkeley, California, jury that the Beretta company was not liable for a teenager's accidental shooting. In *Dix v. Beretta,* the plaintiff had argued that the gun lacked reasonable safety features, and the gun company argued that it had provided adequate safety warnings.

Levin, Myron. "Legal Claims Get Costly for Maker of Cheap Handguns." *Los Angeles Times,* vol. 116, December 27, 1997, p. A1. Reports that Lorcin Engineering, a major maker of Saturday night specials, has filed for bankruptcy, largely because it faces $4 million or more in claims for personal injury or wrongful death arising from use of its products.

Lott, John R., Jr. "Gun Shy: Cities Turn from Regulation to Litigation in their Campaign against Guns." *National Review,* December 21, 1998, p. 46. Reports that the success of states in suing tobacco companies has inspired a similar effort by cities against gun makers. But unlike tobacco companies, gun makers can point to a social benefit: evidence showing that guns have also saved lives and money by deterring criminals.

Ma, Kenneth. "Crusading to Bring Big Gun Makers to Justice." *The Chronicle of Higher Education,* vol. 45, March 19, 1999, p. A10. Describes efforts by David Kairys, a law professor at Templeton University, to develop legal theories for suing gun makers. These include assessing the full costs of gun killings and accidents to cities in the form of police and medical services and showing that gun makers are marketing their products in a reckless or negligent manner, such as by focusing on high-crime areas where their products are most likely to be abused.

McArdle, Elaine. "Lawyers, Guns, and Money: Firearms Litigation Ready to Explode." *Lawyers' Weekly USA,* November 30, 1998, pp. B2–B5. Reports on the first wave of class action suits against gun makers, the legal strategies, and the confidence of proponents that they are on the winning side.

Annotated Bibliography

McClurg, Andrew J. "Handguns as Products Unreasonably Dangerous Per Se." *University of Arkansas at Little Rock Law Journal*, vol. 13, Summer 1991, pp. 599–619. Argues that gun makers should be held strictly liable for firearms injuries, primarily because of the destructiveness of firearms. (This article was presented as a debate with Philip D. Oliver—see Oliver's article below.)

Newbart, Dave. "Made to Kill." *Scholastic Update*, vol. 131, April 12, 1999, p. 4. Describes the arguments being used in negligence suits against gun makers. Written for young people, but is a good, detailed introduction suitable for all readers.

"Ohio Judge Dismisses Gun Suit." *San Francisco Chronicle*, October 8, 1999, p. A5. Reports that an Ohio judge has dismissed one in the growing wave of lawsuits brought against gun manufacturers by states and municipalities. The judge ruled that the legislature, not the court, was the proper body for regulating gun design, and that the risks of gun usage had not been concealed by manufacturers.

Oliver, Philip D. "Rejecting the 'Whipping-Boy' Approach to Tort Law: Well-Made Handguns Are Not Defective Products." *University of Arkansas at Little Rock Law Journal*, vol. 14, Fall 1991, pp. 1–36. Response to an article by Andrew McClurg (see above). Oliver argues that well-made handguns are neither defective nor unreasonably dangerous and that attempting to hold gun makers liable distorts basic principles of tort law.

Olson, Walter. "Firing Squad." *Reason*, vol. 31, May 1999, p. 58. Warns that negligence suits against gun makers may erode the right to obtain firearms by forcing restrictions. A major court victory in any state could have the effect of "legislating" for all. Conservatives may have to suspend their belief in federalism and support national legislation to protect gun makers from lawsuits.

Paige, Sean. "Industries Become Ideological Targets." *Insight on the News*, vol. 14, April 27, 1998, pp. 12ff. Argues that in the wake of the Jonesboro, Arkansas, shootings, opportunistic politicians are demonizing the gun industry. Paige compares this trend to attacks on the alcohol, tobacco, and snack food industries.

Stevens, Susan M. "*Kelley v. R. G. Industries:* When Hard Cases Make Good Law." *Maryland Law Review*, vol. 46, Winter 1987, pp. 486–500. Argues that the court in the *Kelley* case was justified in extending liability law to cover a product (cheap handguns) that the legislature had concluded serves no socially useful purpose. The court was making legitimate social policy in cooperation with the legislature, and the policy may well save lives by curtailing the distribution of dangerous weapons.

Teems, Yvonne. "Minnesota Gun Statute Triggers Liability Fears: Interpretations Vary on How to Notify of No-Gun Policies." *Business Insurance*, vol. 37, June 30, 2003, p. 4. A little-known consequence of "right to carry" laws such as one recently passed in Minnesota is that businesses have to develop their own policies regarding people carrying guns on their premises. Gun incidents could lead to workers' compensation or personal injury claims. Some businesses are banning the carrying of guns on their property (as is permitted by the law). However, the actual extent of the potential problem is unclear.

"Texas Forbids Cities to Sue Gun Firms." *The Washington Post*, June 20, 1999, p. A14. Reports that Texas governor (and then presidential candidate) George W. Bush signed legislation that would prevent cities from suing gun makers; only the legislature could bring such suits. Bush said that manufacturers should not be held liable for the selling of a legal product.

WEB DOCUMENTS

"Fact Sheet: Litigation Is an Important Tool for Injury and Gun Violence Prevention." Johns Hopkins Center for Gun Policy and Research. Available online. URL: http://www.jhsph.edu/gunpolicy/litigation_pht.pdf. Posted in February 2003. Argues that litigation can do more than compensate victims of gun violence: It can induce manufacturers to make their guns safer (or deter unsafe practices). Also, information gathered through trial discovery can be used to justify the creation of new laws or regulations.

Shade, Gary A., and Rod Murphy. "The Ethics of Firearm Industry Lawsuits." Firearms and Liberty.com. Available online. URL: http://www.firearmsandliberty.com (via link). Posted on June 22, 2003. Originally a class paper, it examines the legality of negligence and public nuisance theories used for suing gun makers as well as the morality of using the courts to determine public policy. It concludes that it is problematic for the government to say that a product is legal but allow its manufacturers to be driven out of business even though the product is not defective. Further, the result of such suits (if they destroy the gun industry) might mean that government, rather than protecting people, is depriving them of a measure of protection available through the possession of firearms.

Sullum, Jacob. "Shot Down." Reason Online. Available online. URL: http://reason.com/sullum/051501.shtml. Posted on May 15, 2001. Argues that recent gun lawsuits are "legally and morally bankrupt," as shown by suits in Chicago and New Orleans and other cities being dismissed by courts. The court in New Orleans ruled that the suit was an indirect attempt to regulate firearms manufacture and marketing, a function belonging to the legislature. In Chicago, the court said that the plaintiff had been unable to show that allowing "too many" guns to be sold amounted to a public nuisance. The author suggests that because armed citizens deter crime, marketing firearms might actually create a "public good."

INTERNATIONAL PERSPECTIVES

This final section includes works on gun control in countries other than the United States (especially Canada, Europe, and Australia), international comparisons of gun policies, and the international effort to control the illicit market in firearms and other light weapons.

BOOKS

Crook, John. *Gun Massacres in Australia: The Case for Gun Control.* Chelsea, Victoria, Australia: Gun Control Australia, 1994. An overview of 21 gun killings that took place in Australia during the years 1987 to mid-1994, and an examination of the attempts to control gun misuse as a result of the killings.

Dahinden, Erwin, ed. *Small Arms and Light Weapons: Legal Aspects of National and International Regulations: Proceedings of the UN Conference on the Illicit Trade in Small Arms and Light Weapons.* New York: United Nations, 2002. Proceedings of a 2001 conference on the illegal international arms trade, including the current status of national and international regulations and their effectiveness.

Halbrook, Stephen P. *Target Switzerland: Swiss Armed Neutrality in World War II.* Rockville Centre, N.Y.: Sarpedon, 1998. Argues that Switzerland's armed neutrality during World War II was made possible by its decentralized federal system and its unique system of "citizen soldier" militia. Although the book does not focus on gun rights, the relationship of the Swiss system to the U.S. Second Amendment and collective self-defense makes this book relevant to the gun debate.

Kopel, David B. *Gun Control in Great Britain: Saving Lives or Constricting Liberty?* Chicago: Office of International Criminal Justice, University of Illinois at Chicago, 1992. Analysis of British gun control laws and their effectiveness.

Malcolm, Joyce Lee. *Guns and Violence: The English Experience.* Cambridge, Mass.: Harvard University Press, 2002. Beginning with detailed historical background, the author surveys the development and changes in attitudes toward firearms in British society. She suggests that recent increases in the British crime rate may be correlated with tightened gun control and a loss of the deterrent value of an armed citizenry. (Critics have pointed out that the British method for collecting crime statistics has also changed recently.) She also concludes that compared to the case in the United States, the debate over gun control and gun rights in Britain seems to be just beginning.

Simkin, J., and Aaron Zelman. *Gun Control: Gateway to Tyranny: The Nazi Weapons Law, 18 March 1938*. Hartford, Wisc.: Jews for the Preservation of Firearms Ownership, 1992. Describes Nazi gun control legislation and asserts that it became the model for U.S. gun control efforts starting in the 1960s. The authors generally view gun control as a key element in the totalitarian project.

Simkin, Jay, Aaron S. Zelman, and Alan M. Rice. *Lethal Laws: "Gun Control" Is the Key to Genocide*. Milwaukee, Wisc.: Jews for the Preservation of Firearms Ownership, 1994. Argues that gun control has been a key step in the process of mass murder conducted by the Nazis, Soviets, and other dictatorships of the 20th century. The authors claim that the drafters of U.S. gun laws adopted much of their language from Nazi gun laws.

Squires, Peter. *Gun Culture or Gun Control: Firearms, Violence and Society*. New York: Routledge, 2001. This exploration of gun issues is from a British perspective, comparing differences in the "gun culture" between Britain and the United States, and the resulting differences in the development of social policy. The impact of the 1996 Dunblane, Scotland, shootings on British attitudes is also explored.

United Nations. *United Nations International Study on Firearm Regulation*. New York: United Nations, 1998. A nation-by-nation summary of firearm regulations, including statistics on criminal cases, suicides and accidents related to firearms, and information about international illicit trafficking in firearms.

ARTICLES

"America and Guns." *The Economist*, vol. 346, April 4, 1998, pp. 16ff. Presents a British viewpoint on U.S. gun problems, giving statistics comparing gun deaths in the United States with other countries and expressing incredulity concerning U.S. gun culture.

Arya, Neil. "Confronting the Small Arms Pandemic: Unrestricted Access Should Be Viewed as a Public Health Disaster." *British Medical Journal*, vol. 324, April 27, 2002, pp. 990ff. Argues that physicians throughout the world have seen the terrible consequences of the use of small arms in hundreds of thousands of violent deaths each year; they should now devise strategies to counter gun violence, using sound public health principles. "Supply side" strategies such as weapons buybacks should be pursued, as well as tighter regulations, gun registration, and educational programs. International humanitarian law could also be used to ban certain types of weapons.

Beltrame, Julian, and John Urquhart. "Shootings Mar Canadian Confidence in Tough Gun Laws Curbing Bloodbaths." *The Wall Street Journal*, April 30, 1999, p. B8. Reports that Canadians are discouraged about two recent multiple shootings in their country and are wondering whether the tough new Canadian gun laws can really have an effect on such tragedies.

Bergman, Brian. "Handing Out Heavy Ammo: The Auditor General Blasts Gun Registry." *Maclean's*, December 16, 2002, p. 30. Reports that Canada's universal gun registration scheme is bogged down in waste and mismanagement, with costs ballooning out of control. There has also been considerable local resistance to the program, particularly in the western provinces.

Bergman, Jake, and Julia Reynolds. "The Guns of Opa-Locka: How U.S. Dealers Arm the World." *The Nation*, vol. 275, December 2, 2002, p. 19. The United States is "a one-stop shop for the guns sought by terrorists, mercenaries and international criminals." This is illustrated by the sales of guns to the Colombian ELN terrorist group by a Florida store called Gun Land, and their shipment by "a ragtag South Florida outfit called Lobster Air International." U.S. Attorney General John Ashcroft is criticized for refusing to permit the use of gun purchase records to track crimes and for not pursuing tighter controls on commerce in guns.

Bonner, Raymond. "After Land-Mine Triumph, Groups Combat Small Arms; Weapons Wreak Havoc around the World." *The New York Times*, January 7, 1998, p. A8. Reports that groups that had spearheaded an international campaign to stop the use of land mines are turning their attention to the proliferation of small arms that are involved in violent clashes and crime in many countries.

———. "21 Nations Seek to Limit the Traffic in Light Weapons." *The New York Times*, July 13, 1998, p. A3. Describes an international conference in Oslo, Norway, that is attempting to forge agreements that would reduce the distribution of small arms (mostly rifles) that are plentiful in the world's trouble spots.

Boyd, Neil. "Gun Control: Placing Costs in Context." *Canadian Journal of Criminology and Criminal Justice*, vol. 45, October 2003, pp. 473ff. The author believes that the Canadian firearms laws implemented in 1995 have been reasonably effective, although the ongoing decline in gun ownership is part of a larger cultural trend. The program's well-publicized cost overruns resulted largely from legal action by opponents and lack of cooperation by provincial officials.

"Cambodia's City of Guns." *The Economist*, October 24, 1998, p. 40. Describes the situation of Cambodia's capital, Phnom Penh, where decades of civil war have left the population with 50,000 guns. Afraid of crime and disorder, most people have refused the government's request that the guns be turned in. The article suggests that the government must offer real security and reduce corruption before the populace will cooperate.

Goldring, Natalie J. "The NRA Goes Global." *Bulletin of the Atomic Scientists*, vol. 5, January 1999, p. 61. Argues that gun control will become a reality only when the international flow of arms is stopped. The NRA is using its formidable resources to try to derail efforts of nongovernmental organizations (NGOs) to create international laws that would regulate weapons manufacture and distribution.

"Gun Law in Brazil." *The Economist*, vol. 351, June 19, 1999, p. 29. Reports that Brazil's government is pushing for a total ban on gun ownership but is being opposed by a newly formed gun lobby. Brazil has experienced a high rate of crime and mass shootings in recent years. Police corruption and government inefficiency may undermine the effectiveness of such laws.

Hartnagel, Timothy F. "Gun Control in Alberta: Explaining Public Attitudes Concerning Legislative Change." *Canadian Journal of Criminology*, vol. 44, October 2002, pp. 403–423. Analyzes and draws conclusions from a telephone survey of Alberta residents' attitudes toward the new Canadian gun law. Although nearly half strongly support the laws (and about a quarter strongly oppose them), support may be motivated by a fear of crime such that any increase in crime may erode support for the law.

Hewlett, Bill. "Innocents Lost: The People of Dunblane, Scotland, Bid Farewell to the Victims of a Day That Will Never Be Forgotten." *People Weekly*, vol. 45, April 1, 1996, pp. 42ff. Describes the somber and reflective mood following the killing of 17 kindergarten children and their teacher in Dunblane, Scotland. People wonder how the shooter, Thomas Hamilton, had been able to get a gun permit: Though he had broken no laws, he had frequently been accused of improprieties in supervising youth activities.

"Hey, Anybody Want a Gun?" *The Economist*, vol. 347, May 16, 1998, pp. 47ff. Reports that the United States and 45 other nations have recently begun work on a protocol to control the proliferation of small arms, which often lead to unstable conditions in emerging nations. Opposition by the NRA, however, resulted in outright gun bans being dropped from the agenda.

Kopel, David B. "Japanese Gun Control." *Crime & Justice International*, vol. 19, June 2003, pp. 4–10. The author reviews the history of gun ownership and gun control in Japan. While he acknowledges that Japanese gun control has been very successful (guns are rare and gun crime even more so), Kopel argues that its implementation has depended on practices that would be entirely unacceptable in the United States. In Japan the authorities have extensive and intimate control over individuals, and persons can be searched or arrested and held for long periods without a judicial warrant.

MacQueen, Ken. "Armed, Angry and Defiant: 'Conscientious Objectors' Who Refuse to Register Firearms Say They Are Fighting to Protect Freedoms." *Maclean's*, February 19, 2001, p. 26. Reports that about 300,000 Canadians have refused to meet the January 1 deadline to register their firearms. Resistance seems particularly strong in rural and western areas. Meanwhile, the licensing program has encountered bureaucratic snags and cost overruns.

Malcolm, Joyce Lee. "Gun Control's Twisted Outcome: Restricting Firearms Has Helped Make England More Crime-Ridden than the U.S." *Reason*, vol. 34, November 2002, pp. 20ff. In recent years the British rate for crimes other than murder and rape has overtaken that in the United States. Although Britain has much stricter gun control, it has also historically had a low rate of armed crime. Therefore, the author suggests that disarming British citizens has simply increased their rate of victimization. She suggests that recent legislation is the culmination of a long trend toward taking away an individual's ability of self-defense.

Metaksa, Tanya K. "Global Gun Control Is on the March." *American Rifleman*, vol. 145, August 1997, pp. 42ff. Criticizes the United Nations for adopting a Japanese proposal for international firearms regulations as it is based on faulty data and possibly could result in infringement on Americans' gun rights.

———. "Gun Owners Branded 'A Threat to Mankind.'" *American Rifleman*, vol. 146, April 1998, pp. 38ff. Reports that the United Nations is moving toward institutionalizing an antigun position in international law and relations. The NRA has been trying to become an accredited nongovernmental organization so that it can monitor UN efforts from inside.

Montero, David. "Guns 'R' U.S." *The Nation*, vol. 275, December 2, 2002, p. 20. Argues that lax gun laws and widespread gun shops and gun shows in the United States attract international terrorists and gun smugglers. Examples given include smugglers from Venezuela and Haiti buying large amounts of guns and ammunition from U.S. shops, as well as activities of terrorists, including the IRA, Hezbollah, al-Fuqra, and the Colombian ELN.

Gun Control

Otchet, Amy. "Small Arms, Many Hands." *UNESCO Courier,* November 1998, pp. 37ff. Describes the efforts of a group of nongovernmental organizations waging an international campaign against the proliferation of light weapons (such as automatic rifles) around the world. Otchet also describes the extent of the problem (500 million small arms worldwide) and the politics involved in coming to a consensus for control measures.

"Out of Control: Australia." *The Economist,* vol. 341, November 30, 1996, p. 36. Reports on the mass shooting in Hobart, Australia, where 35 people were killed by Martin Bryant with a semiautomatic rifle. In response, there has been a push for tighter gun control, and all Australian states have banned semiautomatic rifles and shotguns.

Rothenberg, Elliot C. "Jewish History Refutes Gun Control Activists." *American Rifleman,* vol. 136, February 1988, pp. 30ff. Argues that the experience of millions of disarmed Jews being killed by the Nazis as well as the heroic resistance of those who chose to arm themselves and fight back in the Warsaw ghetto is a powerful argument against gun control.

Simonds, Merilyn. "Code of Arms." *Canadian Geographic,* vol. 116, March–April 1996, pp. 44ff. Describes the gun scene in Canada, which has a reasonable number of guns but does not have the emotional attachment to them that many people in the United States have. Simonds reviews the different historical experiences that people in Canada and the United States have had with firearms. She also discusses events that have heated up the gun control debate in Canada. A related article gives a brief chronology of gun control in Canada.

Smith, James F. "Mexican Congress Takes Aim at Illegal Guns from U.S." *Los Angeles Times,* vol. 117, September 7, 1998, p. A3. Reports on Mexican crackdown on people from the United States who smuggle guns into the country, including the jailing of U.S. citizens charged with smuggling.

"Teens under Siege: How Kids Can Go Wrong—And What Parents Can Do." *Maclean's,* May 3, 1999, p. 22. Reports on Canadian reaction to the Littleton, Colorado, high school shootings. Although Canada has fewer guns and stricter gun laws (including registration), gun control is only part of what needs to be addressed in dealing with the social forces that are breeding alienation among youth.

Wilson, Chris Oliver. "Disarming News: Why Bobbies Have No Guns." *U.S. News & World Report,* vol. 124, February 9, 1998, pp. 46ff. Describes the total ban on handguns that Britain put into effect in response to the 1996 school shootings at Dunblane, Scotland, that left 16 dead. Wilson notes that 95 percent of British police officers are unarmed, and four out of five say they do not wish to carry guns.

Annotated Bibliography

WEB DOCUMENTS

"International Homicide Comparisons." Guncite.com. Available online. URL: http://www.guncite.com/gun_control_gcgvinco.html. Updated on October 18, 2003. Discusses the difficulty of drawing valid homicide comparisons between the United States and other countries, and alleged misuse of such data by gun control supporters. The site offers statistics and a variety of related links.

Kates, Don B. "Gun Laws around the World: Do They Work?" National Rifle Association. Available online. URL: http://www.nraila.org/Issues/Articles/Read.aspx?ID=72. Posted in October 1997. Describes gun laws, gun use, and homicide and suicide rates around the world and includes charts. The site argues that peaceful, well-ordered societies do not need gun laws to be that way and that violent, disordered societies do not benefit from gun laws.

CHAPTER 8

ORGANIZATIONS AND AGENCIES

The following organizations are national in scope (a few are international). There are hundreds of local organizations of gun enthusiasts who often take an interest in gun control issues, and there are a growing number of local groups that work for gun violence prevention and gun control. The web sites of national organizations often have links to local organizations, as do some of the web sites listed in Chapter 7 in the Reference section.

Academics for the Second Amendment
P.O. Box 131254
St. Paul, MN 55113
Educational and advocacy organization dedicated to giving the Second Amendment its full and proper place in constitutional discourse; sponsors scholarship and conferences.

Americans for Gun Safety
URL: http://ww2.
americansforgunsafety.com
Phone: (202) 775-0300
Americans for Gun Safety
Washington, DC
An advocacy organization that claims to occupy the middle ground in the gun control debate—supporting the right to own guns but working for

laws to promote gun safety and prevent misuse. Recent issues include trigger locks, closing the gun show loophole and promoting more stringent enforcement of gun laws. There are many affiliated state groups.

American Firearms Industry
URL: http://www.amfire.com
E-mail: afi@amfire.com
Phone: (954) 467-9994
2455 E. Sunrise Boulevard
150 SE 12th Street
Suite 200
Fort Lauderdale, FL 33316
A trade group for firearms dealers. The association has been engaged in trying to counteract liability suits being filed against gun makers by cities.

Organizations and Agencies

**Arming Women Against Rape
and Endangerment (AWARE)**
URL: http://www.aware.org
E-mail: info@aware.org
Phone: (877) 672-9273
P.O. Box 242
Bedford, MA 01730-0242
Promotes self-defense for women through education and training, including firearms training.

**Brady Campaign to Prevent
Gun Violence**
URL: http://www.
bradycampaign.org
Phone: (202) 289-7319
1225 I Street, NW
Suite 1100
Washington, DC 20005
Formerly known as Handgun Control, Inc., the Brady Campaign is the nation's largest and most influential gun control advocacy group. It lobbies for proposed legislation such as requiring trigger locks and closing the "gun show loophole," as well as opposing granting legal immunity to gun makers or liberalizing concealed carry laws. Its web site provides extensive resources on legislation and issues. The group has a research arm, the Brady Center to Prevent Gun Violence; the organization has also merged with the Million Mom March group.

**Brady Center to Prevent Gun
Violence**
URL: http://www.bradycenter.
org
Phone: (202) 898-0792

1225 I Street, NW
Suite 1100
Washington, DC 20005
Emphasizes education about the dangers of handgun possession, particularly involving children; develops programs to educate young people about guns and gun violence; organizes research and legal action projects.

Brass Roots
URL: http://www.brassroots.org
Phone: (520) 270-6941
7272 E. Broadway Boulevard
#301
Tucson, AZ 85710-1407
Arizona-based national gun rights organization.

**Bureau of Alcohol, Tobacco,
and Firearms (ATF)**
URL: http://www.atf.treas.gov
E-mail: ATFMail@atf.gov
Phone: (202) 927-8480
650 Massachusetts Avenue, NW
Room 8290
Washington, DC 20226
The agency of the U.S. Treasury Department that has responsibility for investigation and enforcement of all federal firearms laws.

Cease Fire, Inc.
E-mail: info@ceasefire.org
P.O. Box 33424
Washington, DC 20033-0424
Educational organization dedicated to reducing gun-related deaths of children. Cease Fire, Inc., produces public service announcements and other material urging "handgunfree homes."

Children's Safety Network
URL: http://www.
childrenssafetynetwork.org
E-mail: csn@edc.org
Phone: (617) 969-7100, ext. 2722
55 Chapel Street
Newton, MA 02458-1060
Funded by the Maternal and Child Health Bureau of the U.S. Department of Health and Human Services, the Child Safety Network provides technical assistance, training, and resources to related health professionals in an effort to "reduce the burden of injury and violence to our nation's children and adolescents." Violence and firearms are among the areas covered.

**Citizens Committee for the
  Right to Keep and Bear Arms**
URL: www.crkba.org
E-mail: info@ccrkba.org
Phone: (425) 454-4911
Liberty Park
12500 NE 10th Place
Bellevue, WA 98005
Anti-gun control group emphasizing Second Amendment issues.

**Coalition for Gun Control
  (Canada)**
URL: http://www.guncontrol.ca
Phone: (514) 725-2021
P.O. Box 90062
1488 Queen Street West
Toronto, Ontario M6K 3K3
CANADA
Canadian-based gun control advocacy group that also emphasizes international gun and small arms control issues.

**Coalition to Stop Gun Violence
  (CSGV)**
URL: http://www.csgv.org
Phone: (202) 408-0061
1023 15th Street, NW
Suite 600
Washington, DC 20005
A large coalition of labor, religious, medical, educational, civic, and other groups united to fight gun violence. The coalition "pushes a progressive agenda to reduce firearm death and injury," lobbies and provides technical support to advocacy organizations, and has a separate unit, the Educational Fund to End Gun Violence.

**Federal Bureau of Investigation
  (FBI)**
URL: http://www.fbi.gov
Phone: (202) 324-3691
935 Pennsylvania Avenue, NW
Washington, DC 20525
Performs background checks and gun traces for local authorities and compiles many statistics involving gun violence and guns used in crime.

**Firearm Injury Center
Medical College of Wisconsin**
URL: http://www.mcw.edu/fic
Phone: (414) 456-7676
1000 North 92nd Street
Milwaukee, WI 53226
Dedicated to reducing firearm injuries and deaths by providing "comprehensive, objective, accurate information and analysis of firearms and related morbidity and mortality." Operates the innovative

Violent Injury Reporting System of Wisconsin (VIRS).

Firearms Coalition
URL: http://www.nealknox.com
E-mail: webmaster@
  firearmscoalition.org
Neal Knox Association
P.O. Box 3313
Manassas, VA 20109
A hard-core pro-gun group founded by Neal Knox that reports on legislation in Congress and other gun-related news.

Gun Control Australia (GCA)
URL: http://www.guncontrol.
  org.au
E-mail: pres@guncontrol.org.au
Phone: (+ 03) 5344 9192
Gun Control Australia Inc.
GPO Box 4075
Melbourne VIC 3001
AUSTRALIA
An Australian organization "committed to raising awareness about the gun problem, the gun lobby and issues associated with gun control in Australia."

Gun Control Network
URL: http://www.gun-control-
  network.org
E-mail: contact@gun-control-
  network.org
P.O. Box 11495
London N3 2FE
UNITED KINGDOM
British organization promoting gun control, founded in the aftermath of the Dunblane, Scotland, shootings. The network seeks to change British laws to ban those types of handguns that remain legal to own.

Gun Owners of America (GOA)
URL: http://www.gunowners.
  org
E-mail: goamail@gunowners.org
Phone: (703) 321-8585
8001 Forbes Place
Springfield, VA 22151
Smaller than the NRA but more radical in its advocacy of gun rights, it focuses on activism and lobbying.

Guns Save Lives
URL: http://gunssavelives.com
7481 Huntsman Boulevard
Suite 525
Springfield, VA 22153
Militantly opposes gun control; supports self-defense and the right to carry concealed weapons; provides research, on issues and firearms training.

**The Handgun Epidemic
  Lowering Plan (HELP)**
URL: http://www.helpnetwork.
  org
Phone: (773) 880-3826
Children's Memorial Hospital
2300 Children's Plaza, #88
Chicago, IL 60614-3394
Medically oriented organization that seeks to educate and to strengthen gun control to reduce gun violence. Their web site provides news summaries, policy statements, and help for survivors of shootings.

Handgun-Free America
URL: http://www.handgunfree.
  org
E-mail: info@handgunfree.org
Phone: (703) 465-0474
1600 Wilson Boulevard
Suite 800
Arlington, VA 22209
Works to ban handguns, seeing a ban as the only real solution to the problem of handgun violence. The web site includes extensive news and resource links.

**International Shooting Sport
  Federation (ISSF)**
URL: http://www.issf-
  shooting.org
E-mail: munich@issf-
  shooting.org
Phone: 49-89-5443550
Bavariaring 21, D-80336
München
GERMANY
International organization and governing body for shooting sports.

**Jews for the Preservation of
  Firearms Ownership (JPFO)**
URL: http://www.jpfo.org/
E-mail: webmaster@jpfo.org
Phone: (202) 673-9745
P.O. Box 270143
Hartford, WI 53027
A radical group that sees firearms ownership as bound together with the historical and moral imperatives of Judaism and necessary if future Holocausts are to be prevented. The group often attacks what it considers to be the liberal Jewish establishment's advocacy of gun control.

Join Together
URL: http://www.jointogether.
  org
E-mail: info@jointogether.org
Phone: (617) 437-1500
1 Appleton Street, Fourth Floor
Boston, MA 02116-5223
Education and advocacy group focusing on issues of gun violence and substance abuse. It is a project of the Boston University School of Public Health.

Justice for Shooters (JFS)
URL: http://home.rednet.co.uk/
  homepages/markg/index.html
E-mail: JFS@online.rednet.co.uk
Phone: (01753) 738314
P.O. Box 705
Bourne End
Buckinghamshire SL8 5FS
UNITED KINGDOM
British rights organization.

**Law Enforcement Alliance of
  America (LEAA)**
URL: http://www.leaa.org
E-mail: membership@leaa.org
Phone: (703) 847-2677
7700 Leesburg Pike
Suite 421
Falls Church, VA 22043
An organization that seeks to bring law enforcement officers and citizens together to fight crime. The organization seeks stricter penalties for criminals and promotes victim's rights; it opposes gun control as not being effective crime control.

Legal Community Against Violence (LCAV)
URL: http://www.lcav.org
268 Bush Street
Suite 555
San Francisco, CA 94121
Organization founded after mass shootings in a San Francisco office building in 1993. The group works to strengthen local gun control laws as well as to defend gun control at the state and federal level. The group also maintains the Firearms Law Center web site.

National Center for Injury Prevention/Control
Centers for Disease Control and Prevention
URL: http://www.cdc.gov/ncipc/ncipchm.htm
Phone: (770) 488-1506
Mailstop K65
4770 Buford Highway NE
Atlanta, GA 30341-3724
Division of the Centers for Disease Control that deals with injury prevention, including gun-related injuries. This center has undertaken a considerable amount of research that appears in medical literature.

National Concealed Carry, Inc.
URL: http://www.concealcarry.org
Phone: (630) 660-3935
P.O. Box 4597
Oak Brook, IL 60523
A militant conservative group working to secure the right to carry a concealed weapon in all 50 states.

National Firearms Association (NFA)
URL: http://www.nfa.ca
E-mail: NFAinfo@nfa.ca
Phone: (780) 439-1394
Box 52183
Edmonton
Alberta T6G 2TS
CANADA
Canada's largest gun rights group, the rough equivalent of the U.S. National Rifle Association. The group currently is fighting against gun registration laws.

National Institute of Justice (NIJ)
URL: http://www.ojp.usdoj.gov/nij
E-mail: askncjrs@ncjrs.org
Phone: (202) 307-2942
810 Seventh Street, NW
Washington, DC 20531
The research arm of the U.S. Department of Justice, the NIJ provides invaluable resources on all aspects of criminology and criminal justice, including the National Criminal Justice Reference Service (NCJRS), an online source of summaries, abstracts, and full text documents on numerous subjects, including gun violence.

National Rifle Association (NRA)
URL: http://www.nra.org
Phone: (703) 267-1000
11250 Waples Mill Road
Fairfax, VA 22030
The United States's largest and most effective gun rights group—

what people usually mean when they refer to "the gun lobby." Its political arm is the Institute for Legislative Action (ILA). The NRA has about 4 million members.

National Shooting Sports Foundation (NSSF)
URL: http://www.nssf.org
E-mail: info@nssf.org
Phone: (203) 426-1320
11 Mile Hill Road
Newtown, CT 06470-2359
A large trade organization representing gun manufacturers, distributors, and dealers. The organization promotes hunting, recreational shooting, and gun safety and, as of 1999, was emphasizing greater participation of women in shooting sports.

Pacific Center for Violence Prevention
URL: http://www.pcvp.org
E-mail: tf@tf.org
Phone: (415) 821-8209
San Francisco General Hospital
1001 Potrero Avenue
San Francisco, CA 94110
Addresses prevention of violence; has a section on firearm violence. Its web site presents statistics, fact sheets, and other resources. It is a project of the Trauma Foundation.

Physicians for Social Responsibility (PSR)
URL: http://www.psr.org
Phone: (202) 667-4260
1875 Connecticut Avenue, NW
Suite 1012
Washington, DC 20009

Organization of medical professionals involved in social issues. The group has a section on Violence Prevention that emphasizes gun control issues.

Second Amendment Foundation (SAF)
URL: http://www.saf.org
E-mail: www@saf.org
Phone: (800) 426-4302
James Madison Building
12500 NE Tenth Place
Bellevue, WA 98005
Educational and advocacy organization focusing on the Second Amendment, considered as an individual right to keep and bear arms.

Sporting Shooters Association of Australia (SSAA)
URL: http://www.ssaa.org.au
Phone: 08 9277 6436
P.O. Box 762 Kent Town
South Australia 5071
AUSTRALIA
Australian shooting and gun-rights organization.

Student Pledge Against Gun Violence
URL: http://www.pledge.org
Phone: (507) 645-5378
112 Nevada Street
Northfield, MN 55057
Seeks pledges (commitments) from young people not to bring guns to school and to work to persuade fellow students to avoid guns.

Violence Policy Center (VPC)
URL: http://www.vpc.org
E-mail: info@vpc.org
1140 19th Street, NW
Suite 600
Washington, DC 20036
A "gun control think tank," research education, and advocacy group.

Violence Prevention Research Program (VPRP)
URL: http://www.ucdmc.ucdavis.edu/vprp/
Phone: (916) 734-3539
Western Fairs Building
University of California, Davis
2315 Stockton Boulevard
Sacramento, CA 95817
Researches violence prevention with an emphasis on gun-related violence and the effectiveness of gun laws and policies (such as gun purchase waiting periods).

Women Against Gun Control (WAGC)
URL: http://www.wagc.com
E-mail: info@wagc.com
Phone: (801) 328-9660
P.O. Box 95357
South Jordan, UT 84095
Advocates gun ownership from a woman's point of view.

World Forum on the Future of Sport Shooting Activities (WFSA)
URL: http://www.wfsa.net
Phone: +39 06 5903510
WFSA c/o ANPAM
Viale dell'Astronomia 30
1-00144 Roma
ITALY
An international educational and advocacy group promoting sport shooting. Focuses on combating international gun control efforts in the United Nations.

PART III

APPENDICES

APPENDIX A

STATISTICS AND TRENDS
RELATING TO GUN CONTROL

The following graphs and charts provide background on gun-related crime, types of firearms deaths, and young people as firearms victims. There is also information about gun ownership and public support for various gun control or safety measures.

VIOLENT CRIME TRENDS

The graph "Violent Crime Trends, 1973–2002" provides a measure of trends in violent crime as a whole without regard to weapon (if any) used. In general there is a peak about 1980 and a similar peak about 1993. Since then crime rates have declined substantially, although recorded crimes and arrest rates may be leveling off.

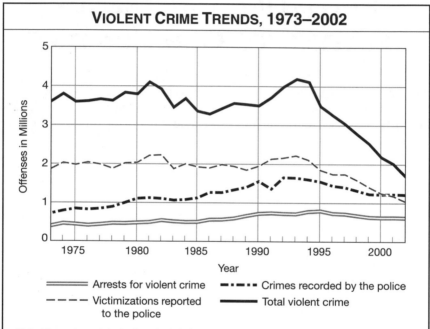

VIOLENT CRIME TRENDS, 1973–2002

Legend:
- ════ Arrests for violent crime
- ▬·▬·· Crimes recorded by the police
- ─ ─ ─ Victimizations reported to the police
- ▬▬▬ Total violent crime

Note: The serious violent crimes included are rape, robbery, aggravated assault, and homicide. Because of changes made to the victimization survey, data prior to 1992 are adjusted to make them comparable to data collected under the redesigned methodology. Estimates for 1993 and beyond are based on collection year while earlier estimates are based on data year.

Source: U.S. Dept. of Justice, Bureau of Labor Statistics, National Crime Victimization Survey, 2002, available online at URL: http://www.ojp.usdoj.gov/bjs/glance/cv2.htm.

Appendix A

CRIME INVOLVING FIREARMS

The graph "Crimes Committed with Firearms, 1973–2002" looks at crimes involving a firearm (which does not necessarily mean the gun was used). Although the shape of the trend is similar to that shown in the preceding graph, the peak around 1993 is about a third higher than the earlier peak around 1980. The rate of gun crimes seems to have roughly leveled off in the last few years.

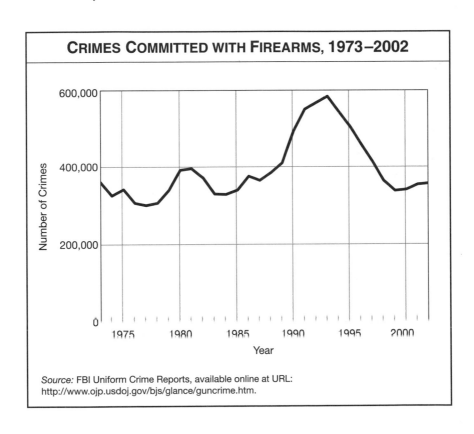

CRIMES COMMITTED WITH FIREARMS, 1973–2002

Source: FBI Uniform Crime Reports, available online at URL:
http://www.ojp.usdoj.gov/bjs/glance/guncrime.htm.

VIOLENCE BY TYPE OF WEAPON

Although gun crimes have a higher potential for serious injury or death than other types of violent crimes, the graph "Violence by Type of Weapon, 1993–2001" shows that violent crimes involving weapons (and firearms in particular) are a relatively small portion of violent crime as a whole. The rate of firearm violence also seems steadier, perhaps reflecting a relatively "hard core" of criminals who decide to regularly use guns.

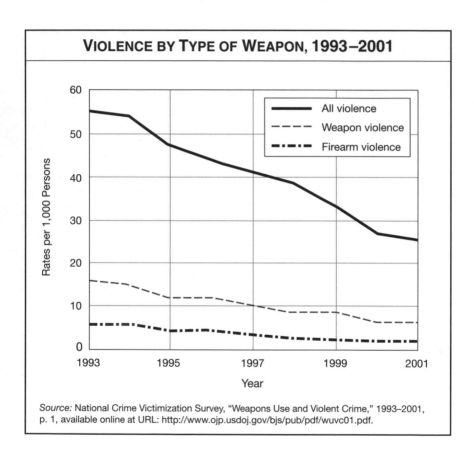

VIOLENCE BY TYPE OF WEAPON, 1993–2001

Source: National Crime Victimization Survey, "Weapons Use and Violent Crime," 1993–2001, p. 1, available online at URL: http://www.ojp.usdoj.gov/bjs/pub/pdf/wuvc01.pdf.

Appendix A

HOMICIDE BY WEAPON TYPE

If a criminal decides to use a weapon with fatal results, the graph "Homicide by Weapon Type, 1976–2000" clearly shows that the handgun is the weapon of choice. However, there has been a gradual increase in the use of other types of guns (such as shotguns or rifles), which are now used about as frequently as knives.

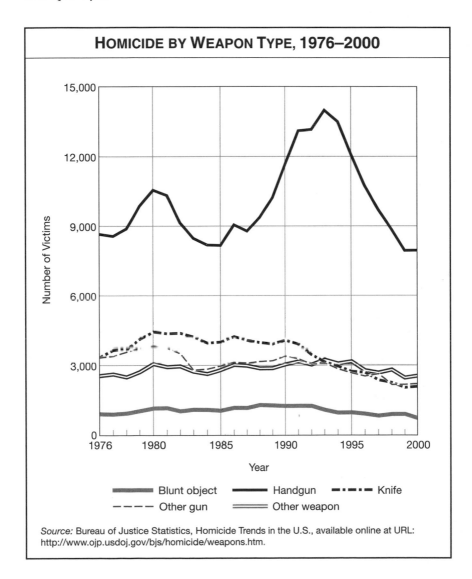

HOMICIDE BY WEAPON TYPE, 1976–2000

Source: Bureau of Justice Statistics, Homicide Trends in the U.S., available online at URL: http://www.ojp.usdoj.gov/bjs/homicide/weapons.htm.

PERCENTAGE OF GUN HOMICIDES BY AGE OF VICTIM

The graph "Percent of Homicides Involving Guns by Age of Victim, 1976–2000" looks at the proportion of homicide victims of each age who were killed using a firearm. The peak appears to be with victims in their late teens, about three-quarters of whom were gun victims. This is followed by a steady decline as victim age increases. One intuitive reason for this peak is that young men in their late teens are more likely than older men to be involved in violent armed gangs and, in turn, to become victims of gun violence themselves.

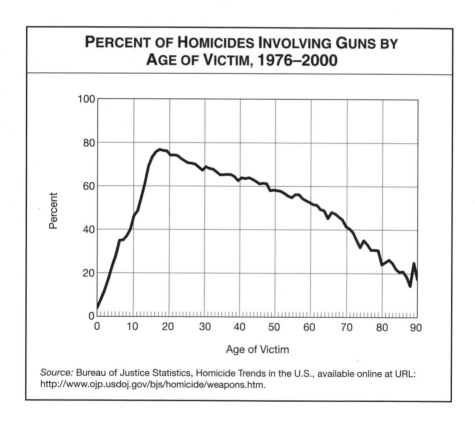

PERCENT OF HOMICIDES INVOLVING GUNS BY AGE OF VICTIM, 1976–2000

Source: Bureau of Justice Statistics, Homicide Trends in the U.S., available online at URL: http://www.ojp.usdoj.gov/bjs/homicide/weapons.htm.

Appendix A

FIREARM VIOLENCE BY AGE OF VICTIM

Another way to look at the effect of gun violence on young people is to consider the graph "Firearm Violence by Age of Victim, 1973–2001." This graph looks at the rate per 1,000 persons in various age groups from 12 to over 65. As in the previous graph we see that the group with the highest victimization rate is late teen/young adult (18–20). While all groups have experienced a general decline in victimization rates since the early to mid 1990s, the two youngest groups (12–14 and 15–17) have experienced the most dramatic declines since 1993: 97 percent and 77 percent respectively.

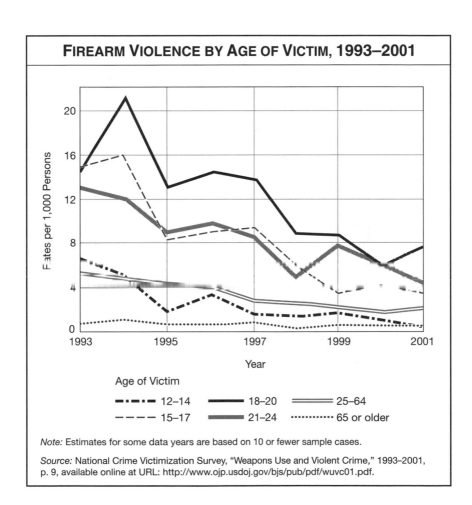

FIREARM VIOLENCE BY AGE OF VICTIM, 1993–2001

Age of Victim

▬·▬·▬ 12–14   ▬▬▬ 18–20   ══════ 25–64

▬ ▬ ▬ 15–17   ▰▰▰ 21–24   ·············· 65 or older

Note: Estimates for some data years are based on 10 or fewer sample cases.

Source: National Crime Victimization Survey, "Weapons Use and Violent Crime," 1993–2001, p. 9, available online at URL: http://www.ojp.usdoj.gov/bjs/pub/pdf/wuvc01.pdf.

FIREARMS AND OTHER CAUSES OF ACCIDENTS

The graph "Firearms Compared to Other Forms of Accidental Death" provides an important perspective. Firearms are only the ninth leading cause of accidental deaths. By far the largest cause are motor vehicle accidents, followed by poisoning, falls, and deaths that do not fit into one of the other categories. In 2000, there were 44,000 people killed in motor vehicle accidents, but only 800 in firearms accidents. Gun rights advocates often say that this fact shows that the gun control forces are exaggerating the risk of firearms accidents in order to promote gun control. Gun control advocates, on the other hand, tend to not draw comparisons to other forms of accidental death. Rather, they ask whether any value in having guns outweighs hundreds of gun accident deaths a year.

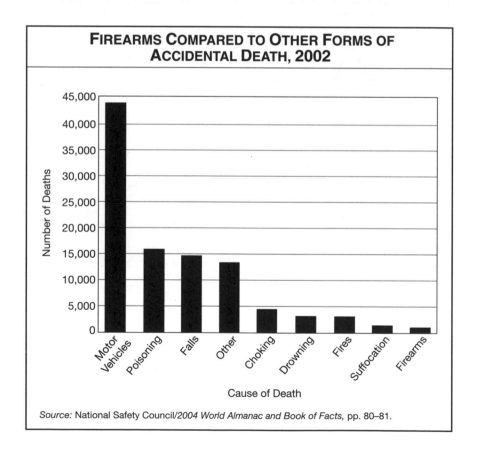

FIREARMS COMPARED TO OTHER FORMS OF ACCIDENTAL DEATH, 2002

Source: National Safety Council/*2004 World Almanac and Book of Facts,* pp. 80–81.

Appendix A

TRENDS IN ACCIDENTAL FIREARMS DEATHS

Looking just at accidental deaths from firearms, one can see a steep decrease from about 1970 to 1990, then a leveling, followed by a more gradual decrease in the late 1990s. Depending on where one stands, this decline can either be attributed to increased adoption of gun safety laws or used as an argument that more such laws are unnecessary.

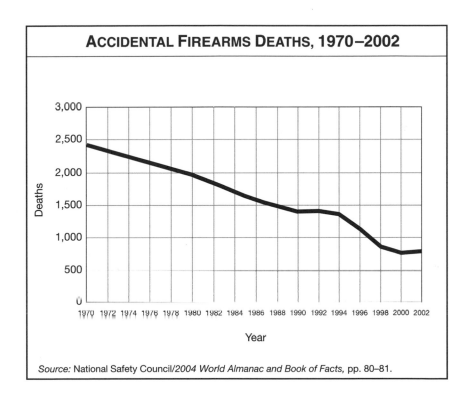

ACCIDENTAL FIREARMS DEATHS, 1970–2002

Source: National Safety Council/*2004 World Almanac and Book of Facts*, pp. 80–81.

FIREARMS DEATHS IN YOUNG PEOPLE

When considering policy initiatives for reducing firearms deaths among young people it is important to know the relative frequency of different "intentions" behind the deaths at different ages. First, it should be noted that the two youngest groups (0–4 and 5–9) have very low numbers of firearms deaths of any type. Gun rights advocates often criticize the lumping of all ages up to 19 (or even 24) under the term *children*. In the early teens (10–14), gun homicides outnumber suicides by about 25 percent, but all numbers are still very low, considering the total population of children. In the late teens (15–19), the numbers go up about tenfold, and homicides are roughly double the number of suicides. Again, gun accidents are actually relatively infrequent.

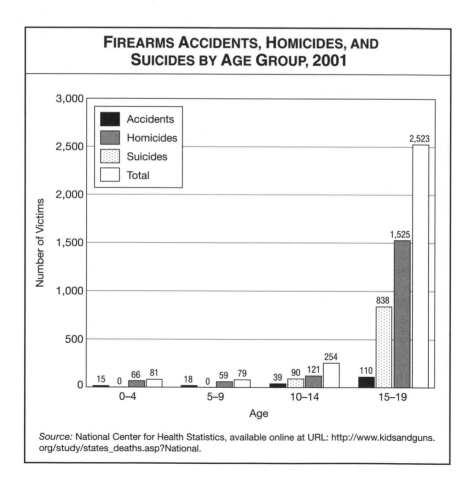

FIREARMS ACCIDENTS, HOMICIDES, AND SUICIDES BY AGE GROUP, 2001

Source: National Center for Health Statistics, available online at URL: http://www.kidsandguns. org/study/states_deaths.asp?National.

FIREARM DEATHS
OF YOUNG PEOPLE—
INTERNATIONAL PERSPECTIVE

The graph "Types of Firearm Deaths in Children, Top Ten Countries" offers a chance to compare both the absolute numbers of firearm deaths of children among different countries and to compare the relative proportions of the different types of deaths (homicides, suicides, and accidents). First, as is generally expected, the rate of firearm deaths of children per 100,000 in the United States is about three times that of the nearest "competitor," Finland. The proportions of homicides, suicides, and accidents vary considerably: In the United States, gun homicides of children outpace suicides roughly three to one, but in Norway suicides seem to dominate by about two to one. (It should be noted that because numbers of gun deaths for children are relatively low, there may be considerable variation in relative proportions from year to year.)

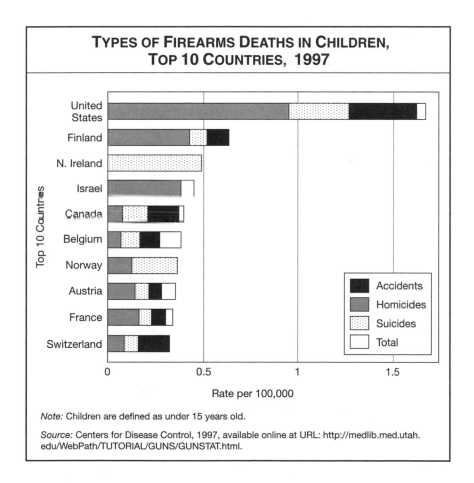

TYPES OF FIREARMS DEATHS IN CHILDREN, TOP 10 COUNTRIES, 1997

Note: Children are defined as under 15 years old.

Source: Centers for Disease Control, 1997, available online at URL: http://medlib.med.utah. edu/WebPath/TUTORIAL/GUNS/GUNSTAT.html.

GUN OWNERSHIP TRENDS

Gun violence can also be viewed in the overall context of gun ownership. The graph "Trends in Household and Adult Firearms Ownership, 1973–2001" shows that since 1980 both the percentage of households with at least one gun and the overall percentage of adults owning at least one gun have declined. The household decline (by roughly a third) is probably the more significant one in terms of gun safety issues, since a house without a gun is unlikely to have a gun safety problem (although it would also be unable to use a gun for defensive purposes). The relatively shallow decline in the percentage of adults with guns might be related to changes in the average size or composition of households.

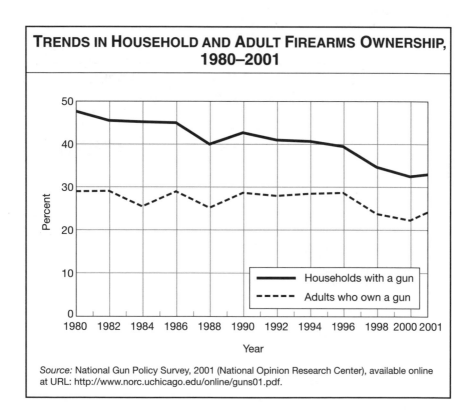

TRENDS IN HOUSEHOLD AND ADULT FIREARMS OWNERSHIP, 1980–2001

Source: National Gun Policy Survey, 2001 (National Opinion Research Center), available online at URL: http://www.norc.uchicago.edu/online/guns01.pdf.

Appendix A

SUPPORT FOR GUN CONTROL AND GUN SAFETY MEASURES

Overall support of gun control is high and remains quite steady. In the chart "Support for Gun Control and Gun Safety Measures, 2001," one can see high support for many existing or proposed gun control measures. Required safety courses and background checks tend to be accepted by many gun rights advocates as well. However, support for such measures as handgun registration and handgun purchase limits remains high but would provoke considerable opposition from a minority. The "concealed carry" item reflects the rough split among the public over whether allowing people to carry concealed handguns would make the community more or less safe. Finally, the one measure that regularly polls only a small minority of support is a total ban on handguns.

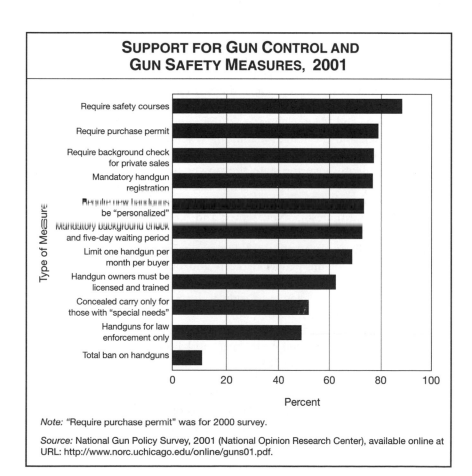

APPENDIX B

FEDERAL AND STATE CONSTITUTIONAL PROVISIONS

Much of the legal debate over gun control measures involves their constitutionality. The federal constitution and many state constitutions contain guarantees of the right to keep and bear arms. When a state gun control law is challenged, it is the state constitution that comes into play because the Second Amendment of the federal constitution has not been applied to the states.

The language of many of the state provisions (such as those of Alaska and Hawaii) matches or resembles that of the Second Amendment, referring to the right to bear arms in the context of the militia. Other state provisions (such as Illinois and Kentucky) refer to the right to bear arms for the defense of oneself and the state, for hunting (Nebraska and Nevada, for example), or for other purposes. A number of state provisions (such as that of Louisiana) explicitly give the state the power to regulate the carrying of concealed weapons. Note that the following states do not have constitutional provisions relating to the right to keep and bear arms: California, Iowa, Maryland, Minnesota, New Jersey, and New York.

Federal: "A well-regulated militia, being necessary to the security of a free State, the right of the people to keep and bear arms, shall not be infringed." (Second Amendment)

Alabama: "That every citizen has a right to bear arms in defense of himself and the state." (Article I, Section 26)

Alaska: "A well-regulated militia being necessary to the security of a free state, the right of the people to keep and bear arms shall not be infringed." (Article I, Section 19)

Arizona: "The right of the individual citizen to bear arms in defense of himself or the State shall not be impaired, but nothing in this Section shall be construed as authorizing individuals or corporations to organize, maintain, or employ an armed body of men." (Article II, Section 26)

Arkansas: "The citizens of this State shall have the right to keep and bear arms for their common defense." (Article II, Section 5)

Colorado: "The right of no person to keep and bear arms in defense of his home, person and property, or in aid of the civil power when thereto legally summoned, shall be called in question; but nothing herein contained shall be construed to justify the practice of carrying concealed weapons." (Article II, Section 13)

Connecticut: "Every citizen has a right to bear arms in defense of himself and the state." (Article 1, Section 15)

Delaware: "A person has the right to keep and bear arms for the defense of self, family, home and State, and for hunting and recreational use."(Article I, Section 20)

Florida: "The right of the people to keep and bear arms in defense of themselves and of the lawful authority of the state shall not be infringed, except that the manner of bearing arms may be regulated by law." (Article I, Section 8)

Georgia: "The right of the people to keep and bear arms shall not be infringed, but the General Assembly shall have the power to prescribe the manner in which arms may be borne." (Article I, Section I, par. VIII)

Hawaii: "A well regulated militia being necessary to the security of a free state, the right of the people to keep and bear arms shall not be infringed." (Article I, Section 15)

Idaho: "The people have the right to keep and bear arms, which right shall not be abridged; but this provision shall not prevent the passage of laws to govern the carrying of weapons concealed on the person, nor prevent passage of legislation providing minimum sentences for crimes committed while in possession of a firearm, nor prevent passage of legislation providing penalties for the possession of firearms by a convicted felon, nor prevent the passage of legislation punishing the use of a firearm. No law shall impose licensure, registration or special taxation on the ownership or possession of firearms or ammunition. Nor shall any law permit the confiscation of firearms, except those actually used in the commission of a felony." (Article I, Section 11)

Illinois: "Subject only to the police power, the right of the individual citizen to keep and bear arms shall not be infringed." (Article 1, Section 22)

Indiana: "The people shall have a right to bear arms, for the defense of themselves and the State." (Article I, Section 32)

Kansas: "The people have the right to bear arms for their defense and security; but standing armies, in time of peace, are dangerous to liberty, and shall not be tolerated, and the military shall be in strict subordination to the civil power." (Bill of Rights, Section 4)

Kentucky: "All men are, by nature, free and equal, and have certain inherent and inalienable rights, among which may be reckoned: . . . Seventh: The right to bear arms in defense of themselves and of the state, subject to the power of the general assembly to enact laws to prevent persons from carrying concealed weapons." (Bill of Rights, Section I, par. 7)

Louisiana: "The right of each citizen to keep and bear arms shall not be abridged, but this provision shall not prevent the passage of laws to prohibit the carrying of weapons concealed on the person." (Article I, Section 11)

Maine: "Every citizen has a right to keep and bear arms and this right shall never be questioned." (Article I, Section 16)

Massachusetts: "The people have a right to keep and bear arms for the common defence [sic]. And as, in time of peace, armies are dangerous to liberty, they ought not to be maintained without the consent of the legislature; and the military power shall always be held in an exact subordination to the civil authority, and be governed by it." (Declaration of Rights, Part I, Article XVII)

Michigan: "Every person has a right to keep and bear arms for the defense of himself and the state." (Article I, Section 6)

Mississippi: "The right of every citizen to keep and bear arms in defense of his home, person, or property, or in aid of the civil power when thereto legally summoned, shall not be called in question, but the legislature may regulate or forbid carrying concealed weapons." (Article 3, Section 12)

Missouri: "That the right of every citizen to keep and bear arms in defense of his home, person and property, or when lawfully summoned in aid of the civil power, shall not be questioned; but this shall not justify the wearing of concealed weapons." (Article I, Section 23)

Montana: "The right of any person to keep or bear arms in defense of his own home, person, and property, or in aid of the civil power when thereto legally summoned, shall not be called in question, but nothing herein contained shall be held to permit the carrying of concealed weapons." (Article II, Section 12)

Nebraska: "All persons are by nature free and independent, and have certain inherent and inalienable rights; among these are . . . the right to keep and bear arms for security or defense of self, family, home, and others, and for lawful common defense, hunting, recreational use, and all other lawful purposes, and such rights shall not be denied or infringed by the state or any subdivision thereof." (Article I, Section 1)

Nevada: "Every citizen has the right to keep and bear arms for security and defense, for lawful hunting and recreational use and for other lawful purposes." (Article I, Section II, Paragraph 1)

New Hampshire: "All persons have the right to keep and bear arms in defense of themselves, their families, their property, and the state." (Part 1, Article IIa)

New Mexico: "No law shall abridge the right of the citizen to keep and bear arms for security and defense, for lawful hunting and recreational use and for other lawful purposes, but nothing herein shall be held to permit the carrying of concealed weapons. No municipality or county shall regulate, in any way, an incident of the right to keep and bear arms." (Article II, Section 6)

North Carolina: "A well regulated militia being necessary to the security of a free State, the right of the people to keep and bear arms shall not be infringed; and, as standing armies in time of peace are dangerous to liberty, they shall not be maintained, and the military shall be kept under strict subordination to, and governed by, the civil power. Nothing herein shall justify the practice of carrying concealed weapons, or prevent the General Assembly from enacting penal statutes against that practice." (Article I, Section 30)

North Dakota: "All individuals are by nature equally free and independent and have certain inalienable rights, among which are . . . to keep and bear arms for the defense of their person, family, property, and the state, and for lawful hunting, recreational, and other lawful purposes, which shall not be infringed." (Article I, Section 1)

Ohio: "The people have the right to bear arms for their defense and security; but standing armies, in time of peace, are dangerous to liberty, and shall not be kept up; and the military shall be in strict subordination to the civil power" (Article I, Section 4)

Oklahoma: "The right of a citizen to keep and bear arms in defense of his home, person, or property, or in aid of the civil power, when thereunto legally summoned, shall never be prohibited; but nothing herein contained shall prevent the Legislature from regulating the carrying of weapons." (Article II, Section 26)

Oregon: "The people shall have the right to bear arms for the defence [sic] of themselves, and the State, but the Military shall be kept in strict subordination to the civil power." (Article I, Section 27)

Pennsylvania: "The right of the citizens to bear arms in defence [sic] of themselves and the State shall not be questioned." (Article I, Section 21)

Rhode Island: "The right of the people to keep and bear arms shall not be infringed." (Article I, Section 22)

South Carolina: "A well regulated militia being necessary to the security of a free State, the right of the people to keep and bear arms shall not be infringed. As, in times of peace, armies are dangerous to liberty, they shall not be maintained without the consent of the General Assembly. The military power of the State shall always be held in subordination to the civil authority and be governed by it. No soldier shall in time of peace be quartered in any house without the consent of the owner nor in time of war but in the manner prescribed by law." (Article I, Section 20)

South Dakota: "The right of the citizens to bear arms in defense of themselves and the state shall not be denied." (Article VI, Section 24)

Tennessee: "That the citizens of this State have a right to keep and to bear arms for their common defense; but the Legislature shall have power, by law, to regulate the wearing of arms with a view to prevent crime." (Article I, Section 26)

Texas: "Every citizen shall have the right to keep and bear arms in lawful defense of himself or the State; but the Legislature shall have power, by law, to regulate the wearing of arms, with a view to prevent crime." (Article I, Section 23)

Utah: "The individual right of the people to keep and bear arms for security and defense of self, family, others, property, or the State, as well as for the other lawful purposes shall not be infringed; but nothing herein shall prevent the legislature from defining the lawful use of arms." (Article I, Section 6)

Vermont: "That the people have a right to bear arms for the defence [sic] of themselves and the State—and as standing armies in time of peace are dangerous to liberty, they ought not to be kept up; and that the military should be kept under strict subordination to and governed by the civil power." (Chapter I, Article XVI)

Virginia: "That a well regulated militia, composed of the body of the people, trained to arms, is the proper, natural, and safe defense of a free state, therefore, the right of the people to keep and bear arms shall not be infringed; that standing armies, in time of peace, should be avoided as dangerous to liberty; and that in all cases the military should be under strict subordination to, and governed by, the civil power." (Article I, Section 13)

Washington: "The right of the individual citizen to bear arms in defense of himself, or the state, shall not be impaired, but nothing in this Section shall be construed as authorizing individuals or corporations to organize, maintain, or employ an armed body of men." (Article I, Section 24)

West Virginia: "A person has the right to keep and bear arms for the defense of self, family, home and state, and for lawful hunting and recreational use." (Article 3, Section 22)

Wisconsin: "The people have the right to keep and bear arms for security, defense, hunting, recreation, or any other lawful purpose." (Article I, Section 25)

Wyoming: "The right of citizens to bear arms in defense of themselves and of the state shall not be denied." (Article I, Section 24)

APPENDIX C

PROVISIONS OF STATE FIREARMS LAWS

The following two charts summarize key provisions of state firearms laws as of early 2004.

The first chart deals with provisions of regulations of gun purchases and includes bans on certain types of firearms, the status of the NICS (National Instant Check System for gun purchasers), waiting periods for handguns and long guns, requirements for a license or permit to purchase handguns or long guns, and the existence of a registration system for handguns or long guns.

The second chart deals with laws concerning the carrying of concealed firearms, including whether carrying is presumptively permitted ("shall issue"), presumptively prohibited ("may issue"), or prohibited outright.

There are several things to keep in mind while looking at these summary charts:

- Many states pass new firearms laws (or modify existing ones) each year.

- Many municipalities or counties have additional gun restrictions, such as bans on the purchase of handguns or the concealed carrying of firearms.

- There are also many federal laws and regulations that affect gun purchase, ownership, or use.

- Stricter federal laws may preempt more lax state laws, but the existence of federal regulation does not generally preclude enacting stricter state regulations.

- Some state firearms laws may preempt localities from legislating on the same topic, but this varies by state and is often the subject of litigation.

Because of these considerations, it is best to view the charts as a "snapshot" of the status of state gun control laws in 2004 rather than as a definitive reference.

Individuals who are directly affected by gun laws (such as gun owners, dealers, or manufacturers) should recheck the web site at http://www. nraila.org/media/misc/compendium.htm and check with the appropriate state agency for up-to-date information.

Key to the following charts:

1. In certain cities or counties.
2. **National Instant Check System (NICS) exemption codes:**

   RTC: Carry permit holders who are exempt from NICS.
   GRTC: Holders of RTC permits issued before November 30, 1998, are exempt from NICS. Holders of more recent permits are not exempt.
   L: Holders of state license to possess or purchase or firearms ID cards and who are exempt from NICS.
   O: Other, See Note 3.

3. **NICS exemption notes: Arkansas:** RTC permits issued prior to November 30, 1998, and those issued on and after April 1, 1999, qualify. Those issued between November 1, 1998, and March 31, 1999 do not qualify. **Indiana:** Personal protection, hunting, and target permits all qualify for exemptions. **Kentucky:** RTC permits issued after July 15, 1998, and prior to November 30, 1998, are exempt. **Maryland:** There are no exemptions for handgun purchases. For long gun purchases, those holding RTC permits issued before November 30, 1998, are exempt. **Michigan:** No exemptions for handguns; license for long guns. **Mississippi:** Permits issued to security guards do not qualify. **Texas:** Texas Peace Officer License, TCLEOSE Card, is valid only if issued prior to November 30, 1998. **Washington:** RTC permits issued after July 1, 1996, and prior to November 30, 1998, are exempt.
4. Chicago only. No handgun not already registered may be possessed.
5. **Arkansas** prohibits carrying a firearm "with a purpose to employ it as a weapon against a person." **Tennessee** prohibits carrying "with the intent to go armed." **Vermont** prohibits carrying a firearm "with the intent or purpose of injuring another."
6. Loaded.
7. New York City only.
8. A permit is required to acquire another handgun before 30 days have elapsed following the acquisition of a handgun.
9. **Maryland** subjects purchases of "assault weapons" to a seven-day waiting period.

10. May be extended by police to 30 days in some circumstances. An individual not holding a driver's license must wait 90 days.
11. Carrying a handgun openly in a motor vehicle requires a license.
12. Every person arriving in **Hawaii** is required to register any firearm(s) brought into the state within three days of arrival of the person or firearm(s), whichever occurs later. Handguns purchased from licensed dealers must be registered within five days.
13. Concealed-carry laws vary significantly between the states. Ratings reflect the real effect a state's particular laws have on the ability of citizens to carry firearms for self-defense.
14. Purchases from licensed dealers only.
15. The waiting period does not apply to a person holding a valid permit or license to carry a firearm. In **Connecticut,** a hunting license also exempts the holder for long gun purchases. In **California,** transfers of a long gun to a person's parent, child, or grandparent are exempt from the waiting period.
16. **Connecticut:** A Permit to purchase or a carry permit is required to obtain a handgun, and a carry permit is required to transport a handgun outside your home. **District of Columbia:** No handgun may be possessed unless it was registered prior to September 23, 1976, and reregistered by February 5, 1977. A permit to purchase is required for a rifle or shotgun. **Hawaii:** Purchase permits, required for all firearms, may not be issued until 14 days after application. A handgun purchase permit is valid for 10 days for one handgun; a long-gun permit is valid for one year, for multiple long guns. **Illinois:** A Firearm Owner's Identification Card (FOI) is required to possess or purchase a firearm, must be issued to qualified applicants within 30 days, and is valid for 5 years. **Iowa:** A purchase permit is required for handguns and is valid for one year, beginning three days after issuance. **Massachusetts:** Firearms and feeding devices for firearms are divided into classes. Depending on the class, a firearm identification card (FID) or class A license or class B license is required to possess, purchase, or carry a firearm, ammunition thereof, or firearm feeding device, or "large capacity feeding device." **Michigan:** A handgun purchaser must obtain a license to purchase from local law enforcement, and within 10 days present the license and handgun to obtain a certificate of inspection. **Minnesota:** A handgun transfer or carrying permit or a seven-day waiting period and handgun transfer report is required to purchase handguns or "assault weapons" from a dealer. A permit or transfer report must be issued to qualified applicants within seven days. A permit is valid for one year; a transfer report for 30 days. **Missouri:** A purchase permit is required for a

handgun, must be issued to qualified applicants within seven days, and is valid for 30 days. **New Jersey:** Firearm owners must possess an FID, which must be issued to qualified applicants within 30 days. To purchase a handgun, an FID and a purchase permit, which must be issued within 30 days to qualified applicants and is valid for 90 days, are required. An FID is required to purchase long guns. **New York:** The purchase, the possession, and/or the carrying of a handgun requires a single license, which includes any restrictions made upon the bearer. New York City also requires a license for long guns. **North Carolina:** To purchase a handgun, a license or permit is required, which must be issued to qualified applicants within 30 days. **Ohio:** Some cities require a permit-to-purchase or firearm owner ID card.

17. Preemption through judicial ruling. Local regulation may be instituted in **Massachusetts** if ratified by the legislature.
18. Except Gary and East Chicago and local laws enacted before January 1994.
19. **Vermont** and **Alaska** laws respect your right to carry without a permit. Alaska also has a permit to carry system to establish reciprocity with other states.
20. "Assault weapons" are prohibited in **California, Connecticut, New Jersey,** and **New York.** Some local jurisdictions in **Ohio** also ban "assault weapons." **Hawaii** prohibits "assault pistols." **California** bans "unsafe handguns." **Illinois:** Chicago, Evanston, Oak Park, Morton Grove, Winnetka, Wilmette, and Highland Park prohibit handguns; some cities prohibit other kinds of firearms. **Maryland** prohibits several small, low-caliber, inexpensive handguns and "assault pistols." **Massachusetts:** It is unlawful to sell, transfer, or possess "any assault weapon or large capacity feeding device" [more than 10 rounds] that was not legally possessed on September 13, 1994. **Ohio:** Some cities prohibit handguns of certain magazine capacities. **Virginia** prohibits "street sweeper" shotguns. The **District of Columbia** prohibits new acquisition of handguns and any semiautomatic firearm capable of using a detachable ammunition magazine of more than 12 rounds capacity. (With respect to some of these laws and ordinances, individuals may retain prohibited firearms owned previously, with certain restrictions.)
21. Local jurisdictions may opt out of prohibition.
22. Preemption only applies to handguns.
23. Requires proof of safety training for purchase. **California:** Must have Handgun Safety Certificate receipt which is valid for five years. **Connecticut:** To receive certificate of eligibility, must complete a

handgun safety course approved by the Commissioner of Public Safety. **Hawaii:** Must have completed an approved handgun safety course. **Maryland:** Must complete an approved handgun safety course. **Michigan:** A person must correctly answer 70 percent of the questions on a basic safety review questionnaire in order to obtain a license to purchase. **New York:** Some counties require a handgun safety training course to receive a license. **Rhode Island:** Must receive a state-issued handgun safety card.

24. "Assault weapon" registration needed **California** had two dates by which assault weapons had to be registered or possession after such date would be considered a felony: March 31, 1992, for the named make and model firearms banned in the 1989 legislation, and December 31, 2000, for the firearms meeting the definition of "assault weapons" in the 1999 legislation. In **Connecticut,** those firearms banned by specific make and model in the 1993 law had to be registered by October 1, 1994, or possession would be considered a felony. A recent law requires registration of additional guns by October 1, 2003. In **New Jersey,** any "assault weapon" not registered, licensed, or rendered inoperable pursuant to a state police certificate by May 1, 1991, is considered contraband.

25. Local governments cannot enact ordinances that prohibit the sale, purchase, or possession of a firearm. Municipalities cannot restrict a person's ability to travel into, through, or within their jurisdiction for hunting or personal protection. Local governments, including law enforcement agencies, cannot maintain a database of guns or gun owners. Municipalities may prohibit open carry in government buildings if such prohibition is clearly posted.

Gun Control

STATE REGULATIONS ON FIREARMS PURCHASES

| State | Gun ban | Exemptions to NICS[2] | State waiting period (number of days) | | License or permit to purchase | | Registration | |
			Hand-guns	Long guns	Hand-guns	Long guns	Hand-guns	Long guns
Ala.	...	...	...	...	...	...	...	...
Alaska	...	RTC	...	...	...	...	...	...
Ariz.	...	RTC	...	...	...	...	...	...
Arkansas	...	RTC3	...	...	...	...	...	...
Calif.	X[20]	...	10[14]	10[14,15]	...	X	24	...
Colo.	...	...	...	...	8,23	...	...	...
Conn.	X[20]	...	14[14,15]	14[14,15]	X[16,23]	...	...	24
Del.	...	...	...	...	...	...	...	...
Fla.	...	GRTC	3[14,15]	...	...	...	...	...
Ga.	...	RTC	...	...	...	...	...	...
Hawaii	X[20]	L,RTC	...	...	X[16,23]	X[16]	X[12]	X[12]
Idaho	...	RTC	...	...	...	...	...	...
Ill.	20	...	3	2	X[16]	X[16]	4	4
Ind.	...	RTC, O3	...	...	...	...	...	...
Iowa	...	L, RTC	...	...	X[16]	...	...	...
Kans.	...	...	1	...	1	...	1	...
Ky.	...	RTC3	...	...	...	...	...	...
La.	...	GRTC	...	...	...	...	...	...
Maine	...	...	...	...	...	...	...	...
Md.	X[20]	O3	7[14]	7[9,14]	8,23	...	...	...
Mass.	X[20]	GRTC	...	...	X[16]	X[16]	...	...
Mich.	...	203	...	...	X[16,23]	...	X	...
Minn.	...	...	7[16]	16	X[16]	X[16]	...	...
Miss.	...	RTC3	...	...	...	...	...	...
Mo.	...	...	...	...	X[16]	...	...	...
Mont.	...	RTC	...	...	...	...	...	...
Neb.	...	L	...	...	X	...	...	...
Nev.	...	RTC	1	...	...	...	1	...
N.H.	...	...	...	...	...	...	...	...

State	Gun ban	Exemptions to NICS[2]	State waiting period (number of days)		License or permit to purchase		Registration	
			Hand-guns	Long guns	Hand-guns	Long guns	Hand-guns	Long guns
N.J.	X[20]	...	...	...	X[16]	X[16]	...	24
N.Mex.	...	...	...	...	...	...	...	...
N.Y.	X[20]	L, RTC	...	...	X[16,23]	16	X	7
N.C.	...	L, RTC	...	...	X[16]	...	...	...
N.Dak.	...	RTC	...	...	...	...	...	...
Ohio	20	...	1	...	16	...	1	...
Okla.	...	...	...	...	...	...	...	...
Oreg.	...	GRTC	...	...	...	...	...	...
Pa.	...	...	...	...	...	...	...	...
R.I.	...	...	...	7	23	...	...	...
S.C.	...	RTC	8	...	8	...	...	...
S.Dak.	...	GRTC	2	...	...	...	...	...
Tenn.	...	...	...	...	...	...	...	...
Tex.	...	RTC[3]	...	...	...	...	...	...
Utah	...	RTC	...	...	...	...	...	...
Vt.	...	...	...	...	...	...	...	...
Va.	X[20]	...	1,8	...	1,8	...	...	...
Wash.	...	O[3]	5[10]	...	...	...	...	...
W.Va.	...	...	...	...	...	...	...	...
Wis.	...	...	2	...	...	...	...	...
Wyo.	...	RTC	...	...	...	...	...	...
D.C.	X[20]	L	...	...	X[16]	X[16]	X[16]	X

Source: National Rifle Association. "Compendium of State Firearms Laws." Available online. Posted on URL: http://www.nraila.org/media/misc/compendium.htm.

Concealed carry codes:

R: Right-to-Carry: "shall issue" or less restrictive discretionary permit system (Ala., Conn.) (See also note #21.)

L: Right-to-Carry Limited by local authority's discretion over permit issuance.

D: Right-to-Carry Denied, no permit system exists; concealed carry is prohibited.

Gun Control

STATE LAWS RELATING TO CARRYING OF FIREARMS

State	Record of sale reported to state or local govt.	State provision for right-to-carry concealed[13]	Carrying openly prohibited	Owner ID cards or licensing	Firearm rights constitutional provision	State firearms preemption laws	Range protection law
Ala.	⋯	R	X[11]	⋯	X	X	X
Alaska	⋯	R[19]	⋯	⋯	X	⋯	X
Ariz.	⋯	R	⋯	⋯	X	X	X
Arkansas	⋯	R	X[5]	⋯	X	X	X
Calif.	X	L	X[6]	⋯	⋯	X	X
Colo.	⋯	R	25	⋯	X	X[25]	X
Conn.	X	R	X	⋯	X	X[17]	X
Del.	⋯	L	⋯	⋯	X	X	⋯
Fla.	⋯	R	X	⋯	X	X	X
Ga.	⋯	R	X	⋯	X	X	X
Hawaii	X	L	X	X	X	⋯	⋯
Idaho	⋯	R	⋯	⋯	X	X	X
Ill.	X	D	X	X	X	⋯	X
Ind.	X	R	X	⋯	X	X[18]	X
Iowa	⋯	L	X	⋯	⋯	X	X
Kans.	⋯	D	1	⋯	X	⋯	X
Ky.	⋯	R	⋯	⋯	X	X	X
La.	⋯	R	⋯	⋯	X	X	X
Maine	⋯	R	⋯	⋯	X	X	X
Md.	X	L	X	⋯	⋯	X	X
Mass.	X	L	X	X	X	X[17]	X
Mich.	X	R	X[11]	⋯	X	X	X
Minn.	⋯	R	X	⋯	⋯	X	⋯
Miss.	⋯	R	⋯	⋯	X	X	X
Mo.	X	R	⋯	⋯	X	X	X
Mont.	⋯	R	⋯	⋯	X	X	X
Neb.	⋯	D	⋯	⋯	X	⋯	⋯
Nev.	⋯	R	⋯	⋯	X	X	X

Appendix C

State	Record of sale reported to state or local govt.	State provision for right-to-carry concealed[13]	Carrying openly prohibited	Owner ID cards or licensing	Firearm rights constitutional provision	State firearms preemption laws	Range protection law
N.H.	...	R	...	...	X	X	X
N.J.	X	L	X	X	...	X[17]	X
N.Mex.	...	R	...	...	X	X	X
N.Y.	X	L	X	X	...	X[22]	X
N.C.	X	R	...	...	X	X	X
N.Dak.	...	R	X[6]	...	X	X	X
Ohio	I	D	1	10	X	...	X
Okla.	...	R	X[6]	...	X	X	X
Oreg.	X	R	...	...	X	X	X
Pa.	X	R	X[11]	...	X	X	X
R.I.	X	L	X	...	X	X	X
S.C.	X	R	X	...	X	X	X
S.Dak.	X	R	...	...	X	X	X
Tenn.	X	R	X[5]	...	X	X	X
Tex.	...	R	X	...	X	X	X
Utah	...	R	X[6]	...	X	X	X
Vt.	...	R[19]	X[5]	...	X	X	X
Va.	I	R	...	...	X	X	X
Wash.	X	R	X[21]	...	X	X	...
W.Va.	...	R	...	...	X	X	X
Wis.	X	D	...	...	X	X	X
Wyo.	...	R	...	...	X	X	X
D.C.	X	D	X	X	NA	...	...

Source: National Rifle Association. "Compendium of State Firearms Laws." Available online. Posted on URL: http://www.nraila.org.

APPENDIX D

THE BRADY HANDGUN VIOLENCE PREVENTION ACT (1993)

H.R. 1025
One Hundred Third Congress
of the
United States of America
AT THE FIRST SESSION
Begun and held at the City of Washington on Tuesday, the fifth day of January, one thousand nine hundred ninety-three

AN ACT

To provide for a waiting period before the purchase of a handgun, and for the establishment of a national instant criminal background check system to be contacted by firearms dealers before the transfer of any firearm.

Be it enacted by the Senate and House of Representatives of the United States of America in Congress assembled,

TITLE I—BRADY HANDGUN CONTROL

SEC. 101. SHORT TITLE.

This title may be cited as the "Brady Handgun Violence Prevention Act."

SEC. 102. FEDERAL FIREARMS LICENSEE REQUIRED TO CONDUCT CRIMINAL BACKGROUND CHECK BEFORE TRANSFER OF FIREARM TO NON-LICENSEE.

(a) INTERIM PROVISION.—

(1) IN GENERAL.—Section 922 of title 18, United States Code, is amended by adding at the end the following:

"(s)(1) Beginning on the date that is 90 days after the date of enactment of this subsection and ending on the day before the date that is 60 months after such date of enactment, it shall be unlawful for any licensed importer, licensed manufacturer, or licensed dealer to sell, deliver, or transfer a handgun to an individual who is not licensed under section 923, unless—

"(A) after the most recent proposal of such transfer by the transferee—

"(i) the transferor has—

"(I) received from the transferee a statement of the transferee containing the information described in paragraph (3);

"(II) verified the identity of the transferee by examining the identification document presented;

"(III) within 1 day after the transferee furnishes the statement, provided notice of the contents of the statement to the chief law enforcement officer of the place of residence of the transferee; and

"(IV) within 1 day after the transferee furnishes the statement, transmitted a copy of the statement to the chief law enforcement officer of the place of residence of the transferee; and

"(ii)(I) 5 business days (meaning days on which State offices are open) have elapsed from the date the transferor furnished notice of the contents of the statement to the chief law enforcement officer, during which period the transferor has not received information from the chief law enforcement officer that receipt or possession of the handgun by the transferee would be in violation of Federal, State, or local law; or

"(II) the transferor has received notice from the chief law enforcement officer that the officer has no information indicating that receipt or possession of the handgun by the transferee would violate Federal, State, or local law;

"(B) the transferee has presented to the transferor a written statement, issued by the chief law enforcement officer of the place of residence of the transferee during the 10-day period ending on the date of the most recent proposal of such transfer by the transferee, stating that the transferee requires access to a handgun because of a threat to the life of the transferee or of any member of the household of the transferee;

"(C)(i) the transferee has presented to the transferor a permit that—

"(I) allows the transferee to possess or acquire a handgun; and

"(II) was issued not more than 5 years earlier by the State in which the transfer is to take place; and

"(ii) the law of the State provides that such a permit is to be issued only after an authorized government official has verified that the information available to such official does not indicate that possession of a handgun by the transferee would be in violation of the law;

"(D) the law of the State requires that, before any licensed importer, licensed manufacturer, or licensed dealer completes the transfer of a handgun to an individual who is not licensed under section 923, an authorized government official verify that the information available to such official does not indicate that possession of a handgun by the transferee would be in violation of law;

"(E) the Secretary has approved the transfer under section 5812 of the Internal Revenue Code of 1986; or

"(F) on application of the transferor, the Secretary has certified that compliance with subparagraph (A)(i)(III) is impracticable because—

"(i) the ratio of the number of law enforcement officers of the State in which the transfer is to occur to the number of square miles of land area of the State does not exceed 0.0025;

"(ii) the business premises of the transferor at which the transfer is to occur are extremely remote in relation to the chief law enforcement officer; and

"(iii) there is an absence of telecommunications facilities in the geographical area in which the business premises are located.

"(2) A chief law enforcement officer to whom a transferor has provided notice pursuant to paragraph (1)(A)(i)(III) shall make a reasonable effort to ascertain within 5 business days whether receipt or possession would be in violation of the law, including research in whatever State and local recordkeeping systems are available and in a national system designated by the Attorney General.

"(3) The statement referred to in paragraph (1)(A)(i)(I) shall contain only—

"(A) the name, address, and date of birth appearing on a valid identification document (as defined in section 1028(d)(1)) of the transferee containing a photograph of the transferee and a description of the identification used;

"(B) a statement that the transferee—

"(i) is not under indictment for, and has not been convicted in any court of, a crime punishable by imprisonment for a term exceeding 1 year;

"(ii) is not a fugitive from justice;

"(iii) is not an unlawful user of or addicted to any controlled substance (as defined in section 102 of the Controlled Substances Act);

"(iv) has not been adjudicated as a mental defective or been committed to a mental institution;

"(v) is not an alien who is illegally or unlawfully in the United States;

"(vi) has not been discharged from the Armed Forces under dishonorable conditions; and

"(vii) is not a person who, having been a citizen of the United States, has renounced such citizenship;

"(C) the date the statement is made; and

"(D) notice that the transferee intends to obtain a handgun from the transferor.

"(4) Any transferor of a handgun who, after such transfer, receives a report from a chief law enforcement officer containing information that receipt or possession of the handgun by the transferee violates Federal, State, or local law shall, within one business day after receipt of such request, communicate any information related to the transfer that the transferor has about the transfer and the transferee to—

"(A) the chief law enforcement officer of the place of business of the transferor; and

"(B) the chief law enforcement officer of the place of residence of the transferee.

"(5) Any transferor who receives information, not otherwise available to the public, in a report under this subsection shall not disclose such information except to the transferee, to law enforcement authorities, or pursuant to the direction of a court of law.

"(6)(A) Any transferor who sells, delivers, or otherwise transfers a handgun to a transferee shall retain the copy of the statement of the transferee with respect to the handgun transaction, and shall retain evidence that the transferor has complied with subclauses (III) and (IV) of paragraph (1)(A)(i) with respect to the statement.

"(B) Unless the chief law enforcement officer to whom a statement is transmitted under paragraph (1)(A)(i)(IV) determines that a transaction would violate Federal, State, or local law—

"(i) the officer shall, within 20 business days after the date the transferee made the statement on the basis of which the notice was provided, destroy the statement, any record containing information derived from the statement, and any record created as a result of the notice required by paragraph (1)(A)(i)(III);

"(ii) the information contained in the statement shall not be conveyed to any person except a person who has a need to know in order to carry out this subsection; and

"(iii) the information contained in the statement shall not be used for any purpose other than to carry out this subsection.

"(C) If a chief law enforcement officer determines that an individual is ineligible to receive a handgun and the individual requests the officer to provide the reason for such determination, the officer shall provide such reasons to the individual in writing within 20 business days after receipt of the request.

"(7) A chief law enforcement officer or other person responsible for providing criminal history background information pursuant to this subsection shall not be liable in an action at law for damages—

"(A) for failure to prevent the sale or transfer of a handgun to a person whose receipt or possession of the handgun is unlawful under this section; or

"(B) for preventing such a sale or transfer to a person who may lawfully receive or possess a handgun.

"(8) For purposes of this subsection, the term 'chief law enforcement officer' means the chief of police, the sheriff, or an equivalent officer or the designee of any such individual.

"(9) The Secretary shall take necessary actions to ensure that the provisions of this subsection are published and disseminated to licensed dealers, law enforcement officials, and the public."

(2) HANDGUN DEFINED.—Section 921(a) of title 18, United States Code, is amended by adding at the end the following:

"(29) The term 'handgun' means—

"(A) a firearm which has a short stock and is designed to be held and fired by the use of a single hand; and

"(B) any combination of parts from which a firearm described in subparagraph (A) can be assembled".

(b) PERMANENT PROVISION.—Section 922 of title 18, United States Code, as amended by subsection (a)(1), is amended by adding at the end the following:

"(t)(1) Beginning on the date that is 30 days after the Attorney General notifies licensees under section 103(d) of the Brady Handgun Violence Prevention Act that the national instant criminal background check system is established, a licensed importer, licensed manufacturer, or licensed dealer shall not transfer a firearm to any other person who is not licensed under this chapter, unless—

"(A) before the completion of the transfer, the licensee contacts the national instant criminal background check system established under section 103 of that Act;

"(B)(i) the system provides the licensee with a unique identification number; or

"(ii) 3 business days (meaning a day on which State offices are open) have elapsed since the licensee contacted the system, and the system has not notified the licensee that the receipt of a firearm by such other person would violate subsection (g) or (n) of this section; and

"(C) the transferor has verified the identity of the transferee by examining a valid identification document (as defined in section 1028(d)(1) of this title) of the transferee containing a photograph of the transferee.

"(2) If receipt of a firearm would not violate section 922 (g) or (n) or State law, the system shall—

"(A) assign a unique identification number to the transfer;

"(B) provide the licensee with the number; and

"(C) destroy all records of the system with respect to the call (other than the identifying number and the date the number was assigned) and all records of the system relating to the person or the transfer.

"(3) Paragraph (1) shall not apply to a firearm transfer between a licensee and another person if—

"(A)(i) such other person has presented to the licensee a permit that—

"(I) allows such other person to possess or acquire a firearm; and

"(II) was issued not more than 5 years earlier by the State in which the transfer is to take place; and

"(ii) the law of the State provides that such a permit is to be issued only after an authorized government official has verified that the information available to such official does not indicate that possession of a firearm by such other person would be in violation of law;

"(B) the Secretary has approved the transfer under section 5812 of the Internal Revenue Code of 1986; or

"(C) on application of the transferor, the Secretary has certified that compliance with paragraph (1)(A) is impracticable because—

"(i) the ratio of the number of law enforcement officers of the State in which the transfer is to occur to the number of square miles of land area of the State does not exceed 0.0025;

"(ii) the business premises of the licensee at which the transfer is to occur are extremely remote in relation to the chief law enforcement officer (as defined in subsection (s)(8)); and

"(iii) there is an absence of telecommunications facilities in the geographical area in which the business premises are located.

"(4) If the national instant criminal background check system notifies the licensee that the information available to the system does not demonstrate that the receipt of a firearm by such other person would violate subsection (g) or (n) or State law, and the licensee transfers a firearm to such other person, the licensee shall include in the record of the transfer the unique identification number provided by the system with respect to the transfer.

"(5) If the licensee knowingly transfers a firearm to such other person and knowingly fails to comply with paragraph (1) of this subsection with respect to the transfer and, at the time such other person most recently proposed the transfer, the national instant criminal background check system was operating and information was available to the system demonstrating that receipt of a firearm by such other person would violate subsection (g) or (n) of this section or State law, the Secretary may, after notice and opportunity for a hearing, suspend for not more than 6 months or revoke any license issued to the licensee under section 923, and may impose on the licensee a civil fine of not more than $5,000.

"(6) Neither a local government nor an employee of the Federal Government or of any State or local government, responsible for providing information to the national instant criminal background check system shall be liable in an action at law for damages—

"(A) for failure to prevent the sale or transfer of a firearm to a person whose receipt or possession of the firearm is unlawful under this section; or

"(B) for preventing such a sale or transfer to a person who may lawfully receive or possess a firearm."

(c) PENALTY.—Section 924(a) of title 18, United States Code, is amended—

(1) in paragraph (1), by striking "paragraph (2) or (3) of"; and

(2) by adding at the end the following:

"(5) Whoever knowingly violates subsection (s) or (t) of section 922 shall be fined not more than $1,000, imprisoned for not more than 1 year, or both."

SEC. 103. NATIONAL INSTANT CRIMINAL BACKGROUND CHECK SYSTEM.

(a) DETERMINATION OF TIMETABLES.—Not later than 6 months after the date of enactment of this Act, the Attorney General shall—

(1) determine the type of computer hardware and software that will be used to operate the national instant criminal background check system and the means by which State criminal records systems and the telephone or electronic device of licensees will communicate with the national system;

(2) investigate the criminal records system of each State and determine for each State a timetable by which the State should be able to provide criminal records on an on-line capacity basis to the national system; and

(3) notify each State of the determinations made pursuant to paragraphs (1) and (2).

(b) ESTABLISHMENT OF SYSTEM.—Not later than 60 months after the date of the enactment of this Act, the Attorney General shall establish a national instant criminal background check system that any licensee may contact, by telephone or by other electronic means in addition to the telephone, for information, to be supplied immediately, on whether receipt of a firearm by a prospective transferee would violate section 922 of title 18, United States Code, or State law.

(c) EXPEDITED ACTION BY THE ATTORNEY GENERAL.—The Attorney General shall expedite—

(1) the upgrading and indexing of State criminal history records in the Federal criminal records system maintained by the Federal Bureau of Investigation;

(2) the development of hardware and software systems to link State criminal history check systems into the national instant criminal background check system established by the Attorney General pursuant to this section; and

(3) the current revitalization initiatives by the Federal Bureau of Investigation for technologically advanced fingerprint and criminal records identification.

(d) NOTIFICATION OF LICENSEES.—On establishment of the system under this section, the Attorney General shall notify each licensee and the chief law enforcement officer of each State of the existence and purpose of the system and the means to be used to contact the system.

(e) ADMINISTRATIVE PROVISIONS.—

(1) AUTHORITY TO OBTAIN OFFICIAL INFORMATION.— Notwithstanding any other law, the Attorney General may secure directly from any department or agency of the United States such information on persons for whom receipt of a firearm would violate subsection (g) or (n) of section 922 of title 18, United States Code or State law, as is necessary to enable the system to operate in accordance with this section. On request of the Attorney General, the head of such department or agency shall furnish such information to the system.

(2) OTHER AUTHORITY.—The Attorney General shall develop such computer software, design and obtain such telecommunications and computer hardware, and employ such personnel, as are necessary to establish and operate the system in accordance with this section.

(f) WRITTEN REASONS PROVIDED ON REQUEST.—If the national instant criminal background check system determines that an individual is ineligible to receive a firearm and the individual requests the system to provide the reasons for the determination, the system shall provide such reasons to the individual, in writing, within 5 business days after the date of the request.

(g) CORRECTION OF ERRONEOUS SYSTEM INFORMATION.—
If the system established under this section informs an individual contacting the system that receipt of a firearm by a prospective transferee would violate subsection (g) or (n) of section 922 of title 18, United States Code or State law, the prospective transferee may request the Attorney General to provide the prospective transferee with the reasons therefor. Upon receipt of such a request, the Attorney General shall immediately comply with the request. The prospective transferee may submit to the Attorney General information to correct, clarify, or supplement records of the system with respect to the prospective transferee. After receipt of such information, the Attorney General shall immediately consider the information, investigate the matter further, and correct all erroneous Federal records relating to the prospective transferee and give notice of the error to any Federal department or agency or any State that was the source of such erroneous records.

(h) REGULATIONS.—After 90 days' notice to the public and an opportunity for hearing by interested parties, the Attorney General shall prescribe regulations to ensure the privacy and security of the information of the system established under this section.

(i) PROHIBITION RELATING TO ESTABLISHMENT OF REGISTRATION SYSTEMS WITH RESPECT TO FIREARMS.—No department, agency, officer, or employee of the United States may—

(1) require that any record or portion thereof generated by the system established under this section be recorded at or transferred to a facility owned, managed, or controlled by the United States or any State or political subdivision thereof; or

(2) use the system established under this section to establish any system for the registration of firearms, firearm owners, or firearm transactions or dispositions, except with respect to persons, prohibited by section 922 (g) or (n) of title 18, United States Code or State law, from receiving a firearm.

(j) DEFINITIONS.—As used in this section:

(1) LICENSEE.—The term "licensee" means a licensed importer (as defined in section 921(a)(9) of title 18, United States Code), a licensed manufacturer (as defined in section 921(a)(10) of that title), or a licensed dealer (as defined in section 921(a)(11) of that title).

(2) OTHER TERMS.—The terms "firearm", "handgun", "licensed importer", "licensed manufacturer", and "licensed dealer" have the meanings stated in section 921(a) of title 18, United States Code, as amended by subsection (a)(2).

(k) AUTHORIZATION OF APPROPRIATIONS.—There are authorized to be appropriated, which may be appropriated from the Violent Crime Reduction Trust Fund established by section 1115 of title 31, United States

Code, such sums as are necessary to enable the Attorney General to carry out this section.

SEC. 104. REMEDY FOR ERRONEOUS DENIAL OF FIREARM.

(a) IN GENERAL.—Chapter 44 of title 18, United States Code, is amended by inserting after section 925 the following new section:

"S 925A. Remedy for erroneous denial of firearm

"Any person denied a firearm pursuant to subsection (s) or (t) of section 922—

"(1) due to the provision of erroneous information relating to the person by any State or political subdivision thereof, or by the national instant criminal background check system established under section 103 of the Brady Handgun Violence Prevention Act; or

"(2) who was not prohibited from receipt of a firearm pursuant to subsection (g) or (n) of section 922,

may bring an action against the State or political subdivision responsible for providing the erroneous information, or responsible for denying the transfer, or against the United States, as the case may be, for an order directing that the erroneous information be corrected or that the transfer be approved, as the case may be. In any action under this section, the court, in its discretion, may allow the prevailing party a reasonable attorney's fee as part of the costs."

(b) TECHNICAL AMENDMENT.—The chapter analysis for chapter 44 of title 18, United States Code, is amended by inserting after the item relating to section 925 the following new item:

"925A. Remedy for erroneous denial of firearm."

SEC. 105. RULE OF CONSTRUCTION.

This Act and the amendments made by this Act shall not be construed to alter or impair any right or remedy under section 552a of title 5, United States Code.

SEC. 106. FUNDING FOR IMPROVEMENT OF CRIMINAL RECORDS.

(a) USE OF FORMULA GRANTS.—Section 509(b) of title I of the Omnibus Crime Control and Safe Streets Act of 1968 (42 U.S.C. 3759(b)) is amended—

(1) in paragraph (2) by striking "and" after the semicolon;

(2) in paragraph (3) by striking the period and inserting "; and"; and

(3) by adding at the end the following new paragraph:

"(4) the improvement of State record systems and the sharing with the Attorney General of all of the records described in paragraphs (1), (2), and (3) of this subsection and the records required by the Attorney General under section 103 of the Brady Handgun Violence Prevention Act, for the purpose of implementing that Act."

(b) ADDITIONAL FUNDING.—

(1) GRANTS FOR THE IMPROVEMENT OF CRIMINAL RECORDS.—The Attorney General, through the Bureau of Justice Statistics, shall, subject to appropriations and with preference to States that as of the date of enactment of this Act have the lowest percent currency of case dispositions in computerized criminal history files, make a grant to each State to be used—

(A) for the creation of a computerized criminal history record system or improvement of an existing system;

(B) to improve accessibility to the national instant criminal background system; and

(C) upon establishment of the national system, to assist the State in the transmittal of criminal records to the national system.

(2) AUTHORIZATION OF APPROPRIATIONS.—There are authorized to be appropriated for grants under paragraph (1), which may be appropriated from the Violent Crime Reduction Trust Fund established by section 1115 of title 31, United States Code, a total of $200,000,000 for fiscal year 1994 and all fiscal years thereafter.

TITLE II—MULTIPLE FIREARM PURCHASES TO STATE AND LOCAL POLICE

SEC. 201. REPORTING REQUIREMENT.

Section 923(g)(3) of title 18, United States Code, is amended—

(1) in the second sentence by inserting after "thereon," the following: "and to the department of State police or State law enforcement agency of the State or local law enforcement agency of the local jurisdiction in which the sale or other disposition took place";

(2) by inserting "(A)" after "(3)"; and

(3) by adding at the end thereof the following:

"(B) Except in the case of forms and contents thereof regarding a purchaser who is prohibited by subsection (g) or (n) of section 922 of this title from receipt of a firearm, the department of State police or State law enforcement agency or local law enforcement agency of the local jurisdiction shall not disclose any such form or the contents thereof to any person or entity, and shall destroy each such form and any record of the contents thereof no more than 20 days from the date such form is received. No later than the date that is 6 months after the effective date of this subparagraph, and at the end of each 6-month period thereafter, the department of State police or State law enforcement agency or local law enforcement agency of the local jurisdiction shall certify to the Attorney General of the United States that no disclosure contrary to this subparagraph has been made and that all forms and any record of the contents thereof have been destroyed as provided in this subparagraph."

TITLE III—FEDERAL FIREARMS LICENSE REFORM

SEC. 301. SHORT TITLE.

This title may be cited as the "Federal Firearms License Reform Act of 1993".

SEC. 302. PREVENTION OF THEFT OF FIREARMS.

(a) COMMON CARRIERS.—Section 922(e) of title 18, United States Code, is amended by adding at the end the following: "No common or contract carrier shall require or cause any label, tag, or other written notice to be placed on the outside of any package, luggage, or other container that such package, luggage, or other container contains a firearm."

(b) RECEIPT REQUIREMENT.—Section 922(f) of title 18, United States Code, is amended—

(1) by inserting "(1)" after "(f)"; and

(2) by adding at the end the following new paragraph:

"(2) It shall be unlawful for any common or contract carrier to deliver in interstate or foreign commerce any firearm without obtaining written acknowledgement of receipt from the recipient of the package or other container in which there is a firearm."

(c) UNLAWFUL ACTS.—Section 922 of title 18, United States Code, as amended by section 102, is amended by adding at the end the following new subsection:

"(u) It shall be unlawful for a person to steal or unlawfully take or carry away from the person or the premises of a person who is licensed to engage in the business of importing, manufacturing, or dealing in firearms, any firearm in the licensee's business inventory that has been shipped or transported in interstate or foreign commerce."

(d) PENALTIES.—Section 924 of title 18, United States Code, is amended by adding at the end the following new subsection:

"(i)(1) A person who knowingly violates section 922(u) shall be fined not more than $10,000, imprisoned not more than 10 years, or both.

"(2) Nothing contained in this subsection shall be construed as indicating an intent on the part of Congress to occupy the field in which provisions of this subsection operate to the exclusion of State laws on the same subject matter, nor shall any provision of this subsection be construed as invalidating any provision of State law unless such provision is inconsistent with any of the purposes of this subsection."

SEC. 303. LICENSE APPLICATION FEES FOR DEALERS IN FIREARMS.

Section 923(a)(3) of title 18. United States Code, is amended—

(1) in subparagraph (A), by adding "or" at the end;

(2) in subparagraph (B) by striking "a pawnbroker dealing in firearms other than" and inserting "not a dealer in";

(3) in subparagraph (B) by striking "$25 per year; or" and inserting "$200 for 3 years, except that the fee for renewal of a valid license shall be $90 for 3 years."; and

(4) by striking subparagraph (C).

Speaker of the House of Representatives.
Vice President of the United States and President of the Senate.

APPENDIX E

UNITED STATES V. MILLER, 1939

UNITED STATES v. MILLER ET AL.

APPEAL FROM THE DISTRICT COURT OF THE UNITED STATES FOR THE WESTERN DISTRICT OF ARKANSAS.

[Note: footnotes and references have been omitted]

No. 696. Argued March 30, 1939.—Decided May 15, 1939.

The National Firearms Act, as applied to one indicted for transporting in interstate commerce a 12-gauge shotgun with a barrel less than 18 inches long, without having registered it and without having in his possession a stamp-affixed written order for it, as required by the Act, held:

1. Not unconstitutional as an invasion of the reserved powers of the States. Citing Sonzinsky v. United States, 300 U. S. 506, and Narcotic Act cases

2. Not violative of the Second Amendment of the Federal Constitution.

The Court can not take judicial notice that a shotgun having a barrel less than 18 inches long has today any reasonable relation to the preservation or efficiency of a well regulated militia; and therefore can not say that the Second Amendment guarantees to the citizen the right to keep and bear such a weapon. 26 F. Supp. 1002, reversed.

APPEAL under the Criminal Appeals Act from a judgment sustaining a demurrer to an indictment for violation of the National Firearms Act.

Opinion of the Court.

Gun Control

Mr. Gordon Dean argued the cause, and Solicitor General Jackson, Assistant Attorney General McMahon, and Messrs. William W. Barron, Fred E. Strine, George F. Kneip, W. Marvin Smith, and Clinton R. Barry were on a brief, for the United States.

No appearance for appellees.

MR. JUSTICE McREYNOLDS delivered the opinion of the Court.

An indictment in the District Court Western District Arkansas, charged that Jack Miller and Frank Layton

did unlawfully, knowingly, wilfully, and feloniously transport in interstate commerce from the town of Claremore in the State of Oklahoma to the town of Siloam Springs in the State of Arkansas a certain firearm, to-wit, a double barrel 12-gauge Stevens shotgun having a barrel less than 18 inches in length, bearing identification number 76230, said defendants, at the time of so transporting said firearm in interstate commerce as aforesaid, not having registered said firearm as required by Section 1132d of Title 26, United States Code (Act of June 26, 1934, c. 737, Sec. 4 [sec. 5], 48 Stat. 1237), and not having in their possession a stamp-affixed written order for said firearm as provided by Section 1132c, Title 26, United States Code (June 26, 1934, c. 737, Sec. 4, 48 Stat. 1237) and the regulations issued under authority of the said Act of Congress known as the 'National Firearms Act', approved June 26, 1934, contrary to the form of the statute in such case made and provided, against the peace and dignity of the United States.

A duly interposed demurrer alleged: The National Firearms Act is not a revenue measure but an attempt to usurp police power reserved to the States, and is therefore unconstitutional. Also, it offends the inhibition of the Second Amendment to the Constitution—"A well regulated Militia, being necessary to the security of a free State, the right of people to keep and bear Arms, shall not be infringed."

District Court held that section eleven of the Act violates the Second Amendment. It accordingly sustained the demurrer and quashed the indictment.

The cause is here by direct appeal.

Considering *Sonzinsky v. United States* (1937), 300 U.S. 506, 513, and what was ruled in sundry causes arising under the Harrison Narcotic Act (footnote 2)—*United States v. Jin Fuey Moy* (1916), 241 U.S. 394; *United States v. Doremus* (1919), 249 U.S. 86, 94; *Linder v. United States* (1925), 268

U.S. 5; *Alston v. United States* (1927), 274 U.S. 289; *Nigro v. United States* (1928), 276 U.S. 332—the objection that the Act usurps police power reserved to the States is plainly untenable.

In the absence of any evidence tending to show that possession or use of a "shotgun having a barrel of less than eighteen inches in length" at this time has some reasonable relationship to the preservation or efficiency of a well regulated militia, we cannot say that the Second Amendment guarantees the right to keep and bear such an instrument. Certainly it is not within judicial notice that this weapon is any part of the ordinary military equipment or that its use could contribute to the common defense. *Aymette v. State*, 2 Humphreys (Tenn.) 154, 158.

The Constitution as originally adopted granted to the Congress power— "To provide for calling forth the Militia to execute the Laws of the Union, suppress Insurrections and repel Invasions; To provide for organizing, arming, and disciplining, the Militia, and for governing such Part of them as may be employed in the Service of the United States, reserving to the States respectively, the Appointment of the Officers, and the Authority of training the Militia according to the discipline prescribed by Congress." With obvious purpose to assure the continuation and render possible the effectiveness of such forces the declaration and guarantee of the Second Amendment were made. It must be interpreted and applied with that end in view.

The Militia which the States were expected to maintain and train is set in contrast with Troops which they were forbidden to keep without the consent of Congress. The sentiment of the time strongly disfavored standing armies; the common view was that adequate defense of country and laws could be secured through the Militia—civilians primarily, soldiers on occasion.

The signification attributed to the term Militia appears from the debates in the Convention, the history and legislation of Colonies and States, and the writings of approved commentators. These show plainly enough that the Militia comprised all males physically capable of acting in concert for the common defense. "A body of citizens enrolled for military discipline." And further, that ordinarily when called for service these men were expected to appear bearing arms supplied by themselves and of the kind in common use at the time.

Blackstone's Commentaries, Vol. 2, Ch. 13, p. 409 points out "that king Alfred first settled a national militia in this kingdom," and traces the subsequent development and use of such forces.

Adam Smith's *Wealth of Nations*, Book V, Ch. 1, contains an extended account of the Militia. It is there said: "Men of republican principles have been jealous of a standing army as dangerous to liberty." "In a militia, the character of the labourer, artificer, or tradesman, predominates over that of the soldier: in a standing army, that of the soldier predominates over every other character; and in this distinction seems to consist the essential difference between those two different species of military force."

"The American Colonies in the 17th Century," Osgood, Vol. I, ch. XIII, affirms in reference to the early system of defense in New England—

"In all the colonies, as in England, the militia system was based on the principle of the assize of arms. This implied the general obligation of all adult male inhabitants to possess arms, and, with certain exceptions, to co-operate in the work of defence." "The possession of arms also implied the possession of ammunition, and the authorities paid quite as much attention to the latter as to the former." "A year later [1632] it was ordered that any single man who had not furnished himself with arms might be put out to service, and this became a permanent part of the legislation of the colony [Massachusetts]."

Also "Clauses intended to insure the possession of arms and ammunition by all who were subject to military service appear in all the important enactments concerning military affairs. Fines were the penalty for delinquency, whether of towns or individuals. According to the usage of the times, the infantry of Massachusetts consisted of pikemen and musketeers. The law, as enacted in 1649 and thereafter, provided that each of the former should be armed with a pike, corselet, head-piece, sword, and knapsack. The musketeer should carry a 'good fixed musket,' not under bastard musket bore, not less than three feet, nine inches, nor more than four feet three inches in length, a priming wire, scourer, and mould, a sword, rest, bandoleers, one pound of powder, twenty bullets, and two fathoms of match. The law also required that two-thirds of each company should be musketeers."

The General Court of Massachusetts, January Session 1784, provided for the organization and government of the Militia. It directed that the Train Band should "contain all able bodied men, from sixteen to forty years of age, and the Alarm List, all other men under sixty years of age, . . ." Also, "That every non-commissioned officer and private soldier of the said militia not under the control of parents, masters or guardians, and being of sufficient ability therefor in the judgment of the Selectmen of the town in which he shall dwell, shall equip himself, and be constantly provided with a good fire arm," &c.

By an Act passed April 4, 1786 the New York Legislature directed: "That every able-bodied Male Person, being a Citizen of this State, or of any of the United States, and residing in this State, (except such Persons as are hereinafter excepted) and who are of the Age of Sixteen, and under the Age of Forty-five Years, shall, by the Captain or commanding Officer of the Beat in which such Citizens shall reside, within four Months after the passing of this Act, be enrolled in the Company of such Beat. . . . That every Citizen so enrolled and notified, shall, within three Months thereafter, provide himself, at his own Expense, with a good Musket or Firelock, a sufficient Bayonet and Belt, a Pouch with a Box therein to contain not less than Twenty-four Cartridges suited to the Bore of his Musket or Firelock, each Cartridge containing a proper Quantity of Powder and Ball, two spare Flints, a Blanket and Knapsack; . . ."

The General Assembly of Virginia, October, 1785, (12 Hening's Statutes) declared, "The defense and safety of the commonwealth depend upon having its citizens properly armed and taught the knowledge of military duty."

It further provided for organization and control of the Militia and directed that "All free male persons between the ages of eighteen and fifty years," with certain exceptions, "shall be inrolled or formed into companies." "There shall be a private muster of every company once in two months."

Also that "Every officer and soldier shall appear at his respective muster-field on the day appointed, by eleven o'clock in the forenoon, armed, equipped, and accoutred, as follows: . . . every noncommissioned officer and private with a good, clean musket carrying an ounce ball, and three feet eight inches long in the barrel, with a good bayonet and iron ramrod well fitted thereto, a cartridge box properly made, to contain and secure twenty cartridges fitted to his musket, a good knapsack and canteen, and moreover, each non-commissioned officer and Private shall have at every muster one pound of good powder, and four pounds of lead, including twenty blind cartridges; and each serjeant shall have a pair of moulds fit to cast balls for their respective companies, to be purchased by the commanding officer out of the monies arising on delinquencies. Provided, That the militia of the counties westward of the Blue Ridge, and the counties below adjoining thereto, shall not be obliged to be armed with muskets, but may have good rifles with proper accoutrements, in lieu thereof. And every of the said officers, non-commissioned officers, and privates, shall constantly keep the aforesaid arms, accoutrements, and ammunition, ready to be produced whenever called for by his commanding officer. If any private shall make it appear to the satisfaction of the court hereafter to be appointed for trying delinquencies under this act that he is so poor that he cannot purchase the arms herein required, such court shall cause them to be purchased out of the money arising from delinquents."

Most if not all of the States have adopted provisions touching the right to keep and bear arms. Differences in the language employed in these have naturally led to somewhat variant conclusions concerning the scope of the right guaranteed. But none of them seem to afford any material support for the challenged ruling of the court below.

In the margin some of the more important opinions and comments by writers are cited.

We are unable to accept the conclusion of the court below and the challenged judgment must be reversed. The cause will be remanded for further proceedings.

MR. JUSTICE DOUGLAS took no part in the consideration or decision of this cause.

APPENDIX F

UNITED STATES V. TIMOTHY JOE EMERSON, 2001

Note: Following are excerpts from the full decision. Because of their relevance to gun control issues, the excerpts focus on issues relating to the interpretation and application of the Second Amendment to the U.S. Constitution. Footnotes have been omitted.

REVISED NOVEMBER 2, 2001
IN THE UNITED STATES COURT OF APPEALS FOR THE FIFTH CIRCUIT

No. 99-10331

Appeal from the United States District Court for the Northern District of Texas

October 16, 2001

Before GARWOOD, DeMOSS and PARKER, Circuit Judges.

GARWOOD, Circuit Judge:

The United States appeals the district court's dismissal of the indictment of Defendant-Appellee Dr. Timothy Joe Emerson (Emerson) for violating 18 U.S.C. § 922(g)(8)(C)(ii). The district court held that section 922(g)(8)(C)(ii) was unconstitutional on its face under the Second Amendment and as applied to Emerson under the Due Process Clause of the Fifth Amendment. We reverse and remand.

DISCUSSION

I. Construction of 18 U.S.C. § 922(g)(8)

18 U.S.C. § 922 provides in relevant part:

"(g) It shall be unlawful for any person-. . .

(8) who is subject to a court order that —

(A) was issued after a hearing of which such person received actual notice, and at which such person had an opportunity to participate;

(B) restrains such person from harassing, stalking, or threatening an intimate partner of such person or child of such intimate partner or person, or engaging in other conduct that would place an intimate partner in reasonable fear of bodily injury to the partner or child; and

(C)(i) includes a finding that such person represents a credible threat to the physical safety of such intimate partner or child; or

(ii) by its terms explicitly prohibits the use, attempted use, or threatened use of physical force against such intimate partner or child that would reasonably be expected to cause bodily injury; or. . .

to ship or transport in interstate or foreign commerce, or possess in or affecting commerce, any firearm or ammunition; or to receive any firearm or ammunition which has been shipped or transported in interstate or foreign commerce.". . .

V. Second Amendment

The Second Amendment provides:

"A well regulated Militia, being necessary to the security of a free State, the right of the people to keep and bear arms, shall not be infringed."

A. INTRODUCTION AND OVERVIEW OF SECOND AMENDMENT MODELS

The district court held that the Second Amendment recognizes the right of individual citizens to own and possess firearms, and declared that section 922(g)(8) was unconstitutional on its face because it requires that a citizen be disarmed merely because of being subject to a "boilerplate [domestic relations injunctive] order with no particularized findings." *Emerson*, 46 F.Supp.2d at 611. The government opines that *stare decisis* requires us to reverse the district court's embrace of the individual rights model. Amici for the government argue that even if binding precedent does not require reversal, the flaws in the district court's Second Amendment analysis do.

In the last few decades, courts and commentators have offered what may fairly be characterized as three different basic interpretations of the Second Amendment. The first is that the Second Amendment does not apply to individuals; rather, it merely recognizes the right of a state to arm its militia. This "states' rights" or "collective rights" interpretation of the Second Amendment has been embraced by several of our sister circuits. The government commended the states' rights view of the Second Amendment to the district court, urging that the Second Amendment does not apply to individual citizens.

Proponents of the next model admit that the Second Amendment recognizes some limited species of individual right. However, this supposedly "individual" right to *bear* arms can only be exercised by members of a functioning, organized state militia who bear the arms while and as a part of actively participating in the organized militia's activities. The "individual" right to *keep* arms only applies to members of such a militia, and then only if the federal and state governments fail to provide the firearms necessary for such militia service. At present, virtually the only such organized and actively functioning militia is the National Guard, and this has been the case for many years. Currently, the federal government provides the necessary implements of warfare, including firearms, to the National Guard, and this likewise has long been the case. Thus, under this model, the Second Amendment poses no obstacle to the wholesale disarmament of the American people. A number of our sister circuits have accepted this model, sometimes referred to by commentators as the sophisticated collective rights model. On appeal the government has abandoned the states' rights model and now advocates the sophisticated collective rights model.

The third model is simply that the Second Amendment recognizes the right of individuals to keep and bear arms. This is the view advanced by Emerson and adopted by the district court. None of our sister circuits has subscribed to this model, known by commentators as the individual rights model or the standard model. The individual rights view has enjoyed considerable academic endorsement, especially in the last two decades.

We now turn to the question of whether the district court erred in adopting an individual rights or standard model as the basis of its construction of the Second Amendment.

B. *STARE DECISIS* AND *UNITED STATES V. MILLER*

The government steadfastly maintains that the Supreme Court's decision in *United States v. Miller*, 59 S.Ct. 816 (1939), mandated acceptance of the collective rights or sophisticated collective rights model, and rejection of the individual rights or standard model, as a basis for construction of the Second Amendment. We disagree. Only in *United States v. Miller* has the Supreme Court rendered any holding respecting the Second Amendment as applied to the federal government. There, the indictment charged the defendants with transporting in interstate commerce, from Oklahoma to Arkansas, an unregistered "Stevens shotgun having a barrel less than 18 inches in length" without having the required stamped written order, contrary to the National Firearms Act. The defendants filed a demurrer challenging the facial validity of the indictment on the ground that "[t]he National Firearms Act . . . offends the inhibition of the Second Amendment," and "[t]he District Court held that section 11 of the Act [proscribing interstate transportation of a firearm, as therein defined, that lacked registration or a stamped order] violates the Second Amendment. It accordingly sustained the demurrer and quashed the indictment." *Id.* at 817–18. The government appealed, and we have examined a copy of its brief. The *Miller* defendants neither filed any brief nor made any appearance in the Supreme Court.

The government's Supreme Court brief "[p]reliminarily" points out that: ". . .the National Firearms Act does not apply to all firearms but only to a limited class of firearms. The term 'firearm' is defined in Section 1 of the Act . . . to refer only to 'a shotgun or rifle having a barrel of less than 18 inches in length, or any other weapon, except a pistol or revolver, from which a shot is discharged by an explosive if such weapon is capable of being concealed on the person, or a machine gun, and includes a muffler or silencer for any firearm whether or not such firearm is included within the foregoing definition.'" (*id.* at 6).

In this connection the brief goes on to assert that it is "indisputable that Congress was striking not at weapons intended for legitimate use but at weapons which form the arsenal of the gangster and the desperado" (*id.* at 7) and that the National Firearms Act restricts interstate transportation "of only those weapons which are the tools of the criminal" (*id.* at 8).

The government's brief thereafter makes essentially *two* legal arguments. *First*, it contends that the right secured by the Second Amendment is "only one which exists where the arms are borne in the militia or some other military organization provided for by law and intended for the protection of the state." *Id.* at 15. This, in essence, is the sophisticated collective rights model.

The *second* of the government's two arguments in *Miller* is reflected by the following passage from its brief:

"While some courts have said that the right to bear arms includes the right of the individual to have them for the protection of his person and property as well as the right of the people to bear them collectively (*People*

v. *Brown*, 253 Mich. 537; *State v. Duke*, 42 Tex. 455), the cases are unanimous in holding that the term "arms" as used in constitutional provisions refers only to those weapons which are ordinarily used for military or public defense purposes and does not relate to those weapons which are commonly used by criminals. Thus in *Aymette v. State* [2 Humph., Tenn. 154 (1840)], *supra*, it was said (p. 158): 'As the object for which the right to keep and bear arms is secured, is of general and public nature, to be exercised by the people in a body, for their *common defence*, so the *arms*, the right to keep which is secured, are such as are usually employed in civilized warfare, and that constitute the ordinary military equipment. If the citizens have these arms in their hands, they are prepared in the best possible manner to repel any encroachments upon their rights by those in authority. They need not, for such a purpose, the use of those weapons which are usually employed in private broils, and which are efficient only in the hands of the robber and the assassin. These weapons would be useless in war. They could not be employed advantageously in the common defence of the citizens. The right to keep and bear them, is not, therefore, secured by the constitution.'" (*Id.* at 18–19).

The government's *Miller* brief then proceeds (at pp. 19–20) to cite various other state cases, and *Robertson v. Baldwin*, 17 S.Ct. 326, 329 (1897), in support of its *second* argument, and states:

"That the foregoing cases conclusively establish that the Second Amendment has relation only to the right of the people to keep and bear arms for lawful purposes and does not conceivably relate to weapons of the type referred to in the National Firearms Act cannot be doubted. Sawed-off shotguns, sawed-off rifles and machine guns are clearly weapons which can have no legitimate use in the hands of private individuals."

Thereafter, the government's brief in its "conclusion" states " . . . we respectfully submit that Section 11 of the National Firearms Act does not infringe 'the right of the people to keep and bear arms' secured by the Second Amendment."

Miller reversed the decision of the district court and "remanded for further proceedings." *Id.* at 820. We believe it is entirely clear that the Supreme Court decided *Miller* on the basis of the government's *second* argument— that a "shotgun having a barrel of less than eighteen inches in length" as stated in the National Firearms Act is not (or cannot merely be assumed to be) one of the "Arms" which the Second Amendment prohibits infringement of the right of the people to keep and bear—and *not* on the basis of the government's *first* argument (that the Second Amendment protects the right of the people to keep and bear *no* character of "arms" when not borne in actual, active service in the militia or some other military organization provided for by law). *Miller* expresses its holding as follows:

"In the absence of any evidence tending to show that possession or use of a 'shotgun having a barrel of less than eighteen inches in length' at this time has some reasonable relationship to the preservation or efficiency of a well regulated militia, we cannot say that the Second Amendment guarantees the right to keep and bear *such an* instrument. Certainly it is not within judicial notice that this weapon is any part of the ordinary military equipment or that its use could contribute to the common defense. *Aymette v. State of Tennessee*, 2 Humph., Tenn. 154, 158." *Id.* at 818 (emphasis added). . .

Nowhere in the Court's *Miller* opinion is there any reference to the fact that the indictment does not remotely suggest that either of the two defendants was ever a member of any organized, active militia, such as the National Guard, much less that either was engaged (or about to be engaged) in any actual military service or training of such a militia unit when transporting the sawed-off shotgun from Oklahoma into Arkansas. Had the lack of such membership or engagement been a ground of the decision in *Miller*, the Court's opinion would obviously have made mention of it. But it did not.

Nor do we believe that any other portion of the *Miller* opinion supports the sophisticated collective rights model.
    Just after the above quoted portion of its opinion, the *Miller* court continued in a separate paragraph initially quoting the militia clauses of article 1, § 8 (clauses 15 and 16) and concluding:
    "With obvious purpose to assure the continuation and render possible the effectiveness of such forces [militia] the declaration and guarantee of the Second Amendment were made. It must be interpreted and applied with that end in view." *Id.* at 818.
    Miller then proceeds to discuss what was meant by the term "militia," stating in part:
    "The signification attributed to the term Militia appears from the debates in the Convention, the history and legislation of Colonies and States, and the writings of approved commentators. These show plainly enough that *the Militia comprised all males physically capable of acting in concert for the common defense* . . . ordinarily when called for service these men were expected to appear *bearing arms supplied by themselves* and of the kind in common use at the time. . ."

These passages from *Miller* suggest that the militia, the assurance of whose continuation and the rendering possible of whose effectiveness *Miller* says were purposes of the Second Amendment, referred to the generality of the civilian male inhabitants throughout their lives from teenage years until old age and to their personally keeping their own arms, and not merely to individuals during the time (if any) they might be actively engaged in actual military service or only to those who were members of special or select units.

We conclude that *Miller* does not support the government's collective rights or sophisticated collective rights approach to the Second Amendment. Indeed, to the extent that *Miller* sheds light on the matter it cuts against the government's position. Nor does the government cite any other authority binding on this panel which mandates acceptance of its position in this respect. However, we do not proceed on the assumption that *Miller* actually accepted an individual rights, as opposed to a collective or sophisticated collective rights, interpretation of the Second Amendment. Thus, *Miller* itself does not resolve that issue. We turn, therefore, to an analysis of history and wording of the Second Amendment for guidance. In undertaking this analysis, we are mindful that almost all of our sister circuits have rejected any individual rights view of the Second Amendment. However, it respectfully appears to us that all or almost all of these opinions seem to have done so either on the erroneous assumption that *Miller* resolved that issue or without sufficient articulated examination of the history and text of the Second Amendment.

C. TEXT

We begin construing the Second Amendment by examining its text: "[a] well regulated Militia, being necessary to the security of a free State, the right of the people to keep and bear Arms, shall not be infringed." U.S. Const. amend. II.

1. SUBSTANTIVE GUARANTEE

a. "People"

The states rights model requires the word "people" to be read as though it were "States" or "States respectively." This would also require a corresponding change in the balance of the text to something like "to provide for the militia to keep and bear arms." That is not only far removed from the actual wording of the Second Amendment, but also would be in substantial tension with Art. 1, § 8, Cl. 16 (Congress has the power "To provide for . . . arming . . . the militia. . ."). For the sophisticated collective rights model to be viable, the word "people" must be read as the words "members of a select militia". The individual rights model, of course, does not require that any special or unique meaning be attributed to the word "people." It gives the same meaning to the words "the people" as used in the Second Amendment phrase "the right of the people" as when used in the exact same phrase in the contemporaneously submitted and ratified First and Fourth Amendments.

There is no evidence in the text of the Second Amendment, or any other part of the Constitution, that the words "the people" have a different connotation within the Second Amendment than when employed elsewhere in the Constitution. In fact, the text of the Constitution, as a whole, strongly suggests that the words "the people" have precisely the same meaning within the Second Amendment as without. And, as used throughout the Constitution, "the people" have "rights" and "powers," but federal and state governments only have "powers" or "authority", never "rights." Moreover, the Constitution's text likewise recognizes not only the difference between the "militia" and "the people" but also between the "militia" which has not been "call[ed] forth" and "the militia, when in actual service."

Our view of the meaning of "the people," as used in the Constitution, is in harmony with the United States Supreme Court's pronouncement in *United States v. Verdugo-Urquidez*, 110 S.Ct. 1056, 1060–61 (1990), that:

"'[T]he people' seems to have been a term of art employed in select parts of the Constitution. The Preamble declares that the Constitution is ordained and established by 'the People of the United States.' The Second Amendment protects 'the right of the people to keep and bear Arms,' and the Ninth and Tenth Amendments provide that certain rights and powers are retained by and reserved to 'the people.' While this textual exegesis is by no means conclusive, it suggests that 'the people' protected by the Fourth Amendment, and by the First and Second Amendments, and to whom rights and powers are reserved in the Ninth and Tenth Amendments, refers to a class of people who are part of a national community or who have otherwise developed sufficient connection with this country to be considered part of that community." (citations omitted). . .

It appears clear that "the people," as used in the Constitution, including the Second Amendment, refers to individual Americans.

b. *"Bear Arms"*

Proponents of the states' rights and sophisticated collective rights models argue that the phrase "bear arms" only applies to a member of the militia carrying weapons during actual militia service. Champions of the individual rights model opine that "bear arms" refers to any carrying of weapons, whether by a soldier or a civilian. There is no question that the phrase "bear arms" may be used to refer to the carrying of arms by a soldier or militiaman. The issue is whether "bear arms" was also commonly used to refer to the carrying of arms by a civilian.

The best evidence that "bear arms" was primarily used to refer to military situations comes from *Aymette v. State*, 2 Humph., Tenn. 154 (1840), a prosecution for carrying a concealed bowie knife. The Supreme Court of Tennessee, in construing section 26 of its declaration of rights, providing that "the free white men of this State have a right to keep and bear arms for their common defence," stated:

"The 28th section of our bill of rights provides 'that no citizen of this State shall be compelled to bear arms provided he will pay an equivalent, to be ascertained by law.' Here we know that the phrase has a military sense, and no other; and we must infer that it is used in the same way in the 26th section, which secures to the citizen the right to bear arms. A man in pursuit of deer, elk, and buffaloes might carry his rifle every day for forty years, and yet it would never be said of him that he had borne arms. . ."

Unlike the Tennessee constitution at issue in *Aymette*, the Second Amendment has no "for their common defence" language and the United States Constitution contains no provision comparable to section 28 of the Tennessee constitution on which the *Aymette* court relied.

Amici supporting the government also cite other examples of state constitutional provisions allowing a conscientious objector to be excused from the duty of bearing arms if he pays an equivalent so that another can serve in his place.

However, there are numerous instances of the phrase "bear arms" being used to describe a civilian's carrying of arms. Early constitutional provisions or declarations of rights in at least some ten different states speak of the right of the "people" [or "citizen" or "citizens"] "to bear arms in defense of themselves [or "himself"] and the state," or equivalent words, thus indisputably reflecting that under common usage "bear arms" was in no sense restricted to bearing arms in military service. And such provisions were enforced on the basis that the right to bear arms was *not* restricted to bearing arms during actual military service. *See Bliss v. Commonwealth*, 13 Am. Dec. 251, 12 Ky. 90 (Ky. 1822).

We also note that a minority of the delegates to the Pennsylvania ratification convention proposed the following amendment to the Constitution:

"That the people have a right to bear arms for the defense of themselves and their own state, or the United States, or for the purpose of killing game; and no law shall be passed for disarming the people or any of them, unless for crimes committed, or real danger of public injury from individuals; and as standing armies in the time of peace are dangerous to liberty, they ought not to be kept up; and that the military shall be kept under strict subordination to and be governed by the civil powers.". . .

We conclude that the phrase "bear arms" refers generally to the carrying or wearing of arms. It is certainly proper to use the phrase in reference to the carrying or wearing of arms by a soldier or militiaman; thus, the context in which "bear arms" appears may indicate that it refers to a military situation, e.g. the conscientious objector clauses cited by amici supporting the government. However, amici's argument that "bear arms" was exclusively, or even usually, used to *only* refer to the carrying or wearing of arms by a soldier or militiaman must be rejected. The appearance of "bear Arms" in the Second Amendment accords fully with the plain meaning of the subject of the substantive guarantee, "the people," and offers no support for the proposition that the Second Amendment applies only during periods of actual military service or only to those who are members of a select militia. Finally, our view of "bear arms" as used in the Second Amendment appears to be the same as that expressed in the dissenting opinion of Justice Ginsburg (joined by the Chief Justice and Justices Scalia and Souter) in *Muscarello v. United States*, 118 S.Ct. 1911, 1921 (1998); viz:

"Surely a most familiar meaning [of carrying a firearm] is, as the Constitution's Second Amendment ("keep and *bear* Arms") (emphasis added) and Black's Law Dictionary, at 214, indicate: "wear, bear, or carry . . . upon the person or in the clothing or in a pocket, for the purpose . . . of being armed and ready for offensive or defensive action in a case of conflict with another person.". . .

d. Substantive Guarantee as a Whole

Taken as a whole, the text of the Second Amendment's substantive guarantee is not suggestive of a collective rights or sophisticated collective rights interpretation, and the implausibility of either such interpretation is enhanced by consideration of the guarantee's placement within the Bill of Rights and the wording of the other articles thereof and of the original Constitution as a whole.

2. EFFECT OF PREAMBLE

We turn now to the Second Amendment's preamble: "A well-regulated Militia, being necessary to the security of a free State." And, we ask ourselves whether this preamble suffices to mandate what would be an otherwise implausible collective rights or sophisticated collective rights interpretation of the amendment. We conclude that it does not.

Certainly, the preamble implies that the substantive guarantee is one which tends to enable, promote or further the existence, continuation or effectiveness of that "well-regulated Militia" which is "necessary to the security of a free State." As the Court said in *Miller*, immediately after quoting the militia clauses of Article I, § 8 (cl. 15 and 16), "[w]ith obvious purpose to assure the continuation and render possible the effectiveness of such forces the declaration and guarantee of the Second Amendment were made." *Id.*, 59 S.Ct. at 818. We conclude that the Second Amendment's substantive guarantee, read as guaranteeing individual rights, may as so read reasonably be understood as being a guarantee which tends to enable, promote or further the existence, continuation or effectiveness of that "well-regulated Militia" which is "necessary to the security of a free State." Accordingly, the preamble does not support an interpretation of the amendment's substantive guarantee in accordance with the collective rights or sophisticated collective rights model, as such an interpretation is contrary to the plain meaning of the text of the guarantee, its placement within the Bill of Rights and the wording of the other articles thereof and of the original Constitution as a whole.

As observed in *Miller,* "the Militia comprised all males physically capable of acting in concert for the common defense" and "that ordinarily when called for service these men were expected to appear bearing arms supplied by themselves." *Id.*, 59 S.Ct. at 818. *Miller* further notes that "'[i]n all the colonies . . . the militia systems . . . implied the general obligation of all adult male inhabitants to possess arms.'" *Id.* (citation omitted). There are frequent contemporaneous references to "a well-regulated militia" being "composed of the body of the people, trained in arms." Plainly, then, "a well-regulated Militia" refers *not* to a special or select subset or group taken out of the militia as a whole but rather to the condition of the militia as a whole, namely being well disciplined and trained. And, "Militia," just like "well-regulated Militia," likewise was understood to be composed of the people generally possessed of arms which they knew how to use, rather than to refer to some formal military group separate and distinct from the people at large. . .

"Perhaps the most accurate conclusion one can reach with any confidence is that the core meaning of the Second Amendment is a populist/republican/federalism one: Its central object is to arm "We the People" so that ordinary citizens can participate in the collective defense of their community and their state. But it does so not through directly protecting a right on the part of states or other collectivities, assertable by them against the federal government, to arm the populace as they see fit. Rather, the amendment achieves its central purpose by assuring that the federal government may not disarm individual citizens without some unusually strong justification consistent with the authority of the states to organize their own militias. That assurance in turn is provided through recognizing a right (admittedly of uncertain scope) on the part of individuals to possess and use firearms in the defense of themselves and their homes . . . a right that directly limits action by Congress or by the Executive Branch. . ." *Id.*, Vol. 1, n.221 at 902.

In sum, to give the Second Amendment's preamble its full and proper due there is no need to torture the meaning of its substantive guarantee into the collective rights or sophisticated collective rights model which is so plainly inconsistent with the substantive guarantee's text, its placement within the bill of rights and the wording of the other articles thereof and of the original Constitution as a whole. . .

6. 19TH CENTURY COMMENTARY

The great Constitutional scholars of the 19th Century recognized that the Second Amendment guarantees the right of individual Americans to possess and carry firearms. . .

Next, Justice Joseph Story:

"§ 1000. The next amendment is:" A well regulated militia being necessary to the security of a free state, the right of the people to keep and bear arms shall not be infringed.

§ 1001. The importance of this article will scarcely be doubted by any persons, who have duly reflected upon the subject. The militia is the natural defence of a free country against sudden foreign invasions, domestic insurrections, and domestic usurpations of power by rulers. It is against sound policy for a free people to keep up large military establishments and standing armies in time of peace, both from the enormous expenses, with which they are attended, and the facile means, which they afford to ambitious and unprincipled rulers, to subvert the government, or trample upon the rights of the people. *The right of the citizens to keep, and bear arms has justly been considered, as the palladium of the liberties of a republic; since it offers a strong moral check against the usurpation and arbitrary power of rulers;* and *will generally,* even if these are successful in the first instance, *enable the people to resist,* and triumph over them. And yet, though this truth would seem so clear, and the importance of a well regulated militia would seem so undeniable, it cannot be disguised, that among the American people there is a growing indifference to any system of militia discipline, and a strong disposition, from a sense of its burthens, to be rid of all regulations. How it is practicable *to keep the people duly armed* without some organization, it is difficult to see. There is certainly no small danger, that indifference may lead to disgust, and disgust to contempt; and thus gradually undermine all the protection intended by this clause of our national bill of rights."

Joseph Story, Commentaries on the Constitution of the United States 708–709 (Carolina Academic Press 1987) (1833) (emphasis added). Justice Story calls the right of "citizens" to keep and bear arms the "palladium" of our liberties. He viewed the private ownership of firearms as reducing the need for the maintenance of large standing armies by promoting the vitality of the militia, and laments that militia participation is on the decline, fearing this will result in fewer Americans being armed.

Appendix F

7. ANALYSIS

. . .Given the political dynamic of the day, the wording of the Second Amendment is exactly what would have been expected. The Federalists had no qualms with recognizing the individual right of all Americans to keep and bear arms. In fact, as we have documented, one of the Federalists' favorite 1787–88 talking points on the standing army and federal power over the militia issues was to remind the Anti-Federalists that the American people were armed and hence could not possibly be placed in danger by a federal standing army or federal control over the militia. The Second Amendment's preamble represents a successful attempt, by the Federalists, to further pacify moderate Anti-Federalists without actually conceding any additional ground, i.e. without limiting the power of the federal government to maintain a standing army or increasing the power of the states over the militia.

This is not to say that the Second Amendment's preamble was not appropriate or is in any way marginal or lacking in true significance. Quite the contrary. Absent a citizenry generally keeping and bearing their own private arms, a militia as it was then thought of could not meaningfully exist. As pointed out by Thomas Cooley, the right of individual Americans to keep, carry, and acquaint themselves with firearms does indeed promote a well-regulated militia by fostering the development of a pool of firearms-familiar citizens that could be called upon to serve in the militia. While standing armies are not mentioned in the preamble, history shows that the reason a well-regulated militia was declared necessary to the security of a *free* state was because such a militia would greatly reduce the need for a standing army. Thus, the Second Amendment dealt directly with one of the Anti-Federalists' concerns and indirectly addressed the other two. While the hard-core Anti-Federalists recognized that the Second Amendment did not assure a well-regulated militia or curtail the federal government's power to maintain a large standing army, they did not control either branch of Congress (or the presidency) and had to be content with the right of individuals to keep and bear arms.

Finally, the many newspaper articles and personal letters cited indicate that, at the time, Americans viewed the Second Amendment as applying to individuals. This is confirmed by the First Congress's rejection of amendments that would have directly and explicitly addressed the Anti-Federalists' standing army and power over the militia concerns.

We have found no historical evidence that the Second Amendment was intended to convey militia power to the states, limit the federal government's power to maintain a standing army, or applies only to members of a select militia while on active duty. All of the evidence indicates that the

Second Amendment, like other parts of the Bill of Rights, applies to and protects individual Americans.

We find that the history of the Second Amendment reinforces the plain meaning of its text, namely that it protects individual Americans in their right to keep and bear arms whether or not they are a member of a select militia or performing active military service or training.

E. SECOND AMENDMENT PROTECTS INDIVIDUAL RIGHTS

We reject the collective rights and sophisticated collective rights models for interpreting the Second Amendment. We hold, consistent with *Miller*, that it protects the right of individuals, including those not then actually a member of any militia or engaged in active military service or training, to privately possess and bear their own firearms, such as the pistol involved here, that are suitable as personal, individual weapons and are not of the general kind or type excluded by *Miller*. However, because of our holding that section 922(g)(8), as applied to Emerson, does not infringe his individual rights under the Second Amendment we will not now further elaborate as to the exact scope of all Second Amendment rights. . . .

VI. APPLICATION TO EMERSON

The district court held that section 922(g)(8) was unconstitutionally overbroad because it allows second amendment rights to be infringed absent any express judicial finding that the person subject to the order posed a future danger. In other words, the section 922(g)(8) threshold for deprivation of the fundamental right to keep and bear arms is too low.

Although, as we have held, the Second Amendment *does* protect individual rights, that does not mean that those rights may never be made subject to any limited, narrowly tailored specific exceptions or restrictions for particular cases that are reasonable and not inconsistent with the right of Americans generally to individually keep and bear their private arms as historically understood in this country. Indeed, Emerson does not contend, and the district court did not hold, otherwise. As we have previously noted, it is clear that felons, infants and those of unsound mind may be prohibited from possessing firearms. See note 21, *supra*. Emerson's argument that his Second Amendment rights have been violated is grounded on the propositions that the September 14, 1998 order contains no express finding that he represents a credible threat to the physical safety of his wife (or child), that the evidence before the court issuing the order would not sustain such a finding and that the provisions of the order bringing it within clause (C)(ii) of section 922(g)(8) were no more than uncontested boiler-plate. In essence, Emerson, and the district court, concede that had the order contained an express finding, on the basis of adequate evidence, that Emerson actually posed a credible threat to the physical safety of his wife, and had that been a genuinely contested matter at the hearing, with the parties and the court aware of section 922(g)(8), then Emerson could, consistent with the Second Amendment, be precluded from possessing a firearm while he remained subject to the order. . . .

VII. CONCLUSION

. . . For the reasons stated, we reverse the district court's order granting the motion to dismiss the indictment under the Fifth Amendment.

We agree with the district court that the Second Amendment protects the right of individuals to privately keep and bear their own firearms that are suitable as individual, personal weapons and are not of the general kind or type excluded by *Miller,* regardless of whether the particular individual is then actually a member of a militia. However, for the reasons stated, we also conclude that the predicate order in question here is sufficient, albeit likely minimally so, to support the deprivation, while it remains in effect, of the defendant's Second Amendment rights. Accordingly, we reverse the district court's dismissal of the indictment on Second Amendment grounds.

We remand the cause for further proceedings not inconsistent herewith.

REVERSED and REMANDED

INDEX

Locators in **boldface** indicate main topics. Locators followed by *c* indicate chronology entries. Locators followed by *b* indicate biographical entries. Locators followed by *g* indicate glossary entries.

Index

Index

Index

Index